Travel Guide
to Europe 1492

D1415803

LORENZO CAMUSSO

Travel Guide to Europe 1492

Ten Itineraries in the Old World

AN OWL BOOK
HENRY HOLT AND COMPANY
NEW YORK

First published in the United States in 1992
by Henry Holt and Company, Inc., 115 West
18th Street, New York, New York 10011.

Originally published in Italy in 1990 under the
title *Guida ai Viaggi nell'Europa del 1492* by
G. Mondadori.

Library of Congress Cataloging-in-
Publication Data

Travel guide to Europe 1492: ten itineraries in
the Old World—
    1st American ed.
        p.   cm.
    "An Owl Book"
    1. Fifteenth century. 2. Europe—Tours.
3. Historic sites—Europe—Guidebooks
CB367.T73   1992
914.04'21—dc20   91-46167
                                        CIP

ISBN 0-8050-2102-7 (An Owl Book: pbk.)

Henry Holt books are available at special
discounts for bulk purchases for sales
promotions, premiums, fund-raising, or
educational use. Special editions or book
excerpts can also be created to specification.

For details contact: Special Sales Director,
Henry Holt and Company, Inc., 115 West
18th Street, New York, New York 10011.

First American Edition—1992

Created by Fenice 2000

Editor in chief: Luca Selmi
Editorial assistance and photo research:
Cecilia Lazzeri, Valeria Chiodo
Tables designed by Marco Giardina
Itinerary maps by Fabrizio Lucioni
Editorial secretary: Orietta Colombai
Translations by Jay Hyams and Sarah
Hilditch
Technical coordination by Renzo Biffi
Color separations by Sebi, s.r.l., Milan
Printed by Amilcare Pizzi S.p.A., Cinisello
Balsamo (Milan)

Printed in Italy

10 9 8 7 6 5 4 3 2 1

Frontispiece: The eye of the 1400s: Visdomini castle at Vincigliata among the Florentine hills, a detail from the Journey of the Magi to Bethlehem, *a fresco by Benozzo Gozzoli in the chapel of Palazzo Medici-Riccardi. Below: An imaginary landscape of the period: a horizon filled with mountains, a city, woods, small boats on water, hunters in clearings, and two travelers resting under a tree; detail from the* Madonna and Child *by Giovanni Bellini.*

Contents

To travel in the past. Is it really such an unusual notion? In modern-day travel markets do they not above all buy and sell the past? Marble worn smooth by the blinding light of Greece; the dizzy terraces of Machu Picchu; sphinxes, pyramids, a people painted in the hypogea along the Nile valley; the Great Wall of China, like a snake sleeping on the crests of hills; the azure cupolas of the madrasahs of Samarkand; even the ghost towns of Arizona. Time and space to be consumed as historic, artistic delicacies.

In this guide only a few more small steps have been taken: a past time and place heretofore consigned to the history books is singled out — the Europe of the few decades before and after the discovery of America — and an attempt is made to plunge the traveler back into that past, not merely to show him a backdrop. Before and after the "visit to the monument" he will find no airplanes, cruise ships, or hotel rooms droning with the low buzz of an air-conditioner, but days in the saddle, inaccessible mountain passes, oceans buffeted by the blow of unforeseeable winds; at sundown inns, landlords, serving maids; the sensation, at least, of all this, a scent of adventure of the "time machine" sort (without the fatigue that could so easily have rendered everything ugly — the journey is only an imaginary one).

The historical moment chosen is obviously selected with the five-hundredth anniversary of Columbus' discovery of America in mind, but not for that reason alone. If one believes Rousseau, Europe was already formed over two hundred years ago; let alone in 1992. "There are no longer, today, Frenchmen, Germans, Spaniards, even Englishmen; there are nothing but Europeans. We all have the same tastes, the same passions, the same customs" (Jean-Jacques Rousseau, Considerations sur le gouvernement de Pologne, *1772). But let us go back another couple of centuries. At the close of 1492, half a millennium ago, and even slightly later, nobody knew that America had been discovered, let alone what was to derive from this discovery on both sides of the Atlantic. An anniversary is like a telephone number, an aid to conversation, not the conversation itself, nor its content. The recurrence of the date is an occasion for reflection, both on the fact that the discovery of America can*

1492
_____
1992

also be considered a starting point, or at least an important passage, in the process of definition, of individualization of Europe (and therefore an opportunity for asking ourselves what it means to be European), and on the fact that the Europe that discovered America was, in an early form, the Europe of today. All the more reason, then, for a highly realistic "journey in time" through that Europe.

The following pages furnish a guide to this journey. According to use, they contain general information and suggested itineraries as well. The former is the same sort that a traveler of those times, at the doorstep of his own home, would have wanted to read (and would have been able to read in the guides of those days): the general configuration of the Old World, who might be his traveling companions, the actual traveling conditions (on horseback and for the most part overland; by boat when following rivers downstream; on the sea in a galley or round-bellied boat), the opportunities for obtaining sustenance and lodging, even the pleasures which could be experienced along the way (naturally, the pleasures; the pessimistic attitude of one of Cervantes' characters — "No journey is bad when it has an end, unless it ends at the gallows" — was not a mirror of general opinion). If the basic introductory information found in any modern guide can be recognized in the items cited above, just think that all, or almost all, of them were already spoken of in a guide which Aimery Picard compiled during the 12th century for pilgrims headed toward Santiago de Compostela.

The "suggested" itineraries are not intended to stifle the fantasy of the traveler, just as the asterisks in a modern guide do not abolish free choice. Here, however, each itinerary refers to a real, or probable, journey. A certain Gerozzo di Jacopo de' Pigli, Florentine, really did set out for Bruges in 1446 (Itinerary 1). In 1480, on the battlefield of Saint-Aubin-du-Cormier, there really were Milanese merchant armorers (Itinerary 4). Might not pilgrims have come to Rome from the distant diocese of Trondheim for the Jubilee of 1500 (Itinerary 6)? The ten itineraries are arranged in chronological order in the hope that the reader might perceive the passage of time and events — of history — during these several crucial decades, particularly as they had a bearing on everyday life.

7

Over mountains to inns

Traveling in the Europe
of five hundred years ago

Which Europe?

If we could fly over the Europe of five hundred years ago, perhaps in a helicopter, and look down on it from our modern contrivance with our modern knowledge, it would seem a marvelous country. On landing, our impressions would probably vary from place to place, here wonderful, here disturbing, here causing absolute anguish.

Looking down on the physical realities of Europe circa 1492, we would recognize much: the Mediterranean, the endless forests, the green hills of France, Castile's rugged plateau, olive trees and birch trees, vineyards and fields combed by plows. We would see many of the monuments by which we recognize cities — the famous bridges and cathedrals — but many others were yet to come (such as the Eiffel Tower). The cities would also seem, to our eyes, somewhat small, perhaps even a bit empty.

The population of Europe around the end of the 15th century is usually given as about 70 million, an increase of 25 million over the course of the preceding hundred years. Other sources give more modest numbers. Let us accept that Columbus, Erasmus, Luther, and Leonardo shared their Europe with about 70 million people; such a figure would mean the population of Europe was about one-tenth of what it is today. This smaller population was distributed in ways much different from today's European population: following the accepted theories, Germany had a population of 20 million, the Low Countries had about 6 million, France had 19, and England 3.

The Europeans: yesterday and today

The population of several states (in millions) at the end of the 15th century and today are provided in a somewhat speculative set of comparisons:

France	*19*	*55.5*
Germany	*20*	*85*
Ottoman Empire	*4.5*	*33*
(European portion)		
England	*3*	*46*
Italy	*7*	*57*
The Netherlands	*6*	*24.6*
Portugal	*1*	*10*
Russia	*9*	*191*
Spain	*7.5*	*39*
Switzerland	*0.75*	*6.4*

The projected size of populations at the end of the 15th century is very uncertain, and the various political entities represented above had different borders than those of today. In order to approach a valid comparison with contemporary population estimates, 15th-century Germany has been compared to present-day post-unification Germany plus Austria, and the Netherlands comprise the present-day Belgium, Holland, and Luxembourg. It should be recalled that both France and Switzerland were smaller than they are today. To estimate the European portion of the Ottoman Empire, a sum of the present data for Greece, Albania, Bulgaria, European Turkey, and part of Yugoslavia has been used. Regarding the figures for Russia, the lands belonging to the grand prince of Moscow in the 15th century occupied only a limited fraction of contemporary European Russia.

One traveled with a different concept of time, in scenery that can be reconstructed only in fragments; the rhythm was that of the horse, the environment that of a Europe with less than one tenth of its present population. On the page opposite the title: Horsemen from the History of the True Cross *by Piero della Francesca in San Francesco, Arezzo, and a landscape from the* Chronica mundi *by Hartmann Schedel (1493).*

The current population of Belgium and Holland — the area included in the Low Countries during the 15th century — is about 24 million; today's Germany, together with Austria, has about 86 million (what was called Germany during the 15th century was an even larger area); contemporary France, larger than the France of the late 15th century, has 54 million inhabitants; the kingdom of Henry VII corresponds to an area that today numbers 50 million inhabitants.

In general, much less of the land of Europe was cultivated then, and roughly one-third of those fields lay fallow each year. There were more trees in the countryside, in many areas bordering the cultivated fields, more marshes, more boggy areas along river courses. There were fewer buildings along the floors of valleys. Mountain areas were more or less deserted. Except for small fishing villages, the areas along sea coasts were sparsely populated. The areas of uninhabited forestland spread enormous distances. Bears wandered through mountain forests, there were wild boar in the underbrush, wolf packs ventured right up to the edges of inhabited areas. When, in 1520, France's Francis I instituted the *grands louvetiers* — royal officers charged with carrying out wolf hunts over the territory of both nobles and peasants — he was only fulfilling his bound duty to protect his subjects.

In the countryside, landowners and the other well-to-do lived in castles — villas had not yet become fashionable

How large were the cities?

The estimated population sizes of several European cities at the end of the 15th century are compared here with figures of today. The historic numbers are at best rough approximations of actual size. City administrators in those days did not engage in accurate census-taking, and the words "about" and "approximately," which should accompany every number, have been omitted for the sake of simplicity.

Antwerp	45,000	480,000
Augsburg	20,000	245,000
Barcelona	40,000	1.8 million
Bruges	35,000	120,000
Cologne	40,000	1 million
Córdoba	40,000	290,000
Florence	100,000	420,000
Genoa	50,000	720,000
Ghent	55,000	250,000
Granada	40,000	260,000
Istanbul	400,000	5.5 million
London	50,000	6.7 million
Naples	100,000	1.2 million
Nuremberg	20,000	460,000
Paris	80,000	8.7 million
Prague	20,000	1.2 million
Rome	50,000	2.8 million
Seville	40,000	670,000
Venice	100,000	320,000
Vienna	20,000	1.5 million

Several omissions may be noted. For example, Madrid and Berlin are not listed above. The former was little more than a village in the 15th century. The latter was to become the first city of Prussia only in the 1700s.

— and such castles did not always enjoy the amenities later found in villas: fireplaces, loggias, orchards, and gardens. All around was a wide variety of animals: deer, wild bison, lynx, wolves, and weasels. Herons and cranes paddled across the waters of ponds, and storks nested in chimney tops.

Bougainvillaea did not yet grow along the shores of the Mediterranean, but everywhere there was countryside still in its natural state — or returned to its natural state. The population reductions caused by plagues during the middle of the 14th century had led to the abandonment of many inhabited areas, and as of yet no one had returned to many of these deserted places. To the north of the Alps and east of the Elbe the vista could easily still fit the description given by Tacitus:

"Together a frightening region because of its primeval woods and horrible swamps."

As many as eight out of ten people — even more in eastern Europe — lived in the country, where houses and small villages seemed to stand unchanged by time. Cities, even the most important, were incredibly small: Cologne then had 40,000 inhabitants, Paris 80,000, Vienna 20,000, Bourges 10,000. The traveler arriving from afar saw the city cowering behind its walls, armed guards before all its gates, and perhaps the less than subtle warning of vultures perched atop a scaffold. Not all cities were walled — Venice was protected by water — and few cities in England and the Ottoman Empire had urban fortifications. Nature made its way over the walls, however, and even inside the walls of

a city one might come upon vegetable gardens tended by citizens. (Some cities already had signs of urban crowding, for even then cities were gathering places of all the desperate and luckless.) In most parts of Europe, within the stone walls of a city, most construction was of wood. Paris, however, had already begun to turn itself into a city of stone.

That the world was more beautiful to look at was certainly not a result of nature conservation carried out by the inhabitants of Europe. Environmental problems, quite simply, did not seem to exist. The effects of destructive practices were not yet evident, and wounds dealt nature seemed to heal (in fact, the damage *was* already beginning: following centuries of human activity, the primary forests of the Mediterranean area were gone forever,

and stone architecture had there become a necessity).

The quality of life enjoyed by the Europeans of this period is more difficult to appreciate. Perhaps what the Russian writer Nikolaj Cernysevskij said during the 1800s — "History has a weakness for its children, offering them the marrow of bones that the preceding generation has broken open, cutting its hands" — applies to all periods of development, and the end of the 15th century was certainly a period of development. Historians believe it probable that personal life during this period and up to the middle of the 16th century was pleasant. When forming such "time-machine" opinions it is a good idea to remember that 50 percent of the children born died during their first year and that the average life expectancy was between thirty

the hair on their heads cut short.

Visitors, whether voluntary or not, arrived in Europe from other continents: Americans torn from their home to serve as objects of momentary curiosity, African slaves, prisoners taken by pirates on the Barbary coast (not all of whom enjoyed the relatively pleasant fate of Hasan al Wazzan, best-known as the Lion of Africa, who after being the guest of three popes

and thirty-five years.

The first Americans to visit Europe arrived with Columbus in 1493, exciting proof of the amazing mission just completed. The Europeans who saw them found them fascinating. What the Americans thought is unknown. The European males the Americans saw — western European males — shaved their beards and wore their hair long in the style of Charles VIII. One generation later, this style changed, and men grew thick beards, took pride in their mustaches, and had

Painting, stated Leonardo, "has no need of interpreters of different languages" and immediately "satisfies the human species." But did nature have the same poetic force for the traveler as for the painter? Below: The landscape from the Agony in the Garden *by Giovanni Bellini. Opposite: Trees in a drawing by Cesare da Sesto (on the left) and in the* Portinari Tryptich *by Hugo van der Goes (on the right).*

was finally returned to his homeland), Turkish hostages and ambassadors, and "Tartars" who somehow made their way from the steppe to the markets of eastern regions.

Although the majority of Europeans lived out their lives without ever venturing any farther than the market square of the neighboring village, a remarkably large number of people regularly moved through Europe, and they did so for a wide variety of reasons.

They traveled for reasons of business or religion — which moved more people would be difficult to determine — they moved in search of employment or to practice a trade, and they moved

15

to study. How many ventured forth
out of pure curiosity cannot be determined, but such people certainly existed. There was, for example, the
Italian traveler Lodovico de Varthema.
Born between 1465 and 1470, probably
in Bologna, he set off from Venice in
1500 to see the world, visiting Cairo,
Beirut, Tripoli, Damascus, Mecca (he
took part in the annual pilgrimage
and provided the first account by a
Westerner), Persia, India, Ceylon, the
Malabar Coast, Sumatra, Borneo, Ja-
va, the Moluccas, and so on, his tracks
sometimes disappearing, sometimes becoming improbable. He had a reason
for his travels: "The same desire that
spurs many others to see the different
kingdoms of the world has driven me
on my way."

Faith moved crowds along routes
other than the three classical pilgrimages to the Holy Land, Rome, and
Santiago de Compostela. But was it
really faith, and only faith, that moved
the pilgrim? Thomas Kempis, author
of the *Imitation of Christ* — who lived
most of his life in the Augustinian
monastery of Mount St. Agnes, near
Zwolle, in the Netherlands — took a
dim view of pilgrims and pilgrimages,
doubting as he did the authenticity of
the pilgrim's faith. The pilgrim may
not have moved always for pure belief,
but faith and religious duties moved
cardinals among their nations and
back and forth to the throne of St.
Peter; moved bishops on visits to the
pope; and moved a host of other people, among them collectors of curial
income, inspectors of monasteries, itin-

erant preachers, and pontifical legates. The German cardinal and theologian Nicholas of Cusa, born on the Moselle, went to Constantinople in an effort to bring about the reunion of the Eastern Church with the Church in the West and traveled throughout Germany as a papal representative. It is difficult to locate a clear division between religious voyages and voyages undertaken for international politics, and such trips were taken by informers, almost spies, performers of secret embassies, weavers of intrigues, those on special missions, those sent to negotiate alliances, such as Philippe de Comines, who experienced such great emotion on seeing Venice. The papacy was itself a political force, and diplomatic personnel in general included many people who had taken religious orders.

The exciting age of adventurous merchants who took off on long trips to find markets for their wares was just about over. The great mercantile entrepreneurs put their strategies into effect by way of lines of information, guiding from afar the activities of associates or "factors." While the man at the top may have stayed put, his employees moved around quite a bit: the heads of the branch offices of the Medici bank, mixtures of merchants and bankers, usually returned to Florence each year to give an account of their business. The cartwrights and mule-drivers who accompanied merchandise from one end of Europe to the other may not qualify as travelers, but the small merchants who went from market to market and fair to fair

certainly do. One such traveling merchant, from Munich around the middle of the 15th century, left account books that reveal that he bought supplies at Nuremberg and Nordlingen, crossed the Alps, and went on as far as Venice. Other traveling merchants joined in caravans and went from Krakow to Istanbul, for example, or from Hungary to trade with Tartars on the lower Don or in Moscow.

Travels undertaken for activities connected to handicrafts or artistic skills could be more or less permanent. When the people in an area sought to set up a new productive activity, they usually tried, understandably enough, to attract already proven masters of the activity. The king of England put his arguments in straightforward terms to attract Flemish weavers: he bragged of the excellent quality of the meat, the wonderful beer, and the large beds, and claimed no one could find women more beautiful than those of his island nation. Typography was introduced into almost every nation of Europe by technicians from the Rhine region. Albrecht Dürer's father was a goldworker who had moved from Hungary to Nuremberg.

The travels undertaken by artists in many ways determined the course of art history. German masons, stonecutters, and master builders were busy at work in Spain; masters of stained glass crossed the Alps to work on Milan's cathedral; the Spaniard Berruguete went to Urbino to paint; the Frenchman Fouquet went to Rome for the celebration of the year of jubilee

Europe had mapped out the world, but uncertainties in the drawing of its specific features long remained. The map of Europe on the following pages, in Latin and showing picturesque mountains and forests, was made by the son of the Flemish cartographer Gerhard Kremer, known as Gerardus Mercator (1512-94). Opposite: The merchant, from the Ständebuch *by Hans Sachs (1568), with woodcuts by Jost Amman.*

during the middle of the century; Leonardo da Vinci ended his professional pilgrimage as a painter and master of many other human activities on France's Loire. There are then Aristotele Fieravanti, the Bologna-born architect called to Russia to help design the Kremlin, and the Venetian Gentile Bellini, sent for reasons of international good will and diplomatic subtlety to Constantinople to paint a portrait of Mohammed II. Fieravanti and Bellini found themselves far from their homelands, but one must remember, for example, that the Tuscan artists who went to Venice to work on the frescoes in the ducal palace, or Antonello da Messina, who traveled to Venice from southern Italy, were all going to work in a foreign country.

Yet another kind of professional journey was undertaken by the men who traveled from country to country to practice the soldiering trade for one or another king or emperor, queen or condottiere. There were thus the Scotsmen who traditionally served as guards for the king of France, the Genoese crossbowmen whose skills were valued by military entrepreneurs throughout Europe, and later the Swiss pikemen and Germanic lansquenets with their swaggering and outlandish ways of dress.

Travels for study: students followed culture from university to university, and famous professors were called from a chair in one place to a chair in another. Such was the case of the Pole Nicholas Copernicus of Torun: he studied medicine, mathematics, and as-tronomy at Krakow, then medicine at Padua and mathematics at Bologna; in 1499, the same year in which the young Michelangelo made his first *Pietà* at St. Peter's in Rome, the 26-year-old Pole taught mathematics in that same city.

Even kings traveled. The idea of a capital city had not taken hold everywhere, and there was the lingering tradition of Charlemagne, who was said to have traveled a distance roughly equal to the circumference of the earth during his forty-five-year reign. Between 1477 and 1492, Ferdinand and Isabella of Spain moved more than forty times, traveling from end to end of Spain and visiting nineteen cities, some of them more than once. The Carolingian monarchs moved in order to consume the products of their lands: 15th-century courts moved for reasons similar to fiscal equity, for the court lived at the expense of the city that hosted it.

The rulers of Europe were then, perhaps, more rash than wary, with ambitions far beyond their means, with states split by various factions, with their ability to govern limited by the lack of bureaucratic apparatus, and with their world fraught with sudden revolts: all in all, a Europe of enemies. Philippe de Comines came up with the bizarre notion that it had been God's divine will to place next to each European state its "natural enemy," an idea that if nothing else mirrors the continuous formation and dissolution of intrigues, alliances, dynastic matrimonies, and military cam-

The emperor and the seven elector princes, from the Chronica mundi *by Hartmann Schedel.*

paigns. If one places a contemporary map of Europe over a map of 15th-century Europe one sees that many borders have changed, and by remaining in the same spot, a European over the centuries would easily have found him- or herself living in more than one country.

England and Scotland were two separate kingdoms, and the English control of Ireland was limited to the eastern coast and diminished as one moved inland from Dublin. France's land holdings were then far smaller, to the north and the east, than they are today. Today, the shape of France is likened to a hexagon; it was then more like a pentagon. Calais belonged to the English, Artois and Franche-Comté were ruled by the Hapsburgs, Strasbourg was 150 kilometers outside the national borders; to the south, Avignon was the property of the popes, Rossiglione and Cerdagna were part of Spain. Spain itself did not then include Navarre, which was an independent reign, but it did include — as belonging to the Aragon crown — Sardinia and Sicily (southern Italy from Calabria to the Aburzzi remained in Spanish hands until 1504). Perhaps the only European nation whose borders have stayed unchanged since the 15th century is Portugal.

In theory, the three Scandinavian kingdoms of Denmark, Norway, and Sweden were united, their king a German of the house of Oldemburg. Denmark, the strongest economically, owned outright part of southern Sweden and controlled the passage between the North and Baltic seas. Sweden, divided between pro-Danish and pro-independence groups, held Finland, but in the great expanses of northern tundra, the Lapps and the Finns knew and cared nothing about sovereigns.

The center of Europe was ruled by an elected emperor, Maximilian I of Hapsburg, who, thanks to family inheritance, was ruler of Austria, Styria, Carinthia, Carniola, and Tyrol, and thanks to his wife's inheritance was ruler of the Low Countries (Belgium and Holland), Luxembourg, and Franche-Comté, governed by his son Philip. Germany, the principal component of the Holy Roman Empire, was composed of thirty-odd principalities, about fifty ecclesiastic territories, a hundred duchies, and a few dozen free cities. Switzerland, at that time a federation of eleven cantons, was part of the Holy Roman Empire only in theory. Also an imperial territory was the duchy of Savoy, which included areas spread across and around the Alps that are today found in Italy, France, and Switzerland.

Italy had become an area of contention between France and Spain, and as the 15th century drew to a close the outcome of their struggle was still unclear. Most of Italy was then composed of five principal states: the duchy of Milan, the republic of Venice, the republic of Florence, the papal lands, and the Kingdom of Naples; Milan was about to be occupied by the French, and Naples was about to become a Spanish possession. Various Italian political entities had their own

foreign possessions: Venice, for example, ruled Dalmatia, Corfu, Crete, and Cyprus. The political forces in Italy included the republics of Genoa (which owned Corsica), Lucca, Siena, the duchies of Modena, Ferrara, and Urbino, and the marquisate of Mantua.

To the east of Germany were the kingdom of Bohemia, the marquisate of Moravia, and the duchy of Silesia, all of which were part of the Holy Roman Empire. Farther to the east were the kingdoms of Poland and Hungary, both outside the empire. Silesia and Moravia had been included in the Hungary of Matthias Corvinus, but with his death Silesia had passed into the orbit of Poland, and Moravia had fallen into that of Bohemia. A vast country, Hungary included the principality of Transylvania (today part of Rumania), Belgrade, and Croatia up to the Gulf of Quarnero. At the end of the century, Hungary and Bohemia, both elected monarchies, were united under Ladislaus Jagellone, son of the dead king of Poland Casimir IV. Poland, too, was an elective kingdom. Its union with the enormous duchy of Lithuania, which extended from the Baltic to the Ukraine, was interrupted in 1492 and then reestablished in 1501. Although in decline, the order of the Teutonic Knights owned eastern Prussia (as a vassal of the king of Poland) and Livonia, part of the Baltic states that until recently were part of the Soviet Union. Farther yet to the east was the expanding principality of Muscovy, which then far from matched in size the future "European" Russia.

Aside from Lithuania, Muscovy included the Mongol khanates of Kazan, Crimea, and Astrakhan.

Southeastern Europe was ruled by the Ottoman Turks: more than fifty years had passed since their capture of Constantinople. They occupied the Balkan peninsula from the Danube to Greece. They had not conquered Belgrade but held Serbia and Bosnia. Past the Danube, their holdings included the protectorates of Valacchia (today part of Rumania), Hungarian Moldavia (today part of Rumania), and Bessarabia (today part of the Soviet Union).

Political boundaries did not coincide with linguistic boundaries, but the fashion already existed of attributing certain talents, superstitions, or faults to each ethnic group. In his *Praise of Folly*, Erasmus holds that just as nature gives each man a "personal vanity," it gives the "various nations and even the various cities, a particular collective vanity." Thus, the English are fiercely proud of the beauty of their country, of their music, and of their sumptuous banquets; the Scots are proud of their nobility, of their "kinship to the ruling family," and of their philosophic faculties. The French boast of their manners and customs (and the Parisians of their theology), the Spanish their courage in war, the Germans their physical prowess and "their magical arts," and all the Italians affirm that their land is the birthplace of poetry and eloquence and congratulate themselves for — "alone among all mortals" — not being barbarians.

Princes and peoples

France

England

Empire

France. A hereditary monarchy. After the reign of Charles VIII (1483-98), the crown had passed to the collateral house of Orleans with Louis XI, who reigned from 1498 to 1515. Louis XI was the son of Charles of Orléans, the poet-prince, and great grandson of Charles V. His queen, Anne, was heiress of the duchy of Brittany and widow of his predecessor, Charles VIII. The country was one of the most populous in Europe, with a population of 19 million. Paris was by far the largest city, probably numbering 80,000. The kings were infrequently in residence in Paris. Louis XII preferred to hold court at the Castle of Blois in the Loire valley, his birthplace.

The Netherlands. From 1482 to 1506 present-day Belgium and Holland were imperial lands of Philip the Fair of Hapsburg, who inherited them from his mother, Mary of Burgundy, together with Luxembourg and Franche-Comté. It was a prosperous land owing to the profitable trade of its cities: Ghent, the most populous, exceeding 50,000 inhabitants; Bruges, with a population of 35,000; and Antwerp, which grew to reach the size of Ghent.

England. A hereditary monarchy. After the Battle of Bosworth Field (1485), in which Richard III was killed, the Wars of the Roses ended, and a Tudor, Henry VII, gained the throne. In 1509 he was succeeded by his son Henry VIII. The country had only 3 million inhabitants, and wealth derived mainly from sheep. London had a population of 50,000; Bristol and York had between 10,000 and 15,000.

Scotland A hereditary monarchy. The reigning monarch since 1488 was James IV Stuart, who married Margaret Tudor, daughter of King Henry VII of England. James IV met his death in 1513 at Flodden Field in battle against the English and was succeeded by his son, James V.

Scandinavia. Norway was a hereditary monarchy; Denmark and Sweden were elective monarchies. The union of these three kingdoms, dating back to the end of the 14th century, existed more in theory than reality. Sweden probably consisted of 800,000 inhabitants. The population of the other two kingdoms is unknown. Denmark was the wealthiest of the three, controlling both banks of the Kattegat. Christian I, the first

of the Oldensburg monarchs, was succeeded in 1481 by his son John I, who died in 1513.

Germany. The sovereign emperor following the death of Frederick III in 1493 was his son Maximilian I of Hapsburg, who reigned until his death in 1519). The principalities (most notably the Platinate, the two Bavarias, Württemberg, Saxony, Mecklemberg, and Brandenberg), the ecclesiastical territories, counties, and cities maintained strong independence. The population totalled 20 million inhabitants. Cologne, with a population of 40,000, was the largest city, followed by Nuremberg, Augsburg, Vienna, Metz, and Strasbourg, each numbering about 20,000. Principal sources of wealth included the merchandise and manufacturing of these cities; mineral resources were also important.

Bohemia and Hungary. Two electorate monarchies of uncertain population size. Prague, the capital of Bohemia, probably numbered around 20,000 inhabitants. After George Podebrady, Ladislav II Jagiello, son of Casimir IV, king of Poland, was elected king of Bohemia in 1471. This same Ladislav was elected to the throne of

The majority of Europeans were the subjects of kings; most (probably four out of five) were Roman Catholics.

Alexander VI

Castile

Moscow

Hungary after the death of Matthias Corvinus in 1490, becoming Ladislav VI of Hungary.

Italy. Four large cities (Milan, Naples, Venice, Florence) contained approximately 100,000 inhabitants; Rome and Genoa were half that number. The republic of Venice was the sole state possessing dominions outside the peninsula. Other states of importance included the duchy of Milan (occupied by France in 1500), the republic of Florence, the Papal States of the Spanish pope Alexander VI (1498-1503). The kingdoms of Naples and Sicily, Spanish possessions from the start of the 16th century, were the most populous entities. Difficult to consider as Italian was the duchy of Savoy, which joined lands on both sides of the Alps.

Switzerland. With the addition of Basel and Schaffhausen in 1501, twelve cantons formed the Swiss federation. The other cantons were Schwyz, Uri, and Unterwalden, which united in 1291; Lucerne, 1332; Zürich, 1351; Glarus and Zug, 1352; Bern, 1353; Fribourg and Solothurn, 1481. Although theoretically subjects of the empire, the three quarters of a million Swiss had fought their

way to independence.

Spain. Spain was formed by the union of several kingdoms. Castile, a hereditary kingdom, numbered 6.5 million inhabitants; Aragon, a second hereditary kingdom, had a population of 1 million. Following the marriage of Ferdinand of Aragon to Isabella of Castile in 1479, these two kingdoms were jointly governed, but were not formally united. The Moorish kingdom of Granada was conquered in 1492. Tiny Navarre, another hereditary monarchy, was joined to Castile, south of the Pyrenees, in 1512. Isabella died in 1504, and Ferdinand in 1516. The crowns the passed to their grandson Charles of Hapsburg (Charles V). Spain never again was divided.

Portugal. A hereditary monarchy of approximately 1 million inhabitants. Reigning monarchs included John II the Perfect, succeeded in 1495 by his cousin, Manuel I the Great. Overseas exploration had been underway for some time. On the other side of the Strait of Gibraltar, the Portuguese had held Ceuta since 1415 and Tangiers since 1471. Madeira was acquired in about 1420, and the Azores circa 1432. Portuguese explorers passed

the Cape of Good Hope in 1488 and reached India in 1498.

Poland and Lithuania
With the marriage (1386) of an Angevin (Edvige, daughter of Louis II of Hungary) to the grand prince of Lithuania (Wladislaus II Jagiello, a pagan), a union between Lithuania and Poland was formed. The Lithuanian grand duchy was hereditary, and the Polish monarchy was elective. Poland had approximately 9 million inhabitants, and Krakow was its capital.

Russia. Although estimates are uncertain, it is believed that 9 million subjects were ruled by the grand prince of Moscow. His dominions, although in expansion, were considerably smaller than contemporary European Russia. Ivan III the Great was succeeded by his son Basil (1505) and grandson Ivan IV the Terrible (1533).

The Ottoman Empire.
Mohammed II, conqueror of Constantinople (1453), was succeeded in turn by his son Beyazid II (1481) and grandson Selim I (1512). On the death of Mohammed II, the Ottoman dominions in Europe equalled those in Asia, and his subjects in the Balkans numbered approximately 5.5 million.

25

At a horse's pace

In 1508, Erasmus wrote to his lifelong friend Thomas More about a recent trip he had made from Italy to England. The Dutch theologian, scholar, and humanist — not to mention restless and curious traveler — related that he had passed his time during the journey meditating on topics and phrases for his *Praise of Folly*, a work he quickly completed on his arrival. This meditation, Erasmus explained, had permitted him to avoid wasting his time in "ignorant conversations during all the time I was forced to spend on horseback."

Such then was travel: interminable hours in the saddle. The horse was at that time the equivalent, although more costly, of today's private automobile. Women too traveled by horse, although whether they straddled the horse as men did or rode seated on the horse's back with both legs over one side is not clear. Fourteenth-century miniatures present Mary, fleeing into Egypt with Joseph and the Christ Child, seated with her legs over one side; they also show empresses following their husbands over the Alps with one leg to the right, one to the left, both lost in full skirts that blend with the rich caparisons of their mount.

Not everyone could afford to travel at a horse's pace, for they cost dearly: a horse's traveling expenses equaled those of its rider. Although slower and less prestigious than the horse, the donkey was was surer footed over difficult terrain and more economical because of its ability to turn wayside grass into energy. Most convenient

The preferred means of travel was above all the horse, prestigious and costly. Below: Horsemen resting, a miniature from the Livre du couer d'amour espris, *an allegorical romance by René of Anjou, illustrated by the anonymous Master of King René (ca. 1460) or, according to some, by the prince himself. Opposite: A horseman approaching a castle, detail from the* Madonna of Jacob Floreins *by Hans Memling.*

and least expensive was the mule, but even then many people considered prestige as important, if not more important, than efficiency.

Most people traveled by foot, the poor moving from place to place when forced by necessity, pilgrims driven on their journeys by the intense yearning for penitence. There were also wheeled vehicles, including a wide range of carriages and carts drawn by oxen, mules, and horses that were used wher-

ever geography favored the existence of passable roadways. Such vehicles were employed primarily to move merchandise, but they also carried passengers, particularly the elderly and those women who could not sit a horse.

Forecarriages, which allowed the carriage's front wheels to turn and follow a roadway's curves, had been in use since around 1470 and were borrowed from military technology (gun limbers were useful for artillery). The carriage itself was still in an early stage, and the version in use during the second half of the 16th century lacked glass and a suspension system; the coach, a closed four-wheeled carriage with inside seats and elevated outside seat for the driver, is thought have been developed in Hungary and to have spread among the royalty and nobility of Europe during the 16th century.

Foot, cart, and saddle were not the only means of travel across land. Giosafat Barbaro, patrician, merchant, and Venetian ambassador, wrote an annotated panorama of travel in Russia in 1487. One could not travel far during the summer, he claimed, because of all the mud and the insects that swarmed out of the immense woods. When everything froze over during the winter, however, one could easily travel using the so-called sano, on which all kinds of merchandise could be loaded. These sanos were sleighs, and Ambrogio Contarini, another Venetian ambassador, used one to travel from Moscow back to Venice during the middle of January 1476. He wrote, "These so-called sanos are somewhat like houses, with a horse before to pull them, and they are used only during the period of ice, and each person has his own. One sits in one of these sanos along with as many blankets as desired and controls the horse, which goes along at a fast pace."

As the primary means of transportation in Europe, the horse led to the establishment of way stations and relay stations. In 1516, Sigmund von Herberstein, diplomat in the service of Maximilian I, using a Hungarian carriage with good horses, was able to make the journey from Vienna to Buda in just a few hours because of the opportunity to change horses at regular intervals. There were, in fact, five post stations, one of which performed services analogous to those of a modern gas station: the horses' shoes and harnesses were checked, and repairs were made to the carriage. Extra horses were always indispensable: the Bohemian baron Lev z Rozmitalu, who traveled in Europe in 1465-67 in a party of forty-odd people, left home with 52 horses and a baggage train.

The Florentine goldsmith, sculptor, and autobiographer Benvenuto Cellini, certainly one of art and literature's most feisty characters, had much to say about way stations and their masters. In 1540, during his second trip to France, he noticed horses ready to be sent back to Siena that could be had for a modest fee provided the traveler dropped them off in that city. Cellini took one. After handing the horse over to the stablehand in Siena, Cellini realized he had left on the horse his stirrups and a saddle cushion. A quarrel arose later when the artist showed up to claim his belongings. The problem, Cellini explained, was the fault of the station master, "the most bestial man ever known in that city." In the end, the station master lay dead, struck by a ricochetting arquebus ball. Even as a traveler, Cellini was a turbulent fellow, and his age was one of violence.

29

The road

All traces of the road disappeared beneath the puddles and mud of spring and autumn rains. When the edges of what had once been the route were no longer visible, one steered by a distant belltower or other landmark. Snow too made travel arduous, but even during the height of summer no clouds of dust rose from the hard-packed roadways — none of the vehicles of the time moved fast enough to create such clouds, leaving only occasional gusts of wind to do so.

The roads melted into the landscape naturally and did not stand out in contrast as artificial creations. Although paving with cobblestones could be found on the streets of certain cities, elsewhere it existed only in short stretches or in the remains of Roman roads. Road maintenance consisted of little more than dumping wheelbarrowfuls of dirt into the larger holes or placing fascines — bundles of sticks — over the mud.

The advent of steam power and rails is often credited with the improvement in overland communication, but some historians have noted a deterioration of those modes until the arrival of the internal-combustion engine and asphalt. The development of improved roads and vehicles is thought to have always lagged behind general progress, never equal to the possibilities offered by new technical discoveries. Even so, people during the period of the passage from the Middle Ages to the modern age made use of advances made during the preceding three centuries to open roads, consolidate routes, and put up bridges. This flury of construction had led to the creation of a few saints, including St. Benedict, a young shepherd celebrated as creator as of the bridge over the Rhone at Avignon, and Dominic, a clergyman who is said to have paved the roads and built the bridges along the *camino frances* route to Santiago de Compostela.

Cities were knots in a net of roadways, and the mesh of routes always became thicker nearer urban centers, particularly in northern Italy, Flanders, and certain parts of France and Germany. The economies of cities, with their changing tides of merchandise, had specified routes according to preferred itineraries, creating a kind of standard map of the principal traffic routes. Even so, the impression emerges from the period that several varying routes were available for each itinerary. Even in far-off northeastern Europe, undoubtedly behind the rest of Europe, there were alternatives: traveling from Vilna in Lithuania to Moscow, Sigmund von Herberstein could choose to avoid the "public road, so well traveled." In truth, there were two recognized routes — the first across Livonia, the second by way of Smolensk — but the German chose yet a third, between the two. Recurrent wars took place along one or the other of the two major routes. In 1537, Benvenuto Cellini, on his way to his first meeting with France's Francis I, found he could not take the usual route through Piedmont and over the Alps because of a war. Instead, he went from Padua along the Via Grigo-

Pollarded trees along a dike, reed fencing, a large house surrounded by an encircling wall, other houses and outbuildings arranged in a line; along the double curve of the road a man passes on horseback. This is a detail from the Nativity *by the Master of Flémalle, perhaps Robert Campin, a painter from Tournai, so the landscape may be that of Hainault (Belgium).*

The building of bridges had begun two or three centuries earlier. Many small- or medium-sized rivers could be forded; for the larger ones it was necessary to depend on ferrymen. Below: A small masonry bridge, from the Epiphany Triptych *by Hieronymus Bosch. Opposite: A little wooden bridge, detail from the* Triptych of Women *by Hans Memling.*

ni, which took him to the Albula and the Bernina where, around the eighth of May, he encountered a great deal of snow before reaching "a lake that is between Valdistate and Vessa [Wallenstadt in the canton of San Gallen and Wesen on Lake Wallen].

"The freezing cold had made the slopes of the mountains so slippery that descending seemed impossible." This is a report from the year 1077; the German king Henry IV (later Holy Roman emperor) was crossing the Alps by way of Mont Cenis in the dead of winter on his way to seek absolution by Pope Gregory VII (the pope had excommunicated and deposed him, but Henry met the pope at Canossa in Emilia-Romagna and won him over with humiliation and penitence — for three days he stood barefoot in the snow before being admitted to the pope's presence). To get down the mountain the emperor and his entourage slid along on their hands and knees, sometimes finding footholds on the shoulders of those beneath them, and when they lost their footing they tumbled down a long way into the valley.

Conditions improved during the four centuries following the emperor's

difficult journey. Lords and landowners along the Alpine slopes had found it profitable to invest in improving the mountain passes, leveling, reinforcing, and enlarging them. Most of all, they invested the labor of their subjects; the profits came from the tolls they charged. The people living in the valleys had discovered they could earn money from the wayfarers by serving as guides and bearers and by transporting, renting, and leading pack animals over the passes. Even so, although the passes had been crossed and recrossed many times, a journey through the mountains was still a matter for much dismay. Clouds surrounded the peaks in the spring, and the traveler's fears included both concern for the risks and hardships soon to be faced and also instinctive, anguished superstition involving — in the words of the *Chanson de Roland* — those "high mountains, gloomy valleys, dark crags, and sinister abysses."

Crossing a body of water presented the roadway traveler with another critical moment. Many bridges had been built during the preceding two or three centuries, and many Roman bridges remained and had been restored. Various feats of stone engineering existed, including the "devil's bridges," so-called because of the incredulous stupor inspired by their unexpected technical prowess. Others, constructed in wood, were intensely picturesque (even so, the Kapellbrucke of Lucerne, built in 1333, was most of all a military defense made to protect the city on its side facing the lake).

In most cases, however, crossing rivers, brooks, and flood waters required finding either a ford — when and where possible — or a ferry. With no permanent bridges over the Rhine between Basel and Rotterdam, the

---

The passes over the Alps

Brenner, *1,370 m, between Trent and Innsbruck. Used in prehistoric times to transport amber from the Baltic, it regained importance as a mercantile pass beginning in the 13th century.*
Great St. Bernard, *2,467 m, between Aosta, Martigny (Vallese), and Geneva. The hospice was founded in the 11th century.*
Mont Cenis, *2,083 m, between Susa and Savoy. The hospice dates back to the times of Ludovic the Pious (815). On the Italian side, travelers rested at Novalesa.*

Col de Genevre, *1,854 m, between the valleys of the Dora Riparia (Po) and Durance (Rhone). This is the pass by which Charles VIII (1494) entered Italy from France.*
St. Gotthard, *2,114 m, between Bellinzona and Lucerne. The hospice dates from 1171 and was founded by the archbishop of Milan Galdino. The pass became a basic commercial route beginning the 13th century.*
Simplon, *2,009 m, between Domodossola and Briga (Vallese). This pass gained importance during the 13th century with the travel of merchants from Milan.*

This singular Flemish miniature gives an accurate depiction of the preoccupation of public authorities with establishing adequate lines of communication. Two laborers work to complete the pavement of a road surface over a bridge using facing-hammers, while farther on woodcutters fell forest trees to open a path for the road that will connect two cities.

ferrymen operating in that area enjoyed a monopoly and liberally hiked their fees, sometimes as a form of blackmail, whenever the river was in flood and presented increased risk. An adventurous moment of another kind is described by the Venetian Ambrogio Contarini, here speaking of a crossing of the Dnieper: "The Tartars began chopping wood and tying the pieces together; they then put branches on top and over all this they put our belongings. The Tartars then went into the river, holding onto the necks of their horses, and we tied cords from the tails of the horses to the wooden structures and then climbed onto them ourselves and drove our horses out into the river, which we all crossed safely, with the help of God."

Surviving texts offer glimpses of what overland travel was like at the time, sometimes dramatic, sometimes idyllic: riding by horse across the wide fields of Lombardy spread with the warm light of dawn, or over Burgundy's rolling hills, the humid greenness of Germany with its horizons of dark woods, the yellow of summer, the high wide sky of Castile with the road shared by flocks of sheep. We can imagine these moments, but we cannot

35

Meetings along the road. Woodcut from the Buch der
Weisheit der Alten Weisen, *Ulm, 1483, translation of a
collection of apologues on moral training for the use of
princes, the work of a Brahman sage from Kashmir, the
minister of an Indian dynasty of the third century B.C.*

establish the size of the traffic.

Two and a half centuries before the
end of the Middle Ages rules for prece-
dence on roadways had already become necessary: the *Speculum* of Saxony, a celebrated text of consuetudi-
nary law, established that an empty
cart must give way to a loaded cart, a
horseman must give way to a cart, a
pedestrian give way to a horseman,
but a cart, empty or full, had to stop
and allow to pass anyone who, on
horse or on foot, was being chased.

This last detail offers a view of the
perils to life, limb, and precious possessions then habitually faced by travelers. In Germany, travelers paid a
heavy tax for an escort: Dürer noted
the amount he paid in the list of his
expenses for a trip in the Low Countries. Other travelers chose to rely on
their own weapons or courage. Whether to travel armed or unarmed was a
difficult choice: to be unarmed was to
be defenseless before the brigands operating the roadways; to travel armed

aroused the suspicions of local authorities. Knowing his personality, it
is not surprising that Benvenuto Cellini
put his faith in traveling armed. "It
was a pleasant trip," he wrote of one
journey, "except that when we got to
Palissa [La Palice], a gang of bandits
tried to kill us, and it took more than
a little skill to save ourselves."

Other unpleasant incidents arose
when travelers exhibited lack of respect
for the "culture" of the host country.
The Bohemian baron Lev z Rozmitalu
and his party passed some dangerous
moments when a crowd, some four
hundred strong, surrounded the inn in
which they were staying. The foreigners defended themselves with crossbow
shots and were eventually rescued by
the arrival of gentlemen sent to save
them by the king himself. The problems had begun when one of the Bohemian knights took the liberty of
caressing a young girl's breasts and
then threw out of the inn a Spaniard
who had protested this behavior.

There were also the anxieties
brought on by imagination. A middle-
class man of Augsburg, traveling
through unknown forests in Hungary,
found himself riding behind two horsemen who then suddenly vanished. In
the deeping shadows of the evening a
distant castle seemed to loom sinister-
ly; then the trail seemed to fill with
snorting, threatening boar. Actually,
these were all products of the traveler's
imagination, and they disappeared
when he made the sign of the cross and
said a prayer. Even so, the man wrote
about this episode in his autobiography.

Rivers

Benvenuto Cellini and his party and horses had to cross Lake Walen, which is "fifteen miles in length," by boat, and they were afraid because "those boats were made of fir, were not very large or strong, were not nailed, and were without pitch." Notwithstanding a furious storm that forced them to make an emergency landing, no one drowned.

When one examines the methods of travel in Europe between the end of the 15th and beginning of the 16th centuries it is difficult to fully comprehend the tight integration between roadways and navigation along internal waters. Lakes and rivers were natural extensions of roads, and vice versa. Traveling from Nuremberg to Antwerp in the summer of 1520, Dürer embarked on the Main at Frankfurt and on the sixth day disembarked at the port of Cologne on the Rhine. The change from horse or cart to boat, barge, or raft took place with a remarkable frequency.

From a general, historical point of view, it seems that the costs and difficulties of moving people and merchandise were greater by land than by sea. The advantages of traveling by water would have applied as well on internal waterways had not those who owned the passage rights — whether lords or city authorities — found the temptation to levy tolls irresistible. In some places these charges reached the level of rendering such travel unacceptable. Even along that wonderful means of traffic that was the Rhine, and across the plains of northern Italy, where the Po had given life to commerce since the distant Middle Ages, many merchants preferred to travel by

---

Navigation by river

Several European rivers are listed below, along with their length and brief notes on their importance as navigation routes at the end of the 15th century.
Arno, *245 km: handled a portion of the traffic between Pisa and Florence.*
Danube, *2,900 km: potentially navigable from Germany to the Black Sea, its traffic was mainly local.*
Elbe, *1,112 km: a large waterway in use from Bohemia to as far as the North Sea.*
Loire, *1,000 km: a waterway running from central France to the Atlantic.*
Po, *672 km: saw a certain amount of traffic from Pavia to the Adriatic coast.*
Guadalquivir, *680 km: primarily made*
Seville an ocean port.
Rhine, *1,250 km: the most important European river, heavily traveled from Basel to the sea.*
Rhone, *775 km: from Lyon downstream, was joined by traffic from the Saône.*
Seine, *776 km: used by traffic within Paris and its surrounding region and for access to the Channel.*
Tagus, *1,008 km: navigable at least along its lower third; using the Atlantic tides it was possible to travel upstream as far as Santarem.*
Thames, *323 km: navigated from the sea to London and beyond.*
Vistula *1,100 km: the outlet to the Baltic for Polish corn, but, because of ice, was navigable only for a few months per year.*

road to avoid paying the tolls charged by everyone who had managed to string a chain from one bank of the river to the other. Dürer was not a poor man, particularly during the time of his trip to Flanders, but he watched his expenses carefully and asked the bishop of Bamberg for papers to exempt him from tolls: the charge for these documents was a florin in bureaucratic fees and a few of his works, with which Dürer, a popular artist, managed to ingratiate himself with the prince-bishop. The letters of exemption and the bishop's letters of recommendation helped him avoid 26 tolls by land between Bamberg and Frankfurt and 10 by water from Frankfurt to Cologne. In some cases he could not avoid paying, and in one instance the tolltaker, delighted to meet a celebrity, offered him a beer. Not all travelers were popular personalities like the Nuremberg painter, and his account provides a vivid sense of how frequently the traveler had to reach into his purse.

The great age of travel by navigable canal, in England, France, and Germany (where, however, navigation was slowed by locks), came later and was the result of a vast amount of work: an immense system eventually united the Bay of Biscay with the Gulf of Lyon, the Mediterranean with the North Sea, the North Sea with the plains of central Europe, and, by way of the Danube, with the Black Sea. Meanwhile, however, as early as the 14th century, there was a canal between the North Sea and the Baltic that permitted many kinds of craft to avoid the circumnavigation of the Danish peninsula. Aside from this, a great many riverways were navigable: the Loire and the Rhone, the Danube, and the Rhine, which, with its tributaries, united Switzerland, northern France, western Germany, and the Low Countries in a vast communications system. Aside from ships, boats, and barges of every type, the Rhine was also used to float timber. Great rafts made of tree trunks descended on the current, carrying merchandise and passengers. At the river's estuary, the wood was unloaded and sent to sawmills, and the sailors began a slow overland return to get another load.

There was also the Guadalquivir, which could be ascended up to Seville and Córdoba, the Ebro with traffic moving from the sea to Tortosa, the Adige, the Po and its tributaries the Adda, Oglio, and Mincio, and lakes Garda and Como connected by them, the Ticino and Lake Maggiore, which in those years was joined to Milan with the system of the Naviglio Grande and the Naviglio Pavese. Enormous rafts of timber with a wooden hut for the sailors descended the rivers of eastern Europe from beyond the Oder, in Poland, and in Lithuania (which at this time extended into the heart of Russia): farther to the east flowed the immense rivers of Russia, a land in which every geographical feature — rivers, forests, plains, empty space — takes on unusual and different size.

Traveling with a river's current made for a speedy journey: the distance

from Lyons to Avignon could be covered in two to five days, sometimes only in twenty-four hours. Traveling down the Po and the Rhine the average distance covered in a day has been estimated at between 100 and 150 kilometers. Unlike the rafts made of trunks, not all the craft were disassembled at the end of the journey, and going against the current required the spreading of sails, the use of oars, or poles pushed against the river bottom. Most craft were simply hauled back up a river, pulled by horses or oxen moving along parallel towpaths. This system allowed for fifteen or twenty kilometers a day; the same barge that had made it from Lyons to Avignon in 24 hours might spend a month on the return trip.

These scraps of information on traveling speeds by river must be taken as general indications. When considering average speeds one must also take into account the caprices of nature: the flood tides and lows of rivers, the winter freeezing in certain areas of Europe that interrupted navigation, as well as such dangerous obstacles as wrecks or sandbars. Finally, one must compare these speeds to the velocity of travel by land.

Thus we return to the horse's pace, which is calculated at a speed of 30 to 50 kilometers a day for the "average traveler," a difficult person to identify. More concrete examples serve here: the journey from Chur to Bellinzona by way of the St. Bernard Pass, one of the most frequently used Alpine crossings and a distance of 80 kilometers

measured by a compass span, took four to six days. However, using the costly system of fast couriers changing horses at frequent way stations a message could travel from Nuremberg to Venice in four days. Other such quick trips include twelve days from Rome to Paris, three from Rome to Venice, and seven from Venice to Turin. These are record speeds from an age that was not enthralled with speed. It was not uncommon during those days to let messages pile up to diminish the high cost of these fast couriers. Here, then, is a normal trip in the daily reality: in 1483, Bernhard von Breydenbach, a canon of Mainz, traveled to Venice to embark for the Holy Land. Traveling by way of Speyer, Ulm, Innsbruck, Vipiteno, Brunico, Cortina d'Ampezzo, Conegliano, and Treviso, his trip took fifteen days, a distance of 750 kilometers, with an average speed of 55 kilometers per day. The canon was a speedy traveler.

Ships

In May 1458 a Venetian galley on its way to the Holy Land found itself off the coast of Sebenico in the Adriatic Sea. On board were the Paduan knight Gabriele Capodilista and a large group of pilgrims. The wind was from the stern, all the galley's large lateen sails were unfurled. As Capodilista wrote, "We were traveling at seven or eight miles an hour." This was the most favorable wind they had yet encountered on their journey, and both the pilgrims and the sailors were happy. "In their joy, they climbed up along the mast, one upon another, each holding his arms outstretched and standing on the shoulders of the one beneath." This little show put on for the passengers (and probably rewarded with appreciative tips) was similar to those so-called Herculean feats performed in Venice's St. Mark's Square during festivals.

One frequently encounters the opinion that travel by sea was faster and more comfortable than travel by land, but such statements must not be taken too literally. Capodilista was remembering a rather luxurious pilgrimage: even the most optimistic accounts of life aboard ship are rife with tales of terrifying moments, and the speed of ships was all a matter of luck. Ships of the period reached a speed of three to five knots with a light breeze, more than nine with a strong and favorable wind (the knot is a marine mile per hour, so the three figures correspond to speeds of 5.5 km per hour, 9.2, and about 17). Ships usually traveled twenty-four hours a day: on one occasion Columbus made 182 marine miles (about 349 km) in one day. But such speed is not to be taken as a rule.

For example, Charles of Ghent (better known as Charles V, the title he

Travel by sea was more rapid and comfortable than that by land. So it was thought, in spite of the well-known risks involved. Below: Miniature showing the loading operations of a ship from Pisa. Opposite: A port, detail from the predella of the Madonna of the Pergola *by Giovanni Boccati (1447).*

later assumed), on his way to Spain to be crowned king of Castile and Aragon, had an altogether different experience. On July 4, 1517, he was at Middleburg in the Low Countries, awaiting the fleet. Although this was during the summer, the most favorable season for navigation, he was able to leave only during the second week of September, having been held up by unfavorable winds. The ships then encountered bad weather and were unable to make the planned landing at Santander, coming ashore instead on a stretch of inhospitable land along the Asturian coast. From there, Charles and his followers, a few hundred women and gentlemen, started on their way to Spain on mules, horses, and carts drawn by oxen. When Charles finally arrived at Tordesillas and greeted his mother, it was November.

The Mediterranean is more benign than the Atlantic, but Francesco Janis, an Italian from the northern city of Tolmezzo, on a journey from Naples to Spain in a ship out of Biscay at the beginning of April 1519, found himself held nine days in the town of Pozzuoli (directly above Naples) because of contrary winds. He found it an emotional experience and included the inevitable reference to local women: "There is a castle on that island where there are few inhabitants, but many beautiful women, who were amazed at the arrival of the ship."

The ships used during the period can be divided into two categories: round ships and long ships, each tied to a different nautical tradition. The long ship was used in the Mediterranean, the round ship in the Atlantic and northern Europe. The round ship was high, wide, used only sails, and required only a small number of crew-members: although no one then knew it, the future of modern ships was to proceed from its design. The long ship was thin and low, filled almost entirely by banks of rowers; it required a large crew, but was fast. The long ship used sails whenever possible. The two nautical traditions had been in contact for a long time, and round ships navigated the Mediterranean and Mediterranean galleys regularly passed through Gibraltar into the Atlantic.

Below: Detail from the Gallery of Geographical Maps painted by Antonio Danti (1580-83), in the Vatican. Opposite: A round-bottomed boat before a city (from the Chronica mundi*). Following pages: The* Contarina, *a galley that carried pilgrims from Venice to the Holy Land; its owner was Agostino Contarini (from the manuscript of the* Pilgerreise von Costanz nach Jerusalem *by Konrad Grünemberg, 1486).*

Much traveling was done by ship in Europe — in the Mediterranean, in the Baltic, along the Atlantic coasts (aside from the communications between England and the Continent) — but there was then nothing that could have been termed a regular passenger service, except for the galleys that made annual trips carrying pilgrims from Venice to the Holy Land. Indeed, most of the surviving information relates to this voyage.

Without doubt, traveling in a galley full of pilgrims was far more uncomfortable than traveling by merchant galley — such as along the regular routes followed by Venetian merchant ships — or by roundship. Aboard a galley en route to the Holy Land with a full load of pilgrims, the traveler was in a confined space crowded with people, most of whom were unfamiliar with sea travel. For the majority of these pilgrims, their first experience of ships came when they stepped aboard the creaking, swaying deck of the galley tied up at Venice's wharf in front of the ducal palace.

According to the Milanese Santo Brasco, who made the trip to the Holy Land in 1480, the pilgrim needed to bring along "two purses, one chock full of patience, the other with two hundred Venetian ducats," along with "plenty of shirts so as to avoid as far as possible the fleas and other unpleasantries." Another pilgrim advised that on boarding a ship one should immediately become fast friends with the captain in order to obtain quarters on the deck rather than beneath it, where the heat and stench canceled all hope of air.

The Dominican Felix Faber of Ulma, one of the few to repeat the voyage to the Holy Land (1480 and 1483), complained that too many people came without changes of clothes, thus leading to noxious odors and infestations of parasites in clothes, beards, and hair. The pilgrim, Faber advised, should feel no shame when asking a traveling companion to aid in delousing his beard. The ship's sanitary facilities presented far the worst aspect of the voyage, for in a galley these were located up against the bow and were thus regularly submerged beneath rolling waves during rough weather; since making a visit to the lavatory often involved the risk of exiting completely soaked, many travelers stripped and

Vetlicher etwas besunders sehen Als das die frowen vnd Junkfrown des gewar
lachten vnd wie wol es yetzund mittag was war doch keiner zum essen der
herberg gedenken Vetlicher sast besunders gesessen haben ich ward da zu
worten bracht den haff ze Jancgestor des kings Artus müsen wichn
von schäme vnd test der frowen vnd Junkfrown

Item hernach stond die ämpter vnd gewon
haiten des schiffs/ vnd die namen aller segel
vnd anders des man sich gebrucht uf
der galleigen

Vnser galleie

went to the lavatory nude. Even in the best of circumstances, one had to wait in line, and these lines reminded brother Faber of those in front of confessionals at Lent when the people standing and waiting their turn became indignant at the lengthy confessions of those ahead of them.

Greater space was the primary advantage offered by a round ship. The chance passenger aboard such a ship enjoyed special treatment by the officers. Letters written in 1573 by the Spaniard Eugenio de Salazar offer a sense of life aboard such a ship: the cabin boy announced the midday meal with a singsong verse that began *"Tabla, tabla, senor capitan y maestra y buena compana"* ("To table, to table, captain, officers, and good company"), went on to extol the virtues of the king of Castile, and concluded with *"Tabla en buena hora, quien no viniere que no coma"* ("To table as soon as possible, who does not come does not eat"). A young sailor placed on the table a large wooden bowl heaped with salted meat, and each diner grabbed his portion and ate, cutting the meat off the bones with his own personal knife.

By this time, sea travel was undertaken almost throughout the year. In the North Sea, navigation was usually suspended after St. Martin's Day (November 11) and began again at the end of January. In the Mediterranean, the period of suspension had changed: during Roman times ships remained in port from October to April; until the end of the 13th century the period ran from St. Andrew's Day (November 30) to the first of March; then it was shortened to from the end of November until January 20. However, lengthening the season of navigation involved increased risks, even in the Mediterranean, which does not always display the gentle characteristics it shows on summertime beaches. A storm that blew a squadron of Spanish galleys out of the Gulf of Lions (some finished along the coasts of Sardinia, one at the island of Pantelleria, another at Agrigento in Sicily, and others sank) occurred between April 19 and 22. One can thus understand what the 16th-century Italian admiral and statesman Andrea Doria meant by his saying, "There are three ports in the Mediterranean: Cartagena, June, and July."

Aboard ship, one was in the hands of sailors before arriving in God's, and sailors, according to Cervantes (in his *Novelas ejemplares*), "are pagans, discourteous, they know no language but that used aboard ship; although diligent in calm weather, they become lazy during storms, and many command but few obey." During storms the sea had always taken its victims; in good weather, on the other hand, sailing could be a wonderful experience, the ship moving quietly forward on a clear summer night, pushed by warm winds under the glow of the moon, the shadow of the sails spread across the tranquil water. And then there were the glorious dawns, with schools of leaping dolphins, and the sails full of an evening breeze as the ship moved toward sunset.

*Opposite: Etching showing people embarking on a ship, an
illustration for* Filocolo *by Giovanni Boccaccio, Naples, 1478.
At Sandwich, in England, Schaseck, one of the companions of
Baron Lev z Rozmitalu, expressed a landsman's amazement at
the mysterious art of navigation: the mariners could predict
the force and direction of the wind, and announce beforehand
which sail to hoist.*

Speeds: possible and improbable

On foot

*Walking at a steady pace it is possible to cover four kilometers
per hour, or slightly more. Walking for ten hours a day, in theory
a traveler could cover 40-45 kilometers, and a journey from
Geneva to Constanz would take eight or nine days on foot.
However, traveling at this speed as a pedestrian, it would be
necessary to walk steadily without days of rest, to go faster on flat
terrain to compensate for slower speed when climbing, hours
could not be lost ferrying accross rivers, and the weather would
always have to be favorable. An average of about 25 kilometers
per day on long journeys is a more reasonable estimate, although
there have been cases of higher speeds.*

On horseback

*At a gallop, a horseman can reach speeds of 25 kilometers per
hour. This is not a particularly reliable figure. It has, in fact, been
known for letters carried by couriers on horseback to travel from
Rome to Venice in one and a half days (a daily distance of 350
km), from Paris in seven, and from Barcelona in eight; but on
these same routes travel times of 9, 34, and 77 days, respectively,
have also been recorded. The normal traveler did not race and
was often forced to keep to the slower pace of the animals
carrying his baggage. Average travel times by horseback are
between 30 and 50 kilometers per day, perhaps as many as 80 on
those stretches permitting regular changes of horse.*

By ship

*On a river flowing downstream a traveler could depend on
covering 100 or even 150 kilometers per day, which would be the
equivalent of traveling from Basel to Cologne in four days. It was
not considered worthwhile to use rivers to travel upstream, with
some exceptions, as, for instance, on the Loire, where it was
possible to make use of ocean breezes. On the sea, on average, a
galley under sail would make 6 knots, a round-bellied boat 4 or 5
knots: over a period of twenty-four hours these ships would travel
260, 170, and 215 kilometers, respectively. However, it was not
always possible to count on constant and favorable winds.*

Inns

In 1496, Johann Burckard, master of ceremonies of the papal chapel, was traveling in northern Lombardy, on his way to a meeting with Maximilian of Hapsburg. He arrived at the town of Carimate around two in the morning, not an opportune hour, he felt, for a royal audience. Unable to find lodgings in that town, he and his party were forced to return the way they had come, traveling about a mile and a half to the small town of Lentate, where they finally found some available beds.

Then as now, late arrivals were not welcome at inns. The hero of the Spanish novel *Guzman de Alfarache*, by Mateo Alemán, puts it quite clearly: "The stranger who arrives with the sun is always the best received and finds something to put in his stomach and a bed on which to lay down."

The inns of the time bore such names as The Crown, The Lion, The Eagle, The Three Columns, The Angel (the traveling master of ceremonies Burckard stayed in an inn of this name in Rimini, on the Adriatic coast), The Moon, The Bell (Burckard encountered two by this name, one in Emilia and one at Monza in Lombardy; there was a celebrated inn of this name in Rome), The Wheel, The Ram (Ariosto immortalized an inn of this name in the square of the Pantheon at Rome in his *Satires*: "In wet and ugly rain, that night I went all the way to The Ram for dinner"). In 1473, an English traveler wrote about an inn known as The Well near Milan's Porta Ticinese; it was still there in 1789,

when another Englishman, the writer on agricultural subjects Arthur Young, visited it. A Milanese traveling merchant recorded the existence of a famous hostelry in Bordeaux known as The Red Cap; it had two stalls, each large enough to hold one hundred horses. Reports of travelers in Spain make frequent mention of *ventas*: there was a *venta* at Alcalde, one at Trabuque, one at Rio. The Milanese merchant explained (1517-19) that a *venta* was like a Lombardy farmhouse, but it had only a fireplace, with neither beds nor straw for sleeping, just a large bench on which one slept fully clothed. The merchant had little to say, however, concerning "a hostelry in the mountains" in Navarre, on the Roncesvalles road.

The names Three Kings, Three Crowns, At the Star, and The Moor — names frequently encountered along the Rhine — are sometimes said to refer in some way to the reliquaries of the Three Magi, which Rainald of Dassel, bishop of Cologne and companion of Barbarossa, took from Milan's Church of Sant'Eustorgio and brought to his city, but this is doubtful, for the names show up everywhere. Even so, such names may well allude to the Three Wise Men in the sense that they were travelers, in a sense early patron saints of those who take to the road. (The patron saint of hostelers was a certain Theodosius, host and martyr.) No doubt exists, however, concerning the name At the Elephant (an inn of that name can still be found in the northern Italian city of Bres-

After a long day's travel on unfamiliar roads, one looked forward to arriving, toward sundown, at a town or village in which a good inn could be found. Speeds were modest, and the stages could not be very long: the cardinal of Aragon, for instance, spent eight nights on the road from Ferrara to Innsbruck. Below: A detail from The Seven Joys of Mary, *a painting by Hans Memling, 1480.*

sanone), which refers to a very real
elephant, gift of Portugal's John III to
his nephew Maximilian of Hapsburg
(later Maximilian II). Maximilian
brought the elephant with him to Vienna from Portugal by way of the Alps
in 1551.

Many inns and pubs (from "public
house") in England claim the honor of
being the oldest. Among the many

that may deserve the honor is the
Saracen's Head in Southwell, the title
deeds of which date back to 1356: it is
said to have been named by crusaders
returning from the Holy Land.

An inn's name usually appeared on
a sign hanging over the entrance, but
the more humble establishments, particularly taverns, announced their presence by simply hanging a leafy branch

or grapevine over the doorway.

Inns varied greatly, but the basic form can be outlined: a building of two or three floors with a large dining room (with separate tables or long, communal ones) used also for drinking and carrying on conversations, a kitchen on the first floor, bedrooms arranged on the second (corridors to separate the rooms did not exist everywhere), a courtyard large enough to handle coaches and carts, stalls for horses and mules. An inn might also serve as a way or post station. A Spanish ordinance of the late 15th century established the minimal furnishings of a hotel, including the kitchen utensils, tablecloths, and crockery. In 1580, Montaigne was astonished to find himself being served from silver plates at the Couronne in Chalons-sur-Marne. Evidently levels of hospitality already spanned a wide gamut.

The literature of the period helps recreate the atmosphere of these inns: tales, chivalrous poems, and a crowd of picturesque personages come together in the inn. Such works offer much insight into the reality of inns. For example, in one of Cervantes's *Novelas ejemplares*, "The Illustrious Dishwasher," the inn of the Sevillian is described as "one of the finest and most popular of Toledo." Like La Couronne it had a good deal of engraved silverware, but it had no pantry, and the kitchen cooked only those foods the guests brought along themselves. One of the host's reliable employees stood in the courtyard and distributed straw and oats to the stableboys of the guests for their mounts (and he tried to cheat the stableboys, as they did him). Another employee had the chore of maintaining a vast supply of water from a nearby river: this was a kind of promotional expense, for all the mule-drivers knew they could water their animals there rather than take them down to the Tagus River, and thus tried to convince their clients to stay at The Sevillian. The inn also had rooms — "fit neither for kings nor for servants, but for

those who fall into the middle area between those extremes." Within earshot of the arriving guest the host would direct in a loud voice one of the maids to put clean sheets on the beds. The two maids, from Galicia, gazed with open lust at the handsome young guests, and the serving girls and mule-drivers danced in the evening to tunes improvised on a guitar by a youth.

The Sevillian was located in Toledo; but then, Germans set up hotels in Venice (in one Venetian hotel even the guard dog was German, or at least knew them by scent and greeted them with glee). Within the writings of Enea Silvio Piccolomini (later Pope Pius II) one encounters the interesting phrase "Germans make hotels; these people make almost all of Italy hospitable." Perhaps before being the "Swiss art,"

that of the hotelier was German.

Traveling from country to country, the traveler encountered, even in inns, different local customs. There was, for example, the subject of beds. Montaigne wrote that a German would get sick if forced to sleep on a mattress, an Italian on feathers, and a Frenchman without bed drapes and a fire. Erasmus evokes the warm greeting encountered in a Stube, a room with a glowing fireplace found in Alps: here "you take off your boots and put on slippers, change your shirt if you wish; you hang your clothes, wet from the rain, near the fire and then draw yourself close to dry."

Don Antonio de Beatis, canon of Molfetta, accompanied the Neapolitan cardinal Luigi d'Aragon on a tour of Europe (1517-18) and wrote about it in a diary. Comparing German hotels to those of France, he claimed that the Germans made extensive use of feathers because Germany was full of geese. German beds were thus large and without fleas or bed bugs, but the Germans had the unfortunate habit of cramming into a room as many beds as would fit. Don Antonio found the rooms in French inns more to his liking, with a large bed for the guest and alongside it a smaller one for a servant, both made stuffed with feathers. And, the canon added, "there was always a good fire."

In the absence of bathrooms with running water, guests resorted to other methods: "In Magna [Germany], there are one or two tin vases in each bed into which one can piss, in Flanders

these are made of clean brass, but in France, having nowhere else, one must piss into the fire, and that is what they do all night long and all day, and the greater the gentleman or master, the more pleasure he takes in doing so openly." In England — according to Schasek, a Bohemian knight who accompanied Lev z Rozmitalu on his voyage and wrote a diary about it — when a stranger arrives at an inn the host greets him with a big kiss; to the English, claimed Schasek, offering a kiss was like extending the right hand, and the English did not shake hands. A German saying held that "Hosts love guests who drink their fill without making too much noise." Of course, guides with special symbols indicating particularly tranquil spots did not yet exist (although all the world was then much quieter).

Presumably unavoidable due to human nature, innkeepers were not all honest. During his early, innocent experiences of the world, Guzman de Alfarache encountered two such, one right after the other; the second says of the first, a woman, "They've given her a hundred lashes and even taken away her license; I don't understand how she stays open without them going back after her." Thus said, the host does his best to cheat the innocent traveler. The diary of the traveling Milanese merchant (1517-19) recounts a far graver incident: two months before his trip to Toulouse an innkeeper, together with an officer of the law and their fifty-odd accomplices, had been executed for murder. The host had regularly put his wealthier guests together in a particular room; at the right moment, the thieves would enter the room and rob the guests. This had gone on for four years, with about one hundred victims, stones tied to their necks, dumped into the Garonne.

But what could an innkeeper do with a guest like Benvenuto Cellini? Traveling from Venice to Florence in 1535 he stopped at an inn between Chioggia and Ferrara. The innkeeper's insistence on advance payment for the room infuriated the proud artist. "We had very good beds, and everything was new and clean," recorded Cellini, but even so he wanted revenge. After setting off the next day, he stole his way back into the inn and carefully cut up the beds, causing damage of more than fifty scudi. Oh, St. Theodosius!

Money

According to their regulations, the tanners of Paris were supposed to work from dawn until the evening darkness made it impossible to distinguish a livre of Tours from one of Paris. In effect, there was the livre from Tours (*livre tournois*) and the livre from Paris (*livre parisis*); they had different values and were abstractions, a system of reference, and the coins actually in circulation were various submultiples.

Money was, in fact, a realm in disorder. Most of the citizens of western Europe were clear on one thing: a pound (*livre* in France, *lira* in Italian) was worth twenty soldi, a soldo was worth twelve pence (hence a pound was worth 240 pence), but no one had ever seen a pound, much less a soldo. This confusion dates back to the reign of Charlemagne. The great Frankish ruler perfected and spread in the Longobard kingdom the monetary system that his father had begun in the French kingdom, and this reform movement was also adopted on the other side of the English Channel. In brief, this reform established a silver monometallic system and created a new coin, the denier. Workers in the mint took a pound of silver (about 410 grams) and made it into 240 deniers — small coins of 1.76 grams of silver at 950 thousandths.

No provisions were made for multiples of deniers — which, besides, would have been impractical — and people got used to thinking in terms of pounds when the sum in question involved a great many deniers. It was easier to say eight pounds and 31 deniers than 951 deniers. The pound thus worked as a counting measure.

The monometallic regime lasted more than five hundred years, and during the period of Charlemagne, the "monetary area" of the silver denier coexisted with two monetary areas based on gold coins, that of the Islamic empire and that of Constantinople. The Byzantine realm, heir to the Romans, used the gold soldo (solidus), the value of which was established at twelve deniers. Thus, instead of 1,951 deniers, or eight pounds and 31 deniers, one said eight pounds, two soldi, and seven deniers.

Things went along like this until the French Revolution. But around the end of the 15th century, the situation was actually more complicated than the pound-solidus-denier system. In the first place, other coins were circulating in Europe. In Germany, and in general throughout the Holy Roman Empire (with the exception of Italy), the mark had come into use, a mark being a unit of weight equal to eight ancient Roman ounces. The mark varied from place to place, however: that of Cologne, weighing about 234 grams, was the most authoritative. In Castile, the coin used was the maravedi, the name of which comes from the Almeravidi, the Islamic Berber dynasty that dominated Spain.

The second factor complicating Europe's money system was a bit more involved. The seven centuries that had passed since the Carolingian reform had seen much monetary change. Beginning around the end of the 10th century, the Carolingian denier began to decline, containing less and less silver. Since 240 deniers still made a pound, there were many different pounds, each corresponding to a different quantity of silver. For example, until the end of the 1400s, the tournois livre was equal to about 22 grams of fine silver; the Genoese pound came in at fewer than 13 grams; the Venetian 6.2 grams; the Florentine 5.7 grams. Italian pounds had declined more than the others.

Other factors contributed to the monetary problems. When international commerce had resumed with the end of the Dark Ages, the meager denier, made of poor silver, had revealed itself an awkward coin for international exchanges. The need was felt for a fatter coin, and in fact the Italian word *grosso* ("fat") shows up in the various names for this coin: German *Groschen*, for example. The first of these coins, the grosso of the doge Andrea Dandolo, also known as a matapan, was minted in Venice in 1194 and weighed 2.2 grams of an alloy of silver of 965 thousandths. Other similar coins gradually appeared. In France in 1266, Louis IX created the tournois. By that time another monetary movement had begun, also in Italy: the return to gold coins and thus the end of silver monometallism.

In 1252, both Genoa and Florence issued a golden coin weighing 3.5 grams: the genovino and the florin. At its birth, the florin was the exact equal of a Florentine lira composed of silver

Gold or silver in one's pocket

Since there was no paper money, money weighed quite a bit. At some point, a traveler could not avoid having several pieces of gold or silver in a pocket or purse. There were also coins made of base silver, an alloy of a little silver mixed with tin or lead, but this was the money of the poor, who did not travel. The best coins were minted with irregular borders (the dishonest trimmed off the edges), and the faces of such coins bore figures, symbols, coats of arms, and Latin mottoes. As is true today, there was doubtlessly confusion among coins of different lands and of different values, but the seriousness of those mistakes were far greater then because a single coin's buying power was much higher. The golden ducat of Callistus III (1455-58) bore on one side St. Peter with the key and St. Paul with the sword and on the other the coat of arms of the Borgias with their bull. The excelente de la Granada, a double ducat, had Ferdinand and Isabella face to face. On the silver teston of Louis XII of France (1480-1515) there was the profile of the king on one side and the other bore the shield with three fleur-de-lis and the crown (the name teston refers to the use of the head of a prince on a coin). The golden Georges noble of Henry VIII of England (1509-47) had St. George and the dragon on one side and a ship on the other. The silver taller of Matteo Schiner, bishop of Sion and count of Vallese (1501), had a stern bishop with crook and sword kneeling at an altar, an angel on one side, the devil on the other.

Below: The minting of coins, a woodcut by Jost Amman for Hans Sachs' Ständebuch (1568). Opposite: One of the banking documents that saved the inconvenience and risk of traveling with cash; issued in Salzburg by Thomas Prantstetter of Landshut, it certifies a credit of 31 Rhenish florins, payable at the Market of Relics at Nuremberg. The date is March 22, 1443.

deniers, but the silver underwent continuous devaluation. In 1284, Venice released the gold ducat (later known as the zecchino), which was worth 576 Venetian deniers: in 1500 it was worth 5,280.

Once again, the monetary innovation spread. In 1325, golden florins were coined by the kings of Hungary and Bohemia. The Holy Roman emperor gave the right to mint the gold coins to the four elected princes of the Rhine (the bishops of Cologne, Mainz, and Trier, and the palatine elector), and in 1386 they released the florin of Rhine gold. In England, the minting of gold coins began with the florin, later replaced by the "ship's noble," the rosenoble, and, in 1489, by a coin twice the weight of the rosenoble: the sovereign. In France, the denier d'or of 1366 took the name of ecu, and in fact its obverse side showed a shield bearing a fleur-de-lis.

The exchange rate between gold and silver had long fluctuated, but from Roman times on it had tended to stay between 1:10 and 1:13. This relative stability collapsed around the end of the 16th century with the influx of large quantities of American silver. The entire history of medieval money was determined by the lack of precious metals, and the situation began to change during the last decades of the 15th century, just before the influence of American metals made itself felt. The Portuguese had reached sources of gold on the African coasts at Guinea (the Portuguese golden cruzado — from the cruz, or "cross," on its obverse

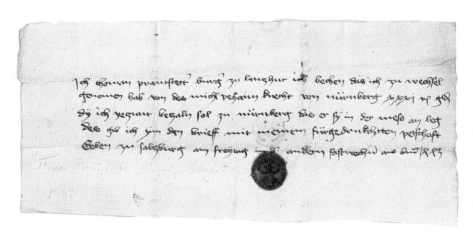

— was made of gold from Guinea and was first minted in 1457; a little later the English used the same gold in the creation of their famous guinea), and silver mines in Saxony, Bohemia, Salzburg, Tyrol, and Hungary began or augmented their production. Many of these new silver coins were minted in sizes larger than any seen before. One such coin was put in circulation by Sigismond of Hapsburg, duke of Austria, in 1484. With the value of a fiorino and made with silver from the mines of the Tyrol in the mint of Joachimstaler, it was called a Groschen, usually abbreviated taler or tallero. This coin, too, was soon followed by imitators (the taller of the Lower Countries during the period of Philip II, also known as a doalder, eventually led to the name dollar).

With such a complex system of coins and values, moneychangers with their scales clearly performed an essential service. In the end, the buying power and relative value among coins were related not to what might be stamped on them but to their actual weight after wear and "shearing" (the illegal scratching away of some of the precious metal, an operation simplified by the coins' irregular shapes). Precisely to prevent this scratching away of gold, the gold coins of Florence circulated in small leather bags sealed by the mint.

The traveler of the period had a method of avoiding some of the complications of the monetary system, the frequent need for moneychangers, and the risk of traveling with a bit too much cash: letters of credit. These could be acquired at a bank and then cashed for the indicated value in another country. Archives include documents relating to such transactions. One, dated June 8, 1474, indicates that a Milan branch office of the Medici bank paid the Fleming Paolo di Battista, a student at Pavia, two hundred ducats, which Stefan van der Gheyst, probably a relative, had previously paid in Antwerp to a representative of the Medici branch in Bruges.

The pleasures of the road

Art, dining, perhaps some pleasant amusement — a feast, carnival, parade, horse or pig race, miracle play, dance, sermon, or criminal execution — and women. Such were the pleasures. Mention of the latter introduces an inequality between the sexes that today seems more than a little unpleasant. But the past cannot be changed: in humanistic philosophy, all of the "human" is male; the Renaissance was a period of rebirth, but not for women. Most historians hold that women's condition got worse with the end of the Middle Ages.

Almost all this period's "travel memoirs" include recollections of emotions — purely masculine — excited by a woman or women. Poggio Bracciolini, the Italian humanist who searched out ancient texts in monasteries beyond the Alps, praised Swiss girls of marriageable age: they had, he claimed, the appearance and dress of goddesses. Don Antonio de Beatis, a canon from the Italian town of Molfetta — located on the Adriatic coast just above Bari — accompanied the Neapolitan cardinal Luigi d'Aragon on a tour of Europe in 1517 to 1518 and wrote about it in a diary, including detailed notes concerning the more striking aspects of the women in Germany, France, and Flanders. Back in his homeland — "beautiful, sweet, agreeable, suave, and sober Italy" — he was attracted only by the women of Genoa, who were tall, with shiny teeth and golden hair worn loose on their shoulders. They were, he claimed, the most graceful and beautiful of all Italy

(he noted beautiful women in Savona, but claimed those on the Riviera were all "very ugly"). Flemish women he found white and red, embodiments of vivacity; they used no rouge; their diet of butter and beer often spoiled their teeth, but when this did not happen, they were among the most beautiful. Frenchwomen were not the equal of the Flemings, but they danced well, displaying "an intelligence to sound." German women stood up respectfully when strangers passed, particularly if the stranger was of the upper class. Certain of his traveling companions revealed to him that the German women were "cold by nature but lascivious."

No one denied that there were also "working women," as they were defined by a diplomatic Milanese in 1492. During the first decades of the 15th century the prostitutes of Paris were put up in houses on the Ile de la Cité, causing King Charles VII, their neighbor, to complain. The whores of Venice were kept confined to the Rialto area until about 1498, at which time they spread throughout the city. The Venetian diarist Marin Sanudo provides a startlingly precise accounting of the city's prostitutes for the beginning of the 16th century: 11,654. A chronicler in Rome in 1490 gave that city 6,800, admitting that the number had reduced somewhat. According to the Milanese merchant who left an account of his trip to Spain, France, the Low Countries, and England in 1517 to 1519, there were few prostitutes in Bruges, but this lack was made up for by maids from local inns who worked at lower prices; in Valencia, on the other hand, an entire quarter of the city was given over to pleasure. No personal weapons were permitted in this quarter, and at night, the women — housed in 150 houses — placed three or four candles beside each doorway, thus creating a "glow that illuminates everything."

The golden age of courtesan literature was the late 16th century (for example, the works of the playwright Pietro Aretino), but as early as 1535 an Italian work was in circulation entitled *The Prices of Prostitutes, a dialogue between a foreigner and a gentleman in which are given the prices and qualities of all the courtesans of Venice along with the names of their pimps.* In his *Journal de voyage* (of a trip to Germany and Italy that took place in 1580 to 1581), Montaigne described a prostitute who, with "absolute lust," was in bed with a certain fellow but upon hearing bells toll the Ave Maria she leapt out of the bed and knelt on the floor in prayer.

Sin and faith; yet sin was then considered the fault only of women. Was it part and parcel of the feminine state? Displaying his habitual absence of emotion, the papal master of ceremonies Johannes Burckard described an incident that occurred in Rome in 1498: a courtesan and the transvestite Moor who lived with her were arrested and carried through the city "as a sign of their scandal," the Moor's dress pulled up over his belly. The woman was let go, the transvestite was strangled at the funeral pyre set up in Campo dei Fiori. The pyre was then set alight, but the flames were soon extinguished by rain.

There was also art. Rarely has our world seen generations of artists as creative as those who ended their work, reached maturity, or began their careers during the last decade of the 15th century: Leonardo da Vinci, Michelangelo, Bramante, Signorelli, Perugino, Botticelli, Giovanni Bellini, Hans Memling, Hieronymus Bosch, el Bermejo, Berruguete, Holbein the Elder, Dürer.

Throughout Europe great artists were busy, but the traveler could not see their works in museums, for there were none. Perhaps there was one: the Conservatori palace set up in Rome's Campidoglio, in which were stored the ancient pieces that Sixtus IV, in 1471, shortly after his election, had donated to the Roman people, thus beginning the age of public collections of art. Most of the collection was bronzes that had originally been atop columns in the pontifical Lateran palace or thereabouts: the Etruscan *She-Wolf* (without the twins Romulus and Remus, who were added in 1509); the highly praised *Spinario*, of which small bronze copies were then being made (one was made for Isabella d'Este) as well as one large copy, by Antonello Gagini, that stood in a fountain at Messina; the so-called *Camillus*, also referred to as the Gypsy; and the *Hercules*, dug up in those years in the Foro Boario. As for "modern" or contemporary art, the owners of such

works had usually commissioned and paid for them themselves and kept them at home. Botticelli's *Primavera* was in a room of the Castello villa, the residence of the cousins of Lorenzo the Magnificent; Giorgione's *Tempesta* (early 1500s) was in the Venetian palace of Gabriele Vendramin, for whom he probably painted it.

The period's interest in art is well known. Important monuments were in public places: the *Fonte Gaia* ("Fountain of Joy"), by the Sienese Jacopo della Quercia, was in the Piazza del Campo in Siena (replaced today by a copy); Donatello's equestrian statue of *Gattamelata* (the condottiere born Erasmo da Narni) was where it is today, in the square in front of the Saint's Basilica in Padua (but the area was then a cemetery); and the signory of Florence was about to put Michelangelo's *David* on display in the entry of their palace (today replaced by a copy; the original is now on display in the city's Academy).

It was in churches that the greatest number of artworks could be seen. This is an emotion that can be experienced today, for those churches that have not been overly changed were then very much as they are today, perhaps only that they then had more walls, their ceilings were often covered with ex-votos, as Erasmus reported, and there were then no dark confessionals, for that ecclesiastic furniture began to spread only with the 16th century. Putting aside devotion, it seems that curiosity for reliquaries was stronger than interest in art, just as sacred images were more important than the way in which they were painted or carved. Even so, the cardinal of Aragon went to see van Eyck's altarpiece with the *Adoration of the Lamb* in the cathedral of Ghent and, in Milan, visited the refectory of the Dominican monastery of Santa Maria delle Grazie to see Leonardo's *Last Supper*. He reported that the work was "wonderfully excellent although it is beginning to spoil, I don't know if because of the humidity of the wall or some other inadvertence." (This was in 1517, and the artist was still alive.) During his temporary conquest of the duchy of Milan, France's Louis XII also went to see the *Last Supper*, and the Italian historian Paolo Giovio noted that the king admired the work greatly and wanted so earnestly to possess it that he inquired if it might not be possible in some way to cut away that portion of the wall so that he could take the painting to France.

The fame of Italian artists was beginning to spread throughout Europe. Happy in the learned atmosphere of his circle of English friends, the Dutchman Erasmus wrote in a letter that he felt no nostalgia for Italy, only for those things one could see there; France's Francis I, having conquered and lost the peninsula, bragged to the Italian artist Benvenuto Cellini that he had seen the best works by the best masters in all of Italy. Perhaps what he had seen in some way compensated for his defeat.

To get an idea of the "pleasures of

Artistically speaking, this was a creative moment. Some travelers went in search of works of art, set down opinions, and visited the studios of artists. Below: The artist at work, a Flemish miniature from Cicero's Retorica *transcribed and illustrated by Raphaël de Mercatel. Opposite: Another painter at work, from the etching* Born under the Sign of Mercury *by Hans Sebald Beham.*

The artists

Hugo van der Goes, Portinari Triptych, *1476, detail*

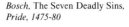

Bosch, The Seven Deadly Sins, Pride, 1475-80

Botticelli, Spring, *1478, detail*

1480

The list of artists who lived, worked, and died during the era spanning the last quarter of the 1400s and the first fifteen years of the 1500s is an eloquent reminder of the stupendous outpouring of genius that was the Renaissance. The three great innovators of Florentine architecture, sculpture, and painting — grand masters of the Renaissance, who had passed away, but whose influence was strongly present — were Filippo Brunelleschi, who died in 1446; Donatello, who passed away in 1466; and Masaccio, who died at the age of 27 in 1428. Along with the flowering of Italian art, the other great artistic movement that came to fruition during the 15th century was Flemish painting. The two schools were aware of, and admired, each other. The first great Flemish masters had also died: Jan van Eyck in 1441, Rogier van der Weyden in 1464.

Jean Fouquet 1420?-1480?

Hugo van der Goes d. 1482

Piero della Francesca 1416?-1492

Hans Memling d. 1494

Pedro Berruguete d. 1503

Andrea Mantegna 1431-1506

Sandro Botticelli 1446-1510

Donato Bramante 1444-1514

Giovanni Bellini 1431?-1516

Hieronymus Bosch d. 1516

Leonardo da Vinci 1452-1519

Albrecht Dürer 1471-1528

Michelangelo 1475-1564

Titian 1477?-1576

Giorgione 1478?-1510

Raphael 1483-1520

The great artistic personalities of Europe between the end of the 1400s and the start of the 1500s

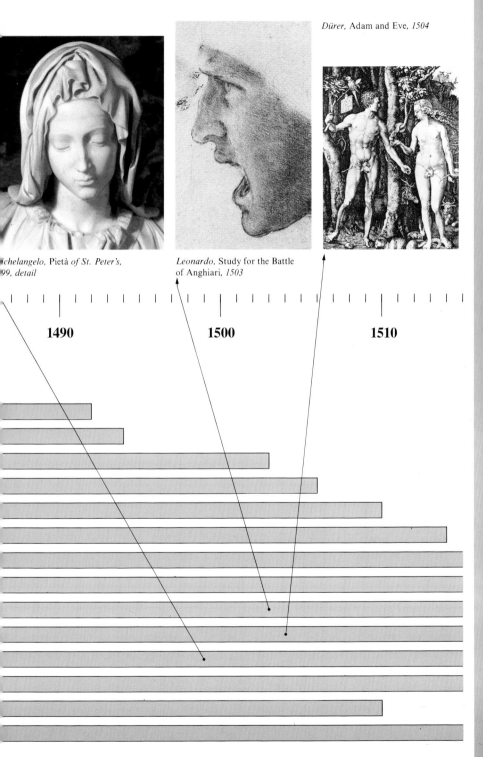

Dürer, Adam and Eve, *1504*

Michelangelo, Pietà *of St. Peter's, 99, detail*

Leonardo, Study for the Battle of Anghiari, *1503*

1490   1500   1510

At the common table in a tavern: these are the pilgrims of
Chaucer's Canterbury Tales, *in an edition by Caxton,*
Westminster, 1484. Could good food be numbered among the
pleasures of the journey? The adventurous gastronomic
experience was perhaps suffered rather than searched after,
but in Cervantes' Novelas ejemplares *a Spanish soldier recalls*
"the pleasant suppers in the inns" of Italy.

the table" available to a traveler during this period, one must imagine on the one hand an austerity bordering on malnutrition for the majority of mortals during most of the year (soups, mushes, little meat, a great deal of bread made from various grains and sometimes including, as a result of ignorance, such hallucinogenic grasses as darnel), and on the other the excesses of rare feasts or the ostentatious opulence of banquets: bewildering numbers of servings, the preparation of vast quantities, heaps of wild game — birds, boar, deer, and in northern Europe even seals and whales — exotic or even bizarre spices (in Venice and the French court use was made of gold dust, also believed to do the heart good). Various moralistic laws were passed against certain excesses. In 1460

the Venetian senate outlawed banquets at which more than a half ducat was spent for each guest. Like all such sumptuary legislation, this law too was passed only in vain. Thus, if the traveler was of the social rank to enjoy elevated hospitality, he or she might have the opportunity of experiencing a true gastronomic event.

Refined — it might be better to say luxurious — cooking called for the abundant use of Oriental spices. Only during the 1600s did French travelers appear who turned up their noses and suffered disturbed palates from overly spicy foods, and such foods were still put on tables in the rest of Europe. In fine dining, the so-called noble roasts of the Middle Ages had been composed of poultry and game; during the 15th century the use of meat from butchers — until then limited to broths and pieces for pies — came into increasing use for roasts and stews. At the same time, the art of carving meat was beginning to be refined, together with the hierarchy of various cuts of beef. Feathered game included birds still considered treats (partridge, quail, larks, pheasant), but that age's preferred birds are no longer considered appetizing: herons, egrets, swans, peacocks, storks, even cormorants. These big birds arrived on the table feathered: in the kitchen the cooks and their helpers carefully removed the feathers, roasted the birds, and then replaced the feathers and served the birds in dignified poses.

Many of today's cheeses were already in wide use during the 15th century. There were the so-called junket cheeses (fresh cheeses wrapped in reeds to prevent dripping), the large rounds of Candia sent to Venice, and Italian Parmesan, which became stylish in France after the return of Charles VIII from his Neapolitan campaign. The traveling canon from Molfetta who wrote so much about the women he saw during his travels also reported on the cooking styles of the countries he visited. He wrote with appreciation of a cheese of Flanders that was green and spicy, its flavor coming from the "juice of odoriferous herbs," but claimed that no Italian would eat a similar cheese that he had encountered in Germany. German cheeses in general did not please him, and he claimed, "The Germans don't like cheese unless it's rotten."

Even then, eating habits aroused varying reactions. De Beatis, the Molfletta canon, gushed with joy about a shoulder of lamb roasted "in its stew" in the French style (the great age of French cuisine came much later), while Montaigne was annoyed that the only eggs available in German inns were hard-boiled and quartered in salads. In any case, it seems that one ate well and abundantly during the last years of the 15th century and first of the 16th. There is considerable nostalgia for these by-gone days, when the tables groaned under the weight of the food, someone was always giving a banquet, and the plates were heaped with food, everyone ate meat every day, and wine was drunk like water. Many and varied chroniclers remembered these years

---

Invitation to a banquet

A royal banquet from the times in which the French court graced the castles of the Loire: three gargantuan courses succeeded one another. For the first course: honey and herb pastry; salted ham; smoked meat puddings; sausages; salted and smoked tongue served with green salad; fricassee of small birds; and minced veal with egg yolk. For the second course: pie; stewed cockrels with lettuce; beef; veal; pork; mutton; and soups; some vegetables, one made with eggs and flavored with saffron and verjuice. With the third course came roast meats (chicken, pigeon, goose, suckling pig, shoulder of mutton); and game pies; with side dishes of broad beans and peas cooked in the pod; and followed by servings of trout, pike, fried fish, and river prawns. Vinegar and capers, lemon, orange, olives, and sorrel sauce were used as garnishes. For dessert: cheeses, cakes, rice pudding made with milk and sugar, peaches, figs, grapes, dates, and melon. Delicacies also uncovered by removing covers of platers: sweet confectionary made with aniseed, fennel and coriander. White, "gray," and red wines accompanied the meal. The courses were brought to table with great ceremony by the butler, the head baker, pages, knights of the kitchen, and the keeper of the plate. The meal was enjoyed from ten o'clock in the morning to midday. A meatless banquet offered to an army leader at Ferrara: sweets of five sorts; salads; stuffed cannelloni; pike, sturgeon, eels, tench, carp, and frogs (either stewed, fried, grilled, or roasted on spits).

with great fondness.

Wine was a great pleasure for everyone, then as now easy to abuse. Although prohibited by Islamic law, wine was on sale even in Constantinople, at least to Greek sailors. This was always young wine, transported in barrels by cart or ship, sometimes over great distances. The Italian wine Montepulciano was already celebrated and in use on the pope's table. Erasmus enjoyed the wines of Burgundy (Luther countered by loving beer most of all). Even the Molfetta traveling companion of the Neapolitan cardinal praised the wines of France: both those red and those white, he claimed, were exceptional, but the rarest, lightest, and freshest were the "cherry-red wines, which they call clarets." Also good and delicate were the German wines, both white and red, "some flavored with sage, elder, or rosemary." It was during the 15th century that cider production, originally based in Biscay, became centered in Normandy. Aqua vitae — distilled liquor — had been used most of all as medicine: it was believed to prevent plague, cure gout, and aid the voice. During the 15th century it changed from a prescribed medicine to a liberally consumed beverage that soon had to be curbed. Coffee, tea, and chocolate did not yet exist in Europe, nor was there tobacco, which Columbus would see natives "drink" during his first days in America.

In most cases, the traveler seated at table in an inn faced not a plate but a wooden cutting board — a trencher — or a thick slice of bread on which food, snatched off a serving plate by hand, was placed. For utensils, each guest had his knife. The fork was a 16th-century invention that spread from Venice only very slowly through the rest of Europe. Even during the first years of the 17th century there were people who expressed surprise at seeing little pieces of meat delivered to a diner's mouth at the end of a "small bifurcated instrument," the diner stretching his neck to reach the piece. Such people also smiled at the unusual skill with which fork users could pierce artichokes, asparagus, or even peas from the serving plate. Ten years later one finds instructions to diners that

The pleasure of travel has always included the possibility of looking around at the world and its inhabitants. Below: A fishing expedition at the court of William VI, count of Holland, Zeeland, and Hainault, in a Dutch-Flemish watercolor from the 15th century. Opposite: A market scene from Contrasto di Carnesciale e la Quaresima, *Florence, 15th century. Following pages: Pieter Brueghel,* Wedding Procession, *1566; beneath the overcast summer sky of Flanders the affianced couple, relatives, and townsfolk make their way to the church.*

they should clean their spoon if, after putting it in their mouth, they wish to use it to take something else from the serving plate. Good manners required that a diner cut bread with a knife rather than simply tearing off a hunk, but that very breaking of bread by hand would become good manners and a symbol of natural elegance beginning during the 1700s.

There were other amusements, both cultural and not. The one thing every traveler seems to have done immediately upon arriving in a foreign city was to climb to the top of some building — a municipal tower, belltower, cathedral tower — to get a sense of the lay of the city from above and to look out over the countryside. This can still be done, but not all of the medieval towers seen today were then complete. The towers of the gothic cathedral of Cologne were built during the last century after the happy discovery, in 1842, of the original plans; the pinnacle designed by Amadeo on Milan's cathedral was completed only during the first years of the 1500s, and the spire with the statue of the Madonna that stands atop the cathedral was erected in 1774.

The reports of travelers contain a remarkable number of references to

*For nobles on a journey, joining in a hunting party with their noble hosts was as much a pleasure as a social obligation. Below: Detail of a Florentine chest from the 15th century with hunting scenes. Certainly no ear was given to the irony of Erasmus (*The Praise of Folly*) on hunters who, "convinced that they are conducting the life of princes," in the exercise of their enjoyment, only manage "to become like beasts themselves."*

fortifications, but such curiosity could be viewed with suspicion by local authorities. In Calais — then an English city — the Milanese merchant (1517-19) noted that foreigners were prohibited from getting near the city's moat and that the death penalty awaited anyone who climbed the city's walls.

Games of chance were available, widespread, and perilous. At night, the rolling of dice was done in secret, either in some building or out in the open in a place beyond the eyes of the city's nightwatchmen — the players all huddled around a small circle of light. During the day, it was done openly in

marketplaces or at fairs, where such things were tolerated. One played without fear even in the presence of princes, even among nobles and merchants, but there was always the danger of incidents, mistaken gestures, or risky words followed by blows, as nearly happened in Paris to the Florentine merchant and writer Buonaccorso Pitti — often a heavy loser at the tables — when the viscount of Meaux addressed him thus: "Oh, Lombard villain and traitor, what are you going to do? Win all evening, you wild sodomite?" Peace was made the next day by the duke of Berry in the presence of his brother, the king. Parents of the age feared their young sons would fall into bad company and get a poor start in life. One of Cosimo de' Medici's recommendations for the instructions given the men sent to direct the branch offices of his bank was that they stay away from gambling.

It must also be said, however, that in the medieval economy all possibility for financial gain came from taking high risks, each business undertaking much like a toss of the dice or a bet, such as those constant bets concerning who would next be made cardinal, when a certain king would finally pass on, how many offspring a wedding would bring, or when the plague would return. Certain economic historians have wondered if the origin of maritime insurance, at that time hardly in wide use, should be seen as nothing other than a bet between the insured and the insurer as to whether a given ship would complete its journey without mishap.

Travelers from the Mediterranean to northern Europe were often dismayed by the promiscuity of public baths. The Spaniard Pero Tafur (1435-39) related that in Flanders it was as natural for men and women to bathe naked together as it was for men and women in his country to go to Mass together. Steam baths were an ancient tradition among the Slavs and Germans, and in villages the doorway to the installation was marked with a sign of branches and leaves during the days the bath was open. During the 1400s these so-called ovens were in use

even in Rome, having been brought there by some German, but they became little more than branch offices of brothels. The water offered pleasure and therapy, though public baths were a holdover of the Middle Ages that was about to disappear (partly, it seems, for fear of the newly arrived venereal diseases).

Around the beginning of the century, Poggio Bracciolini made a pleasing sketch of a thermal bath: half a mile from Baden, near Zurich, a conglomeration of bathing places built along a river, with magnificent hotels and about thirty bathing places, some public and some private. Anyone who wished could even go into the private baths to visit, chat, divert oneself "while the women allow themselves to be seen going in and out of the water almost completely naked." Meals could be eaten on a kind of floating canteen. One passed one's time in song and dance.

The various contests of the period can be likened to today's sports spectacles. Siena's celebrated palio, a horse race that has been run without interruption since 1656, is only the most noted example of a tradition that dates back through the ages and has always been popular. The usual prize with such contests in Italy was the palio, a banner of silk cloth that had for the winner both real and symbolic value. For each contest, chroniclers carefully note the color, the length, and the quality of the cloth of each palio. Rome provides an example: during the city's carnival celebration many

palios were held, involving different groups: boys under fifteen years; Jews under twenty; men over fifty. These participated in races involving colts, stallions, mares, even donkeys and buffalo. There were even races involving pigs. These spectacles took place in the streets, with intense and turbulent popular participation. Irregularities often occurred, and each required that the competition be halted and begun again. Cardinals and other notables sometimes took part in such races masked, and the winners were often from the humblest ranks: the winner of one donkey race was a cheese-and-salami vendor from Via Paradiso.

In Rome, center of Christianity, as in Spain, there were also spectacles involving bulls. During one held at Testaccio, two bulls got loose and fled by swimming across the Tiber. For the celebration of St. John's Day in 1500 St. Peter's Square was closed off with barriers and a bullfight was held with six bulls being hit with swords and arrows by mounted men. Cesare Borgia ("Valentino") and his cronies took part in bullfights, and Erasmus witnessed one in Rome; he did not enjoy himself and judged the spectacle a remnant of barbarism.

Various tournaments and jousts were another form of sport. The habit of associating such contests with the knightly world of northern Europe and with the remote past is incorrect: it was precisely during these years that Burckard wrote about a contest "using lances in the Italian manner" held in St. Peter's Square. Philippe de Comines records with a certain disappointment that Charles VIII, returned from his Italian campaign and at risk of losing every benefit of the undertaking, spent much time at Lyon "*a faire tournais et joustes.*" This was in 1496. Lev z Rozmitalu and his companions did not lose any opportunity to "break a lance" whenever such was offered by some king or prince. In Brussels, at the Burgundy court, the baron Jan Zehrovsky, uncle of Rozmitalu, took part in a mass combat. Tournaments were usually held for the pleasure of the organizers and their circle, but the nobility loved to show off, and so it is unlikely that the public was not permitted to attend. It is known that in Rome the public regularly attended such events.

Although no theaters existed, there was a great deal of theatricality: groups of idlers performed farces; religious confraternities staged the so-called miracle or mystery plays, tales of ordinary lives at the end of which a saint or even the Virgin Mary appeared to solve the story's plot, inevitably by way of a miracle. There was also religious intent within the morality tales, edifying theatrical games involving personifications of such abstract concepts as life, death, and virtue. The rebirth of classical theater was about to take place. The first signs of this came at the Este court in Ferrara, where, beginning in 1486, all dance festivals ended with five or six theatrical spectacles each season, stagings of Italian translations

The sport of gentlemen was still the tournament. As nobles among nobles, travelers did not fail to participate. Below: Knights and the walled area for the "charge"; from the frescoes by Marcello Fogolino (or Romano Girolami, known as "il Romanino"), 1520, in the castle of Malpaga near Bergamo; they recall the celebrations Colleoni offered Christian I of Denmark in 1474. Opposite: Another tournament scene from the Traité de la Forme et Devis d'un Tounois, *by René of Anjou, 15th century.*

of Plautus or Terence, which were performed in a room or in the castle's courtyard. The audience sat on steps covered with rich velvet, the performers were court literates who acted both the male and female roles. Between the acts were intervals featuring mimes and dances. The audience was composed of court members and their guests, but a traveling gentleman would certainly have been welcome.

The *sacre rappresentazioni* ("sacred representations") were popular spectacles that could involve entire cities and could last one day or could go on, in installments, for weeks. The subjects were taken from the Bible or the lives of saints, but the profane mixed freely with the holy, as did the serious with the comic, and — to the horror of city authorities — they often ended in farce. The country most given to *sacre rappresentazioni* during the late 15th century was France, but in 1491 Florence was the site of a *Representation of Saints John and Paul*, written by Lorenzo the Magnificent. The Italian humanist poet Politian put on a representation of *Orpheus* at Mantua in 1480. The form of the *sacre rappresentazioni* suited the elegiac tone, or a lyrical elegance, or, as in the case of *Orpheus*, a mythological subject.

In Flanders, there were companies — called *chambres de rhétorique* in the French-speaking provinces and *Rederijkerskammers* in those with German stock — whose role was to prepare actors for the performance of miracle plays. At meetings governed

with rigid ceremony, the members of these associations had to compose verses and recite them within a certain time period, the subject having been chosen by the president.

The great sermons of the preachers, itinerant or not, were psychodramas open to absolutely everyone. Such characters as Savonarola, Bernardine of Siena, John of Capestrano (the first finished burned at the stake; the other two were made saints) and many others filled churches and city squares, shaking each listener to the bone. When the square filled to overflowing, the people climbed out onto rooftops, causing damage that could require many days to repair. For civic authorities, such religious commotions had the same consequences as today's rock concerts. In 1499, in Rome during Lent, a ten-year-old Dominican preached in various churches and also before the pope with clamorous success. During his stay in the city, he rode a mule accompanied by four members of the same order who acted as his retinue, also on mules, riding behind him in pairs.

From Florence to Bruges

Powerful business interests tied Florence to Bruges, the most important banking and financial centers in Europe. This itinerary across the lands of the duke of Savoy and the duke of Burgundy is more or less that traveled by a Florentine of the bank of Cosimo de' Medici to reach his new office.

**Florence ● Milan ● Vercelli ● Aosta
Great St. Bernard Pass
Geneva ● Besançon ● Nancy ● Brussels
Ghent ● Bruges**

*On the page opposite the title: Florentine youths
against a background of city houses, detail from the fresco of*
St. Peter Healing the Cripple and Raising Tabitha *in the*
Brancacci Chapel in Florence. *The merchant Felice Brancacci
commissioned the decoration of the chapel (1425), at the
height of 15th-century painting, to Masolino da Panicale
(certainly the author of the figures in this detail), who was
later assisted by Masaccio (who may have done the
background).*

Cosimo de' Medici, the master

Cosimo, 57 years of age when this voyage took place, was banker, merchant, textile entrepreneur, and careful cultivator of farms in which his profits were invested. Having been recalled twelve years earlier from a brief exile, he was the undisputed master of Florence. He presented himself modestly as a private citizen—which was, in fact, his legal status—and had the bearing of someone who occasionally served as an official. In actuality, he held the reins of power through his wealth, his skills at financial management, his "liberality" and "prudence," as Machiavelli described. Enea Silvio Piccolomini (Pope Pious II), who was politically astute, testifies in the Commentari *that everything passed through Cosimo's hands, including war and peace, laws, and the designation of magistrates. The affairs of the republic were decided in his house. It lacked only the title as well as the pomp and circumstance to be a kingdom. Medici was also the largest contributor to the city's coffers. According to the register of deeds for the year 1457, his household (with its dependents, a total of fourteen persons) was taxed for 576 florins (two kilos of gold). The size of this taxation can be appreciated by noting that the second and third largest contributors paid 132 and 102 florins respectively, while all the others were taxed at sums below 100. It is also known that Cosimo managed to manipulate the land tax (through fiscal controls) to favor his political allies and damage his adversaries. Some took offense at his brand of tyranny — sweet and patronizing.*

In 1446, Gerozzo di Jacopo de' Pigli, 40 years old, set out from Florence for London. He had already done business in London's Lombard Street, spoke English, and was now being sent by Cosimo de' Medici to London to transform the office there, then an annex of the Bruges office, into a full-blown branch of the Medicean bank. He was to take direction of this new office himself. Gerozzo had invested over three hundred pounds sterling of his own money toward the total two thousand five hundred that formed the capital of this new unit in the banking system of Cosimo, and his contract guaranteed his compensation as one-fifth of the profits. When he rode his horse out through the San Gallo Gate, heading for the Apennines, he carried in his bags a "record," detailed instructions prepared by the heads of the Florentine bank, on how to face the journey and perform the task assigned him. Because of the young men traveling with him (the "errand boys" for the new office), it had been recommended that he proceed by moderate stages, passing through Milan and Geneva, then crossing the lands of the duke of Burgundy as far as Bruges, where he was to embark for London. For his dealings in Milan he had been furnished with a letter of introduction to those who would be able to provide him with money and, above all, with information on the credit of those Milanese merchants who did business in the English city; in Geneva and Bruges he was to observe how things were going in the two Medicean branch offices.

The city Gerozzo di Jacopo de' Pigli was leaving was almost entirely medieval. Several red-hued private towers still stood, although they had all been pollarded at the height of fifty arms (29 meters) in anti-Ghibelline fury halfway through the 13th

*Below: The San Frediano Gate in Florence and a glimpse of
its surroundings, detail from the* Madonna and Child *by
Filippino Lippi (ca. 1490), in Santo Spirito, Florence.
Following pages: The documentary interest of the extremely
detailed painting from the 1800s reproduced here lies in the
fact that it is a faithful reproduction of the so-called chain
print by Francesco Rosselli, 1472. It was thus that the city of
Florence, surrounded by the walls of its seventh circle, then
presented itself.*

century. There was a prevalence of hard
stone or sandstone and brick walls, which
were more often left exposed than plastered.
Among the closely packed houses of the
center were numerous bridges, of masonry
or wood, by which the buildings held one
another up, and walkways or vaults joined
the homes of members of the same family
or political association. Marble (white from
Carrara, green from Prato, and red from
Maremma) could be seen in the religious
heart of the city, the triad of baptistry,
belltower, and cathedral. In that very year
of 1446, Bernardo Rossellino had started
construction of the house of Giovanni Rucellai, following a drawing, all precise
rhythms and classical elements, by the aris-
tocratic intellectual Leon Battista Alberti,
who was to determine the future of architectural taste while himself keeping clear of
the dust of the building site. But the other
glorious Renaissance houses, with the exception of that of the Medici-Riccardi family
in Via Larga, which had been under construction for two years and was the work of
Michelozzo, did not yet exist. There was
neither Palazzo Pitti (Brunelleschi's project
lay buried in one of Luca Pitti's chests,
awaiting the moment when Luca Fancelli
was to take it up for the land near the Via
Romana), nor the house of the Strozzi
family, which was to rise in all its grandeur
from among the modest medieval buildings
in the area around the Old Market, where
various retail trades were spread over seventeen small squares.

Along the Arno River stood rows of
waterwheels, which provided energy for the
factories and drying shops (a kind of large
warehouse) in which bolts of wool were laid
out to dry during certain phases of production. Upstream of the first bridge, logs tied
together to form rafts and floated down

from Casentino were hauled ashore; while below the last bridge, at the wharves of Pignone, near the San Frediano Gate, and at the little port of Prato, flat-bottomed boats traveling upstream from Pisa, loaded with imported wools or iron from Elba, were tied up and unloaded.

There were four bridges. The disastrous flood of 1333 had destroyed all pre-existing bridges save that which had borne the name of the podesta (chief magistrate) Rubaconte da Mandela, a Milanese who had laid its first stone in 1237. This bridge was now known as "alle Grazie" because of the little church of Santa Maria delle Grazie that stood on it along with other structures (up to 1424 the bridge had been inhabited by cloistered nuns, the "Murate"). The Carraia Bridge was the first to be rebuilt (1334-37), possibly based on a plan by Giotto. The

other two bridges were those of the Holy Trinity and the Ponte Vecchio. The latter had been built in 1345, with two rows of shops built in masonry instead of wood, all of them the same and arched. The repair of the bridge had been financed by the rent of these shops, but an open space had been left in the center of the bridge so that one could admire the view of the river and the sur- rounding hills, of which the people of Flor- ence had always been proud.

The outer ring of walls (the sixth from the foundation) encircled almost the whole of the city, which was spread on both banks of the Arno in unequal measure. This ring of walls had been built over the course of half a century, starting in 1284, partly with materials recovered from the cutting down of the family towers. It was eight and a half kilometers in length and had seventy-three

FIORENZA

towers and fifteen gates. The Florentines had planned it for a city undergoing expansion, but shortly after its completion the plague of 1348 had broken out, and so in truth the space encircled by the walls sufficed until the 1800s. Although some of the city's suburbs extended out into the surrounding countryside (for instance, outside the Prato, Faenza, and San Frediano gates), there was also plenty of open land within the walls. The city common at Ognisanto, for example, along the ancient course of the Mugnone River (which had been diverted so that it flowed outside the walls), had been turned into a pubic walk and livestock market, and in the Oltrarno there was the hillside that was to become the Boboli Gardens. Although in the ancient part of the city, that corresponding to the walls of Countess Matilda (the fourth circle of walls

in the history of Florence), there was a prevalence of crowded, vertical building, farther into the suburbs there were gardens and vegetable plots owned by religious institutions or wealthy private citizens. Isolated within its magnificent green frame of hills stood St. Miniato, with its façade built in compartments of green and white marble.

Building projects went ahead for generations, and the completion of church façades was often delayed. The Francescan Santa Croce was still without one in 1446, while that of the Dominican church of Santa Maria Novella was incomplete (the upper part was commissioned from Alberti by Giovanni Rucellai in 1470). At Santa Maria del Fiore, at that time the second largest church in the world, smaller only than Milan's cathedral (also incomplete), only the bottom third of the façade (demolished in 1587) was visible. Even Santa Maria del Carmine was without a facade: an anonymous mass of stone and brick surrounded Masaccio's frescoes, a "textbook" for all Renaissance painters. Brunelleschi's two great churches, San Lorenzo and Santo Spirito, still a long way from completion, were also to remain without façades.

The ingenious imprint Brunelleschi left on the city remained in evidence even after his death, with the completion of his works (the portico of the Spedale degli Innocenti, completed twenty years earlier, was still without the tondos by Luca della Robbia depicting children in swaddling clothes; they were added beginning in 1487). Michelozzo's version of Brunelleschi's language was to form a point of reference for later architects: Michelozzo was then in the process of rebuilding the Church of the Annunziata, taking his inspiration for the rotunda from Brunelleschi's Santa Maria degli Angeli. He was also working at the convent of St. Mark, where Fra Angelico—the Dominican from Fiesole later known as il Beato Fra Giovanni Angelico—was painting some of his earliest known works (the year before, another brother had left the convent to become archbishop of Florence: he was later to become St. Antonino). Michelozzo himself, on the other hand, had not yet renovated the courtyard of the Palazzo Vecchio, of which only the part designed by Arnolfo di Cambio existed. Opposite the palace, which with its lofty belltower, is the "laical" image of the Florentine state, the aerial loggia of three great arches, used for the ceremonies of republican power, was not yet known as the Loggia dei Lanzi.

In the Green Cloisters of Santa Maria Novella (so-called because of the predominant color of their decoration) Paolo Uccello, lover of the perspective that was the new invention of Florence, had painted that very year the *Deluge and Noah's Sacrifice.* The door of the baptistry that looks toward the cathedral is the work of Andrea Pisano; Ghiberti was then working on the gilded panels of the door later known as the Paradise Gate. He had been commissioned for the work in 1425 by the Guild of Merchants. Santa Maria del Fiore already contained the portrait of Sir John Hawkwood (known as Giovanni Acuto), painted by Paolo Uccello (1436). Above the sacristy doors on each side of the altar were the two choristers' tribunes, one by Luca della Robbia (1438), the other, amazing in its fantasy, by Donatello (these are now in the Museum of the Cathedral Building). Even the immense dome, awesome symbol of Florence old and new, had been completed (1436). The city had only just begun its wonderful artistic renaissance. In one of his *Chronicles* (1472), Benedetto Dei was to state that Florence had the seven things without which a city could not truly call itself perfect: freedom; a numerous, rich, and well-dressed populace; a river; lordship over cities, castles, lands, and peoples; learning, from the abacus to the Greek language; "banks" (merchant and banking branch offices) throughout the world; and "every form of art, whole and in perfection."

To cross the Apennines, Gerozzo probably chose the route that passed through Cafaggiolo, Mugello, and Scarperia—the Giogo of Scarperia, at a little less than 900 meters, is the dividing line between the Sieve valley (and the Tyrrhenian Sea) and that of Santerno (and the Adriatic)—and on through Firenzuola and Covigliaio. Cafaggiolo was a small Florentine fortress that Michelozzo was soon (1451) to transform into a summer residence for Cosimo; Scarperia, home of cutlers, and Firenzuola

were two villages founded by the people of Florence in the early 1300s in order to control the feudal lords of the mountains and gain a foothold in Romagna. From there one climbed to the Raticosa Pass, and finally descended toward Bologna.

In the plain beyond the Apennines, Gerozzo found a landscape as different from that of his native Tuscany as was the language different from his version of Italian. Without doubt he already knew this; the man of business and financial affairs learned his trade by traveling. Philippe de Comines, the French historian and diplomat who traveled for reasons of state, and who passed through the Apennines farther west with the retreating army of Charles VIII (1495), described "the flat land of Lombardy, which is among the most beautiful and goodly in the world, and one of the most populous. Although it is said to be flat, it is inconvenient to cross on horseback as it is traversed by many ditches, like unto Flanders, or even more so; but it is much better and

*Below: The exchange bench (Florentine woodcut, 15th century).
Opposite: The countryside around Florence, from an altar
showing the* Flight into Egypt *by Gentile da Fabriano: on
departing Florence the traveler left this countryside behind in
order to climb into the Apennines range. On the road to Flanders
a large city was soon to be encountered, Milan. De Beatis, after
having "well considered" the city from the cathedral belltower,
judged it to be no larger than Paris.*

more fertile, both in good grain and in good
wine and fruits."

Like the rest of Italy, the land Gerozzo
crossed in 1446 was troubled. Before the
arrival of the celebrated few decades of
virtual peace during the second half of the
15th century (the period between the Peace
of Lodi, 1454, and the Italian campaign of
the king of France, 1494-95), other wars
had yet to be fought. City states, "lords,"
and captains of armies of mercenaries (the
famous condottiere) employed themselves
in intrigues, military exploits, alliances,
moves and countermoves, armed incursions,
conquests, sackings, skirmishes, and battles:
an enormous and treacherous game.

The private consequences of this turbulent public atmosphere, or at least the consequences that related to the traveler, ended
in stories that were told of an evening in the
inns in a mixture of proud boasts and
frightened shivers. Gerozzo certainly knew
of the famous little episode attributed to
Facino Cane (later included in vivacious
Latin by Poggio Bracciolini in his *Facezie*):
when a certain man complained that one of
a certain captain's soldiers had stolen his
cloak the captain in question, seeing that
the man was wearing a rich doublet, and
having ascertained that he had also been
wearing it at the time of the theft, dismissed
the man's statement with the sarcastic com-
ment, "If someone has stolen from you, it
was certainly not one of my men. None of
them would have let you go away wearing
such beautiful clothes."

The rich and industrious cities along the
Emilian way, such as Parma, were natural
stopping-off points along the road to Milan.
The course of the Roman Via Emilia ran
on, unchanged over a period of more than
1,600 years. The duchy of Milan, perhaps
the most prosperous land in Europe, was

under the lordship of the astute, gloomy,
and pertinacious Filippo Maria Visconti.
Like all well-informed men of his time,
Gerozzo would have been aware of the fact
that on the death of Filippo Maria Visconti
(which in fact occurred in 1447), the duchy
would pass into the hands of his daughter
and sole heir, Bianca Maria, married to the
adventurous Francesco Sforza. Cosimo de'
Medici was to finance the latter, and thus
it was that Michelozzo came to build in
Milan, in honor of the new duke, a beautiful
head office of the Medici bank (of which
there remains, in a museum, nothing more
than the graceful and famous main door).
At that moment, in the midst of the humid
flatlands, under a blue sky toward which
the chimney smoke of wood fires rose, the
walls of the cathedral lifted themselves
above the housetops.

The countryside around Novara, the
lands of a viscounty, reminded the French-

As is still true today, one was aware of immense change at the crossing of the Alps; the opposite sides were totally different worlds, geographically, atmospherically, linguistically, and culturally. Below: A detail from the Mourning for the Dead Christ, *1500, by Albrecht Dürer. The mountainous landscape in all probability recalls the Alps. Opposite: The Arc of St. Maurice, the work of various goldsmiths (12th-13th century) from the Abbey of Saint-Maurice d'Agaune.*

man Philippe de Comines of Flanders: deep ditches on both sides of the road, a great quantity of mud during the winter, dust in the summer. Among other things, it was in these years that rice began to be cultivated in Lombardy. At Vercelli one entered the lands of the duke of Savoy. Francesco Janis tells us that in the taverns red and white wines of "sweet flavor" were sold; these came from Monferrato, still famous today for its wines.

The distance between Florence and Bruges spans nearly eight degress of latitude. It is a journey from the Mediterranean to northern Europe, with everything that this signifies. There in summer the days are longer, and the dusk sets in more slowly, while in the winter it is the nights which are longest; the sun is less intense, the sky more frequently opaque. On the one hand a continuously gathered-in panorama of hills, with whispering olive trees and cypresses along the roads, the colors intense; on the other, the colors are softer, the horizons wider, but dull and often invisible through mist. It is easy to imagine these, or similar sensations, when following Gerozzo's horse. It is much harder to orient ourselves in the political geography of his time. For us, the journey means passing through Italy, Switzerland, France, and Belgium. Italy and Belgium at that time did not yet exist as political entities; the part of Switzerland to be crossed was not yet Switzerland; the part of France was not entirely France. From Vercelli to Bruges one traveled through two separate and entirely unique political formations: the Savoy states and those of Burgundy. The duchy of Savoy—the Savoy family had been dukes since 1416 by the concession of the Emperor Sigismund—was a bizarre dynastic and feudal construction, at that time at the peak of its power:

a collection of not particularly fertile lands, thick with castles nesting in impervious valleys, and with a limited number of urban centers, communual and sparsely populated. It extended on both sides of the Alps between the sea at Nice and Lake Neuchâtel, from Vercelli to a short distance from Lyon and the course of the Saône.

At the crossing of the Alps, one climbed from Aosta, still closed within its Roman perimeter. Several noble families, having taken possession of the Roman walls, had interspersed among them the towers of their castles. The Great St. Bernard Pass (2,473 meters) is covered with snow nine months of the year. The hospice in the bitter and desolate gorge forming the pass—founded four hundred years earlier by an archdeacon of the Aostan church, Bernard di Mentone, when the area had only recently been purged of Saracens—was the highest along the route, but not the only one. The road was not easy, but Amadeus VIII had crossed it with his artillery, and in the month of December (1434). The young men of Saint-Rhemy, which nestled in a gorge

ten kilometers before and eight hundred meters below the pass, had exchanged their feudal obligation to bear arms for that of keeping the road clear of snow and providing for the safety of travelers.

In the Rhone valley (the Valais), into which the road descended, on the left bank, in the shadow of the sheer cliff face, was the abbey of Saint-Maurice d'Agaune. It had been built in memory of Maurice and the Martyrs of Agaunum, Christian soldiers of the Theban Legion who had been martyred eleven centuries earlier for refusing to take part in heathen sacrifices, and it already possessed its precious treasure: reliquary coffers of embossed silver or gold and enamel, an Oriental ewer that belonged to Charlemagne, and a case containing one of the thorns from Christ's crown, donated by St. Louis.

At Lake Geneva one could proceed by water or else pass along the shoreline, either that of the town of Vaud, covered with vines in the sun, or that of Chablais on the opposite side. Gray castles dominated the edges of the lake, Chillon and Morges on one side, Evian and Thonon on the other. These castles were only a few of those to and from which the Savoy family wandered continuously, moving about their lands, taking with them equipment and furnishings, as their homes were somewhat bare. Beds and other furniture were often kindly loaned to the princes and their followers by their subjects.

Geneva, between the lake, the Rhone, and the Arve, with the icy sparkle and chill air of Mont Blanc, was a city under episcopal sovereignty (the bishop at that time was another Savoy, the ex-duke Amadeus VIII, then serving as the antipope Felix V). It was a municipality, with an active middle class obstinate in the defense of its liberties. Though well known for the availability of cloth, cheese, spices, and salt as well as the products of tanners, leatherworkers, and goldsmiths, Geneva's commercial importance was due in large part to its position as a crossroads for the routes from Italy to Flanders and from southern Germany to Spain. Perhaps even more important were its four trade fairs—at Epiphany, Easter, St. Peter in Bonds (August 11), and All Saints. Men of business from all parts of Europe gathered at these fairs, which served as the marketplace for letters of exchange— at that time the principal instrument of credit—and in substance became a clearinghouse for international finance. The Italian bankers had moved there at the beginning of the century, after the decline of Paris during the worst of the Hundred Years War. Gerozzo here found a taste of home and of his profession among registers, letters

of exchange, merchants, and men of finance, both shrewd and avid. Then, having checked into the state of affairs at the Medici branch office, he set off once more, this time to cross the Jura Mountains, climbing at the Col de la Faucille (1,320 meters).

Gerozzo would have found himself immediately in the lands of the duke of Burgundy. The Burgundian states were not lacking in similarities with those of the duke of Savoy; they were a bizarre conglomeration of fiefs held together only by their intermittent fidelity to their overlord. They were, however, immense, even though not perfectly continuous. From north to south they ran from Mâcon on the Saône as far as Holland; from the Jura to the North Sea; in part they were lands theoretically belonging to the crown of France, in part they were imperial lands. At the moment when the misadventures of Charles the Bold had brought about the fall of Burgundy, Philippe de Comines celebrated the house (a branch of the French Valois) as "esteemed as none other in all Christianity," one that had lasted for one century, counting four princes in "continuous felicity and prosperity." The state was now held by the penultimate duke, Philip the Good. His court showered the land with the golden dust of luxury, languid chivalry, a style of living that was mirrored in its literature.

The itinerary of the Florentine might have passed through Besançon, Nancy, Moselle, and the Ardennes. Besançon is in the Franche-Comté, one of the Burgundian dominions that was to pass over to the Hapsburgs through the marriage of Maximilian to Mary, daughter of Charles the Bold. It was to become French only in the time of Louis XIV, after the siege of 1674. It was then, as today, a picturesque site in which the Doubs River takes a wide bend

*In the lands of the duke of Burgundy. Below: A rich city acts
as background for an execution in a square. Even the
moderate curiosity that surrounds the horrible beheading is an
indication of the times; a miniature by Liédet Loyset in the*
Chroniques *by Jean Froissart (15th century). Opposite:
Wooded hills, a town, a bridge, horsemen, and country folk,
detail from the* Adoration of the Magi, *1470, by the painter
from Ghent Hugo van der Goes.*

around the rock on which the citadel rises,
but it was not yet enclosed by the proud
bastions designed by Vauban, nor was it
possible to see the palace that Nicolas de
Granvelle, minister to Charles V, built (1534-
47) in the Renaissance style. Entering by
the Porte Noire, a Roman arch, one arrived,
as today, at the gothic cathedral of Saint-
Jean, with its unusual opposed apses.

Nancy, capital city of the duchy of Lorraine, is well known as one of the most
beautiful cities of 18th-century France. It is
hard to imagine it as it must have looked to
Gerozzo, on the left bank of the Meurthe
River, between the moat and the walls

under which Charles the Bold perished,
along with the fortunes of Burgundy (1477).
When his counsellors pointed out to him
the great disproportion of forces, which
were strongly in favor of the enemy, the
duke, *"aveques parolles d'home insensé"*
("with the words of an insane man"; this
according to Philippe de Comines), is said
to have replied, *"Si je debvois combattre
seul, si les combateray-je"* ("Even if I had to
fight alone, I would fight them"; this according to Molinet in his *Chroniques*).
Naked and disfigured, his corpse was found
two days after the battle in the mud of the
pond of Saint-Jean.

Below: Well-tended garden plots outside a well-to-do home.
This tidy angle of a Flemish city is from a detail of a Virgin
and Child *by Dirc Bouts, a painter of Haarlem active at*
Louvain (d. 1475). Opposite: The outline of Ghent in a detail
of the Adoration of the Mystic Lamb *(1432) in St. Bavon in*
Ghent. A note in Latin on the frame says the work was begun
*by Hubert van Eyck (*maior quo nemo repertus; "of whom
there was none greater"*) and completed by his brother Jan.*

This was a tragedy reserved for the future. At the present moment, Gerozzo, who had traveled from Geneva and would continue to travel as far as Bruges almost entirely across the lands of the duke of Burgundy, was crossing an extremely rich terrain. This richness was squeezed from the fruit of the countryside, over which small and intermediate nobles presided on their own account or on behalf of overlords, each from his own small castle. But the richness came most of all from the commerce and manu-

facture of the cities: Arras, Lille, Ypres, Ghent, Bruges, Brussels, Louvain, Antwerp, Malines (present-day northern France and Belgium).

Crossing the Ardennes and the immense forest of large oaks and wild heathland, the Florentine was about to arrive at the economic heart of the dominion and, in a certain sense, the economic heart of all Europe. Here are Brabant and Flanders described in a few brief lines taken from the traveling impressions of De Beatis: gardens near almost all the houses with "herbs, roses, carnations, and a quantity of lavender," the fronts of the houses themselves built with a wooden framework filled in with bricks, the wooden parts "so ingeniously worked that not only do they not offend the eyes but rather delight them," roofs covered with "certain tablets of black stone." Across the country, which from Brussels onward is all flat, were "tall and sharply pointed belltowers" and women who all "go around with fine veils upon their heads."

The region is well known as the home of great painting, and this was its moment. In the year in which Gerozzo made his journey to Brussels, in that splendid example of gothic architecture which is the townhall (the tower of which was yet to be constructed), the paintings of Rogier van der Weyden could be seen (they were destroyed during the bombardment of 1695). In the castle of the dukes of Brabant (which no longer exists), Lev z Rozmitalu and his Bohemian companions were to see the Burgundian court of Philip the Good in all its splendor. They were fascinated above all by the figures traced by the ice skaters on the frozen lake in the park.

Ghent was a city in an extremely strong military position. It boasted of never having had to close its gates, either by day or by night, even during sieges. In actual fact, using the water from its four rivers, it could,

93

A country village, the windmill on the riverbank, the city port in the background; in this detail from the Rest during the Flight into Egypt *by Joachim Patenier, about 1520, the whole scene speaks of the painter's homeland (Patenier was born in Dinant and died in Antwerp). In reality the painting tells of the "Murder of the Innocents" in Bethlehem and the "Miracle of Grain" grown overnight, which led the pursuers of the Holy Family to turn back.*

A Burgundian atmosphere

Duke Philip the Good was a strange person, and his complex personality was a mirror for the sensibilities of those times and places: impetuous and astute, immersed with literary notions of chivalry and the immeasurable arrogance of his class. He was capable of breaking off delicate negotiations of state and departing in a rage, to get the better of a beer-vendor of Lilles whose daughter he wished to betrothe to one of his archers. When the dauphin of France (later Louis XI) set out for Brabant, the duke ended the siege of Deventer in order to arrive in Brussels before the prince to give him a suitable welcome. Courtesy was also a point of honor. At his court there were banquets, tournaments, ceremonies, amorous languor, and continual literary misinterpretation. As an example, the Order of the Golden Fleece was founded on the occasion of the duke's third marriage (to Isabella of Portugal in 1430) "for love of chivalry and to spread the Christian faith." The knights were dressed in scarlet robes with sable lining and wore golden collars; the "fleece" was that of Colchis, which had been sought by Jason and the Argonauts (but later, this seeming too pagan a symbol, reference was made to the biblical fleece of Gideon). Court habits with symbolic formalism were the basis of etiquette, especially in Madrid and Vienna. The knight Olivier de la Marche wrote a treatise on this subject at the request of Edward VI of England, discussing problems such as rank among the kitchen staff: were bakers superior to carvers?

in only three hours, flood all the land around the city for the space of one league. This, at least, is what is affirmed by a Milanese merchant (1517-19) in the diary of his travels. All around the city were a great number of windmills, and one went to the Cathedral of St. John (later renamed St. Bavon) to see the polyptych of the *Adoration of the Lamb* by Jan van Eyck, "a stupendous painting, full of intellect," as Dürer was later to note.

Sea fogs and the damp green of the gardens and sands... situated in the plain where the straw yellow dunes hide the North Sea, Bruges had the form of an almond, surrounded and crossed by slow-moving waters. The interwoven city streets intermingle with the maze of canals and seem to ignore all form of logic. "It is a great collection of merchandise and a great assembly of foreign nations," wrote Philippe de Comines, "and it happens that more goods are sent there than to any other city in Europe, and it would be a great damage if it were to be destroyed."

At least in part, the fortune (and decline) of the city was a consequence of the fluid mechanics of sea and wind. The Reye flowed into an arm of the sea that reached inland. Bruges, on the banks of this river, had always been connected to the sea, but then in 1134 one of those savage storms that occur in the North Sea, and that the people of the Netherlands know so well, carved a gulf, the Zwin, to within a mile of the city. This had been provided with an outer harbor, called the Damme, connected via canal with the Reye and the city. When the Zwin began to silt up, the unloading point for merchandise was brought forward, to Sluis. According to local chroniclers, one hundred and fifty foreign ships came in on a single tide in 1468, but the long sleep of the city

was about to begin, due to the progressive inaccessibility of the port, competition from Antwerp, and changing commercial routes. When Gerozzo arrived there, it was still in its prosperous period. There were merchants from seventeen nations in the city who gathered together to discuss business in the "bourse," the house of the van der Beurs family. A short distance away was the Markt, next to which were the houses of the Genoese and Florentine merchants—the first Italian galleys, from Genoa, had arrived in 1277, and the Venetian "galee di marcato" had begun to stop there regularly—and the warehouses of the English and Germans from the Hanseatic cities. Beginning in the second half of the 1300s, the Spanish and Portuguese had also begun to arrive. There was dealing in Italian and Oriental cloth, wines from the Rhine, Bohemian and German metals, English cheeses and wool, and the inevitable spices. No less worthy of note was the importance of Bruges as a banking center, of which London at that time was only a satellite.

The financial situation in which Gerozzo was to immerse himself at Bruges and later run from London was characterized by the structural deficit of the commercial accounts of the Netherlands with respect to Florence and other Italian cities. Flemish tapestries and Dutch paintings were not sufficient to balance the import of alum, spices, silk, and other luxury products from Italy. The difference was made up in Flemish wool, "which is like silk," as De Beatis was to say, but above all in English wool. The English, on the other hand, even with the credit given them by Bruges, more and more favored exporting finished rather than raw materials thanks to the development of their own textile manufacturing, competing with the Flemish and the Italians.

The city was picturesque, with innumerable canals, straddled by hump-backed stone bridges, mirroring nearby houses and trees whose branches bent over the water. As a safeguard against fire, it had for a long time been prescribed that all roofs be tiled. Along the main streets stood lines of beautiful patrician homes with narrow fronts and stepped pediments. The focal points of the city were the Burg and the Markt. The Burg was the place in which, on the banks of the Reye, between sand dunes and marshes, the count of Flanders had built a castle in the 9th century. It now had the appearance of a closed square, bounded by the city hall (completed in 1420) and the Basilica of the Holy Blood, in which could be found an extremely rare relic, a few drops of the blood of Jesus Christ, donated by the patriarch of Jerusalem to the count of Flanders during the 12th century (the blood is today held in a reliquary made by 17th-century goldsmiths). Until the 1300s, this blood performed a miracle by liquefying each Friday. On the other side of the Reye, in the Markt, above the 13th-century Halle, rose the tower. It is now eighty meters high, but at that time it was still missing its upper octagonal portion (built in 1482). In this square, the largest in the city, the fish market was held; two nearby squares were used as the markets for grain and furs. Also on the Markt was perhaps the most unusual building in the whole city, the Waterhalle, dating back to the end of the 1200s, which was built across the river so that boats actually went into it to load and unload their wares under cover. It was demolished in the 1700s.

In the beautiful and luminous gothic church of Our Lady, work proceeded slowly on the construction of its extremely high brick tower. It was to reach 122 meters, but

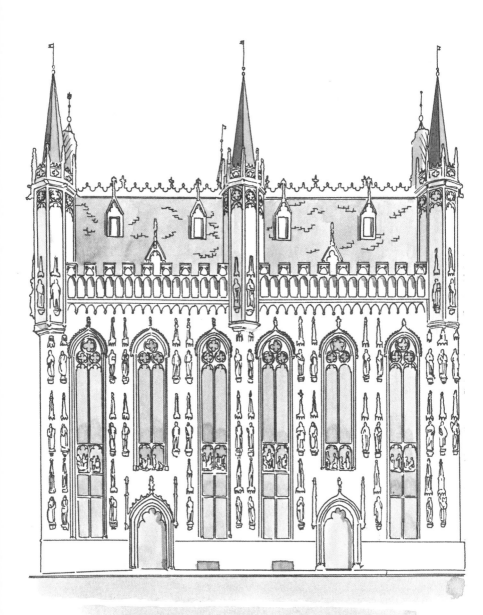

Left: The city hall of Bruges, a proud gothic construction (1376-1420), seat of the city government, looks onto the square known as the Burg. Between its high, narrow windows, forty-eight statues stand in memory of the counts and countesses of Flanders. Below: This 16th-century engraving depicts the little square, not far from the Markt, in which stood the houses of the Genoese and Florentine merchants operating in Bruges.

would not be completed until 1549. Memling had not yet arrived to paint his masterpieces at the nearby hospital of St. John (it is probably only a legend that nuns took him in as a wounded soldier). A man like Gerozzo, from the cultured circle of Cosimo de' Medici, would certainly have had his curiosity aroused by what was traditionally known as the Bruges school of painting, which is to say the great Flemish artists of the 15th century who joined the city's guild of painters, but who were for the most part not born in Bruges itself (Jan van Eyck was probably born in Maaseik, Hugo van der Goes at Ghent, Memling in the Mainz region).

The merchant from Lucca Giovanni Arnolfini, dubbed knight by Philip the Good, and his wife, Giovanna Cenami, kept in their house the splendid portrait they had commissioned twelve years earlier from Jan van Eyck (now in the National Gallery in London). In the church of St. Donation hung a painting by the same artist, the *Madonna Enthroned with Child* (the child holds a green parrot), in which the Virgin sits between St. Donatian and the donor of the work, a canon of the church named van der Paele, who had died at a great age three years earlier.

On May 3, the entire city held a procession, each corporation preceded by three silver trumpets. The celebration lasted four hours. Also participating was the "king of archers and crossbowmen," who had won his title two days earlier, shooting at a wooden parrot in one of the two gardens outside the city to which the specialists in this sport went every feast day to practice their aim.

From Lübeck to Novgorod

The ships of the Hanseatic League sailed the Baltic, loaded with grain, amber, furs, and much other merchandise. This is the voyage of a merchant from the most important Hanseatic city to the great Novgorod, a city of prosperous commerce until the great prince of Moscow subduded it and changed its destiny.

**Lübeck ● Danzig ● Riga
Pskov ● Novgorod**

"In this sea, they do not navigate by compass and chart but by soundings." This note appears in a corner of the Baltic Sea on the famous "planisphere" (1459)—a projection of the entire sphere of the earth on a flat circle of parchment—created by Fra Mauro, a monk and cartographer living on Venice's island of San Michele. The Baltic was a sea of strange, low-lying coasts that were difficult to sight, particularly in the south, the area most often navigated. The sun did not rise very high above the horizon, not even during the summer, and the waters were cold. The port of Riga was blocked by ice from the end of November to early April. The sea was shallow, reaching a depth of 500 meters at only one point, with an average depth of only 70. Fra Mauro's note does not mean that the Baltic sailors had no knowledge of the magnetic needle, but simply that in practice they found it more effective to read the sea bottom using a sounding lead with a socket filled with sticky wax that was dropped overboard whenever necessary. The lead line gave a measure of depth, and the socket provided samples of sand and mud from the seabed, information an experienced sailor could use to estimate position. In some areas, use of the lead was essential to navigation. In 1449, English authorities held a ship from Danzig in the harbor of Plymouth, and to make certain the ship would not escape they merely confiscated its sounding lead.

The kind of ship used in the Baltic—the ship that had accompanied the growth of the Hanseatic League—was the cog or cogge. The seals of the cities of the Hanseatic League showed cogs: it had a single mast with one large, square sail and rigging made of hemp, which had some time before replaced fiber and walrus-skin for the making of rope. A 15th-century seal from the city of Danzig shows new details: the two castles, fore and aft, which were at first merely attached structures, have begun to join the hull, while atop the masthead is a round crow's nest reached by climbing the ratlines (transverse ropes attached to a ship's shrouds to form steps).

Alongside the cog was the hourque, or hulk, which was of greater capacity, had two more masts, and eventually supplanted the cog. Sometimes, however, the two names are used for the same kind of ship, for the evolution of construction was more rapid than that of language during the 15th century. The movement was from a single-masted vessel to one with three masts, and the hulk may have been similar to the carrack, the vessel that was the typical example of a three-masted ship at the end of the 15th century. The hold capacity of Baltic ships was calculated in lasts, a unit for measuring the volume of grain that originally corresponded to the load of a four-wheeled wagon and was thus in line with the nature of Baltic trade. The Hanse exploited east-to-west commercial routes, from Novgorod to Bruges or London (with another branch toward Bergen, Norway). The flow of trade from Flanders to Italy connected the Hanseatic world to the Mediterranean and from there to the routes taken by precious goods brought from the Levant to the ports of Venice and Genoa. This—in an extremely simplified version— was the structure of medieval trading. Hanseatic trading led to the circulation of certain essential commodities in the North Sea and the Baltic: copper and iron loaded at Bergen; dried cod and salt herring; English wool; cloth from Flanders; beeswax from Livonia; amber from Prussia (sold by the Teutonic Knights and used to make rosaries); furs from Russia; grain from Poland, sent by

*Ships and merchants. Opposite: The warehouse of a German merchant, an engraving by Hans Weiditz, early 16th century. Below: A carrack in a drawing by a Flemish master, about 1470. Next to the mainmast the artist's monogram (W.A.) can be seen, along with the word indicating the type of the ship (*kraek*). On the page opposite the title: The same kind of ship in the form of a table decoration; the work of goldsmiths from Nuremberg, 1503.*

farmers or their lords to cities on Baltic estuaries and from there distributed to wherever necessity—the endemic famine of Europe, even in its richest areas—was creating the highest prices.

The Hanse grew up in an atmosphere of colonization of the unknown, following the German settlements along the Baltic coasts. It had used to advantage or exploited— sometimes with ostentatious arrogance hardly distinguishable from ordinary piracy— the natural resources of northern and central-eastern Europe, acting as intermediary among areas with various levels of development. It had been the cause of lucrative and, for those times, large-scale currents of trade, taking advantage of the weakness of the states lying along the Baltic coast, beginning with the German world of which it formed a part. The merchant and naval competition from the English and Dutch that would

eventually supplant the league of German merchant cities had, however, already begun. There had been a war with the English, finally settled at Utrecht in 1474, when a delegation of twenty-six Hanseatic burghers, led by the *Burghermestier* of Lübeck, Heinrich Castorp, had met with English negotiators. Now, halfway through the 1470s, journeys between Lübeck and Novgorod involved the sensation of moving in an environment not without audible sinister and threatening creaks and groans. Among other things, at the eastern end the German community at Novgorod was facing increasing threats from the ambitious grand dukes of Moscow. The Hanse had begun as a union of German merchants who traded with foreign markets. This original association had drawn merchant guilds and towns into the league, and there were about ninety Hanseatic towns at the point of maximum prosperity, distributed from Friesland to Reval (Tallinn) on the Finnish Gulf, from the shores of the Baltic southward as far as Göttingen, Halle, Breslau, and Krakow. The city of Lübeck was custodian for the archives of the league (the decisions of which were subject to review by the individual towns) and was the site of the irregularly held diets (many towns never sent representatives, and participation was always scarce). Lübeck's importance was the result of several factors: it had been the first German commercial city on the Baltic (its name comes from that of a Slavic village, Liubice), it was the starting point for all those who ventured forth to build other cities or settlements along the Baltic coasts, and its position was critical. Situated in the extreme southwestern corner of the northern inland sea, it was where merchants coming from the east along the route from Novgorod to Bruges would disembark to

continue their journey overland to Hamburg and then the Elbe estuary, where they could reach the North Sea.

Like Hamburg and Bremen, the other two great Hanseatic cities, Lübeck, although a port, is not on the sea but is about twenty kilometers inland, at the point where the Wakenitz flows into the Trave in a natural environment of marshy flats where lime trees and birches cast long shadows under the northern sky (as early as the 14th century a canal joined the Trave to the Elbe). In these surroundings, there was originally an oval island bordered by small lakes on which had arisen buildings made of red brick, the austere material of Baltic architecture (what little granite or limestone was used together with the bricks came from across the sea). The entire city was built in brick and was amiably gothic: sober houses with stepped gables, some mirrored in the waters of the Trave, over which the willows bent, or else lined up in severe streets; the town hall, the most imposing civil structure in all medieval Germany; the shops and homes of tanners, leatherworkers, weavers, cobblers, spice vendors, blacksmiths, swordsmiths, silversmiths. There was a cloth market, a coal market, a hay market. Warehouses for salt overlooked the water near the newly constructed (1476) Holstentor, a proud monument with three lines of ogived windows in its curved walls and two conical pinnacles roofed in tile. The city's profile of pinnacles and pointy towers stood out sharply against the broad

*The city of Lübeck (from the atlas of Janssonius or Jansson), surrounded by walls and water. Swans swim in the river, ships are at anchor in the port. Among the pointed towers of the churches the Town Hall (*Dar Rade hus, *in the key) can be seen; this is the heart of the "free imperial city," the principal city of the "illustrious Hanseatic society," as can be read in the Latin script of the scroll.*

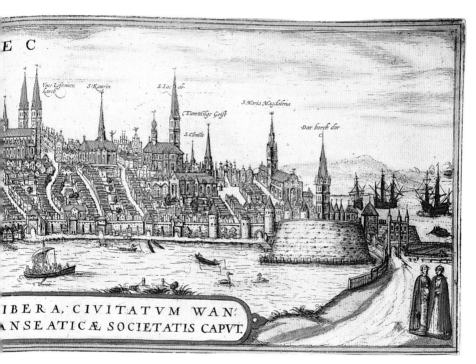

expanse of plain leading to the city. The model had been given by the towers of the cathedral located at the southern tip of the island. Its interior was Romanesque, but its exterior had been transformed by gothic restoration. Rising above the rest of the general panorama were the two square towers with needle-sharp octagonal spires belonging to the Marienkirche. This 13th-century structure (its towers from the 12th), solemn and bare, was the model for all the brick churches of northern Germany. Inside it, the gothic sculpture the *Beautiful Madonna* (1420) had been enchanting the faithful for many years. The kinds of people living in the city and the sense of mercantile business that animated them can be gleaned from the story of the Kulich brothers, which

takes place during the final decades of the 1400s and the beginning of the 1500s. The four Kulich brothers—Kunz, Hans, Paul, and Matteus—were originally from Nuremberg, but had moved to Lübeck. They established a trading network that stretched from Livonia to Scandinavia and southern Germany. The catalog of wares they offered clients included paper, pepper, arms, dyes, and fifteen types of cloth, from gold brocade to cloth from Ulm to seven colors of velvet from Milan. They made money, and at the start of the 1500s the youngest of the brothers, Matteus, became a patrician, which is to say he entered the oligarchy that presided over the diet. He married well, became related to the most important families, and received a fief from the king of Denmark.

Below: Drawing showing the Holstentor, the western gate of the city of Lübeck, erected in 1476, and the two square towers with octagonal cuspids belonging to the Marienkirche, the best-known church in the city, built over a period of one hundred years. Opposite: The altar of Corpus Domini, in carved wood, painted and gilded by the Lübeck artist Henning von der Heide, 1496, previously in the Burgkirche.

One can imagine one of these merchants from Lübeck as, within sight of home, he gives the orders to cast off from the docks. Then, as his well-provisioned ship moves through the meanderings of the Trave, he finds himself occupied with the contradictory feelings caused by departure, sadness at his coming separation from loved ones, the anticipated gains from this venture, curiosity for adventure, and, perhaps, the sweet taste of a Lübecker Marzipan—the confection made from almonds and sugar that had recently been invented—still in his mouth.

What lay before his prow? When the Italian historian Paolo Giovio—who lived in the papal curia and had seen the arrival in 1525 at Pope Clement VII's court of the learned Dmitrij Gerasimov, ambassador of Basil II, grand prince of Moscow—wrote his *Letter on Moscow* to the archbishop of Cosenza, he inserted mention of the great distances between Novgorod and Lübeck: "From Novgorod to Riga, a port close to the shores of the sea of Sarmatia," he wrote, one must travel five hundred miles across a region in which each place is better than the last, with forests and "grassy solitudes," on

toward Moscow, "since there are very often villages"; from Riga to Lübeck, on the other hand, the distance is of over one thousand miles and is "of dangerous navigation."

From the Trave one entered the Gulf of Lübeck and then the wider Mecklenburg Bay. Keeping close to the German coast, the low Danish islands of Lolland and Falster were probably never even sighted.

Once past Rügen, the island close to the German shore that protected another Hanseatic city, Stralsund, the route, in order to give a wide berth to Cape Rixhoft (Cape Rozewie), the northernmost point of Pomerania, probably led within view of the tree-covered slopes of the island of Bornholm (162 meters high). Beyond Rixhoft was a long ribbon of coast that hid the semicircle of dunes forming the Gulf of Danzig. Originally a Slavic settlement, Danzig lay between the Mottlau and Vistula rivers, between the marshes and the last hills of Pomerania leading up to the coast. The Vistula, which freezes for only a few days each year, at that time made a wide bend westward before finding a gap in the chain of dunes to bring it to the sea. It was the city's communication link with the Baltic. (Today, this branch of the river is known as the Dead Vistula; during a flood in the 1800s the river found a more direct route.) The city was one of the strong points of the Hanse. In 1454 it had rebelled against the Order of the Teutonic Knights, the prior rulers for one and a half centuries, and had destroyed the fortress built by the order on the Altstadt ("old city"). This free city, with the right to mint its own coins, make peace and war, and be represented in the diet, had placed itself under the protection of the Polish crown. Having secured Danzig and eastern Pomerania at the Peace of Torun (1466) after defeating the Teutonic Knights, the Polish subjects of Kasmir IV Jagiello had returned to the shores of the Baltic (the Teutonic Knights still held eastern Prussia, but only as subjects of the king of Poland). Danzig (along with Hamburg and Königsberg) was queen of the grain business, which the Hanseatic traders had brought into the Dutch and Flemish markets. Grain was collected at Torun and transported down the Vistula. During a period of shortage in 1481, an estimated hundred thousand grain ships left Danzig. Danzig was a gothic city built of brick, with red towers that served as landmarks along the waterways and plains. In the Rechtstadt ("legal city"— the principal section), the city hall with its square tower dominated the Langmarkt ("long market"). Next to it, reconstruction work was going on at the Artushof (1476-

The galleys, the pirate, the painting

In order to take part in the crusade proclaimed by Pope Pius II against the Turks, Philip the Good, duke of Burgundy, built two galleys at Porta Pisano with funds from the Medici family. When the crusade amounted to naught, the Burgundians neither knew what to do with the ships nor were able to find a willing buyer. Tommaso Portinari, partner and agent of the Medici family, enticed his reluctant patrons into the enterprise of sailing the ships with Florentine crews under the flag of Burgundy (thus affording an opportunity to ignore the dictates of the Florentine marine authorities). The galleys sailed from Pisa on the route to Flanders. On April 27, 1473, off Gravelines, disaster struck: the two ships, returning to Italy, were attacked by Paul Beneke, a pirate from Danzig. One of the two galleys, the San Marco, *managed to escape, while the second, the* San Giorgio, *was boarded and captured. There was no compensation for the mariners who lost their lives in that action, for the lost ship, for the plundered cargo (mainly alum and silk), in spite of claims made by Portinari to the delegates of the Hanseatic League at Utrecht, the protests of Charles the Bold for the insult to his flag, and the papal excommunication of the pirate (the alum, which came from Tolfa, was the property of the Curia). The cargo of the* San Giorgio *included Memling's* Last Judgment, *commissioned by Angelo Tani and destined for a church in Florence; the excommunicated pirate had it placed in the Mariakirche of his city.*

81), seat of the guild of King Arthur, in which the patrician citizens forming this corporation met for their assemblies and feasts. In the Altstadt, another municipal building housed the royal courts. The tower of the Mariakirche rose to a height of 76 meters. The church itself, built during the 13th century and enlarged during the 14th, had an aisle, transcept, and choir with three naves, each nave with a double-sloped roof, in accordance with a detail of the late gothic in Danzig. Inside the church, the triptych of the *Last Judgment*, by Hans Memling, had recently begun to attract attention.

On leaving the Vistula for the sea, the ship from Lübeck would turn its prow to the northeast, following the coasts of Prussia and Kurland until finding the passage, only about fifteen miles wide, between Cape Saare, the southernmost point of the island of Osel (Saaremaa), and Cape Domesnes (Kilkasrags), which forms the entrance to the Gulf of Riga.

The city of Riga was not then old, having been founded only three centuries before. The site had long been occupied by Baltic tribes when the German monk Meinhard built a monastery among those heathen sometime around 1190. Bishop Albert von Buchoewden had then transferred his seat there in 1201 and founded the Livonian Brothers of the Sword, also known as the Livonian Knights, a German military-religious order later joined to the Teutonic Knights. The city was founded at a point on the wide Daugava (or Western Dvina) estuary where a right-hand tributary (the Riga) allowed the creation of a port. Behind the inhabited area, a canal from the Dvina to the Riga made the city into an island in a landscape of enormous spaces and white nights. As everywhere else on the shores of the Baltic, the city meant respite to weary

Stat to der Ryghi, *or "city on the Riga": this is how Riga was known in the oldest documents. The Riga was a tributary of the Dvina. The moat, walls, and bastions that can be seen partially in this perspective view (from Janssonius' atlas) date from the first half of the 16th century. Ships are moored in the middle of the Dvina and along its banks, and a crane can be seen on the wharf.*

Danzig - Riga

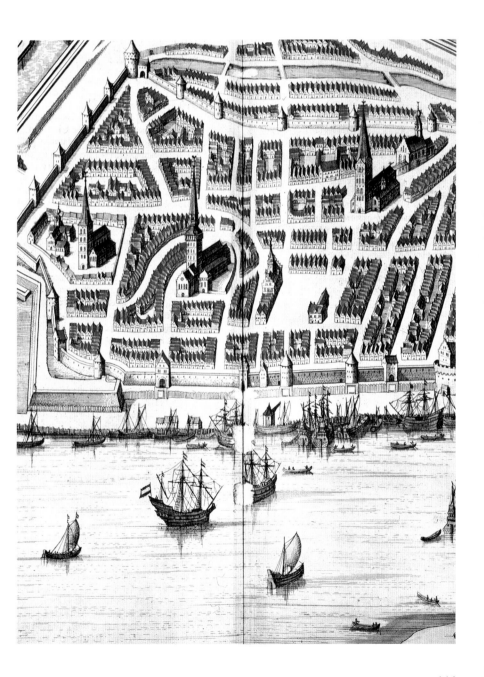

travelers, who scanned the horizon for sight of its spires.

A free city, Riga formed part of the Hanse and was alive with trade. At least a quarter of the population was Lithuanian, another Russian minority. "The Muscovites bring there the white skins of bears, which they obtain from the freezing lands of the northern peoples," states the Veronese Alessandro Guagnino, who during the 16th century fought under the banner of Poland and compiled a description of European "Sarmatia."

The trader from Lübeck would leave his ship at Riga and begin the journey overland into Livonia. The country is described as abounding in wheat and rye, with rivers rich in fish, and much wildlife, such as bears, elk, fox, lynx, martin, beaver, and hares with fur that is snow-white in winter and gray-brown in summer. The peasants—Guagnino found them "rough and barbarous"—were ruthlessly exploited and lived in conditions barely above slavery, wearing shoes of lime bark, eating wheat mixed with rye flour. The women, according to Guagnino, were "most skilled in enchantment and all aspects of the magic arts." Their lords, both noble and not, were all German, the women were married wearing a crown of gilded silver, accompanied by maids in red mantles, the men given to drinking malt and hops beer that Guagnino found "of most bitter taste."

Moving inland, the first Russian city to be reached was Pskov, on the Velikaya River near the southeast shore of Lake Pskov, the southern arm of Lake Peipus and part of a waterway that continued, via the Narva River, into the Gulf of Finland (navigation was blocked by certain reefs in the river). In Russia, travelers found themselves faced with a different form of Christianity among men who did not shave their beards or cut their hair (as for the women, it was difficult to see them at all). Finally, there was the great city of Novgorod. In his treatise on Sarmatia (1517), the Polish humanist, historian, and doctor Matthew of Miechow states that this city was somewhat larger than Rome but was built in wood as well as in stone. In the summer, he wrote, the sky was so light that from sunset until dawn tailors, cobblers, and all other artisans could continue their work without need of lamps. The city stood on the two banks of the Volkhov River, which feeds first into Lake Ilmen and then into Lake Ladoga, from which the Neva River flows down to the Gulf of Finland, this being one of the

Forests and skins. Northern Russia was more than ever a land of forests, and skins were the most highly prized of its riches. Opposite top: Timber merchants, French woodcut, 1501. Opposite bottom: Artisans making up furs, from an edition of the Historia de gentibus septentrionalibus *by Olaf Magno, 1558. Below: Drawing of the church of St. Sophia in Novgorod.*

routes taken by traders. The two parts of the city were surrounded by moats supplied by the river and by wooden walls interspersed with towers. The left bank was the "Santa Sophia side" (Sofijskaja Storona), with the cathedral and kremlin, or castle. The church was very rich, owning hunting rights on all fur-bearing animals, together with fishing rights. The land belonging to the archbishop and the many fortified monasteries lying in a triple ring around the city amounted to more than one-fifth of the immense territory of the state. The archbishop was chosen from among the clergy of the popular assembly, the *veche*, the supreme organ. Santa Sophia had been built in stone during the 11th century on the site of an oak church dating back to the previous century. It had whitewashed walls in the Russian national style derived from the Byzantine, with five cupolas of a shape between swollen and conical on high cylinders with narrow windows. Among its treasures were the brass knockers on the three doors. Those on the Korsun door, the oldest, were Romanesque and had come from distant Magdeburg, where they had been cast during the middle of the 12th century. The Santa Sophia part of the city was divided into three sections. In the castle section, especially along the Prussian Road, which was a continuation within the city of the road from Pskov and Riga, lived the boyars, the great landowners who became rich by selling wax and fur—tribute paid them by their vassals—to foreign traders. The potters' quarter was home to potters, blacksmiths, and silversmiths. The roads to Narva and Carelia left from the Nerevskij quarter. A single bridge led to the city on the right bank of the river, the commercial side, the Torgovlja Storona, formed by the two sections of Slavno and

that of the carpenters. Riverboats rocked in the current along the German wharf. Novgorod was on the most important river route, which united northern Russia with the south. Near the great marketplace could be seen the castle of Jaroslav (son of St. Vladimir, who had converted Kiev to Christianity), the fortification of which had been demolished. It had become a meeting place for the *veche* and the headquarters for the *posadnik* (elected governor). A bell in the castle called the people to assembly. The state was governed by a council of lords, presided over by the bishop. The social structure comprised three classes, apart from the numerous slaves: the lords, or landed gentry; the merchants; and the working class, comprising manual workers and artisans—many of whom had the right to attend the assembly when called to do so by the castle's bell. However, when making decisions, the boyars and merchants always dominated the *veche*. Nearby was the complex of buildings of the Church of Good Friday, built by the Russian merchants who carried on foreign trade; the Church of St. John the Baptist, put up by another

St. George and the Dragon, *an icon of the Novgorod school, 15th century. Novgorod was one of the two great Russian schools of painting with Byzantine inspiration (the other was that of Moscow, which, during the 15th century, was illustrated by Andrej Rublev); it had been formed in the 13th century and during the second half of the following century profited from the teaching of the famous Theophane Greco, who later moved to Moscow.*

guild of Russian merchants; and the Church of St. Peter, built by German merchants of the Hanseatic League. A porticoed enclosure all around this church served as warehouse, archives, and treasury for the commercial community. During the night the weights and scales used for trading were locked into it. The Russians were not permitted to enter, probably to keep them from seeing the quantities of goods in store—the amount of stock available influenced price—and every evening, throughout the period in which they were present in the city, the Hanseatic merchants, one at a time in turns, slept in the church to protect it. When the trading season ended, the keys were handed over to the local authorities in a sealed casket.

For the Germans, Novgorod was the trading center for supplies of wax and, above all, furs. Furs were an important commodity used throughout Europe during those unheated winters and made precious by fashion and the desire for social status. There were sables—these were already rare and, according to the ambassador Sigmund von Herberstein, sold for as much as thirty gold ducats per skin—ermine, fox, and martin, which Venetian gentlewomen wore draped graciously across their shoulders, the muzzle of the animal decorated with precious stones and gold chains, lynx, wolf, and beaver. But in the city markets there were also shipments of Baghdad silk, as well as other silks and extremely rare goods from distant China, even spices. The goods brought from the west by the Hanseatic merchants might seem banal in comparison—cloth from Flanders, salt from Lüneburg—but great riches were to be had from their trade.

The world of the Russians, however, remained inscrutable to the foreign merchants and their diplomats. Herberstein recorded the confidential remarks of a German blacksmith who had emigrated and married a Russian woman; these anecdotes have the flavor of a novel. The wife, it seems, protested that she did not feel loved, which was to say she had never seen any signs of affection, which was to say she had never been beaten. Although greatly taken aback, the German rectified his omission. His wife loved him more and more, but in the end found herself with a broken neck and broken legs.

Novgorod had never been conquered by the Mongols, and this had proved its fortune. It was taken by Ivan III, grand prince of Moscow, and this proved to be its end. The merchants whose journey we have followed from Lübeck probably thought of themselves as witnesses to something that was about to come to an end. In 1471, the forces of Novgorod were beaten by the Moscovites, assisted by the people of Pskov. Ivan had taken advantage of cannons the Italian architect Aristotele Fieravanti had cast and taught them how to use, and of the bridge of boats that the Italian had rapidly constructed to allow the army to cross the Volkhov. The leaders of the Novgorod party that had sought to join forces with Lithuania to avoid the Muscovite conquest were executed. The conditions that Ivan wished to impose—which brought an end to the city's autonomy—were not immediately accepted, but the grand prince did not loosen his grip. The agony lasted several years, but in the end Novgorod was bent to his will. The bell from the castle of Jaroslav, which had once called the people to assembly, was taken to Moscow in 1478. Several texts relate that Ivan took from the city three hundred cartloads of nothing but gold, silver, and jewels.

The pilgrim's shell

From Vézelay to Santiago de Compostela

Pious and courageous Christians visited the tomb of the apostle St. James the Greater from every corner of Europe. According to ageless tradition, they followed certain special itineraries, one of which, the "alms road," is delineated here. Starting in France pilgrims eventually crossed the Pyrenees, then ventured along the *camino francés* from Navarre to Galicia.

**Vézelay ● Bourges ● Limoges ● Périgueux ●
Port-de-Cize ● Roncesvalles ● Pamplona
Burgos ● León ● Santiago de Compostela**

In observation of Christian precepts, the pilgrim found hospitality along his road in the houses of religious orders. On the page opposite the title: Welcoming Strangers and Pilgrims, *detail of the enameled terracotta bas-reliefs from the "Seven Works of Mercy" that the administrator Leonardo Bonafede had made by the Della Robbia workshop for the Ospedale del Ceppo in Pistoia (16th century).*

The pilgrim wore a long robe gathered in at the waist and a cape known as a pelerine, which served as a blanket at night; on his head he wore a wide-brimmed hat that kept the rain from dripping down his back and protected his face from noonday sun; in his knapsack were bread and cheese, perhaps a letter of safe-conduct, money, flints in case the need for a fire arose, wine in a flask made of a gourd, of leather, or even pottery; and in his hand the pilgrim grasped a staff, to lean on when climbing uphill, to test the depth of fords and assist in leaping streams, to drive away stray dogs, even to defend himself if necessary. At the start of the journey, the pilgrim's clothes were blessed.

There were badges to show what pilgrimages one had made (these had been a feature of medieval dress): the palm badge, for example, symbolized the visit to the Holy Land, and its wearer was called a palmer. For pilgrims to Rome, there was a badge showing the keys of St. Peter, or one showing a reproduction of the so-called Veronica veil, the cloth with which Veronica, filled with compassion at the sight of Jesus' suffering on his way to Calvary, had wiped his sweating brow. An image of his features had been left on the cloth. Veronica's name, usually translated as meaning "true image," was given to this relic (vernicle in English), which she brought to Rome so that Tiberius could be cured by it and which, from the time of Pope Boniface VIII, had been displayed in St. Peter's every year during Holy Week. And there were the Jacobins. According to Dante, these "did call themselves pilgrims, as they go unto the house of Galicia, since the burial place of St. James was farther from his homeland than that of any other apostle." As their badge they had the famous rayed shell, the St. James scallop (*Pecten jacobaeus*).

Santiago de Compostela

León

118

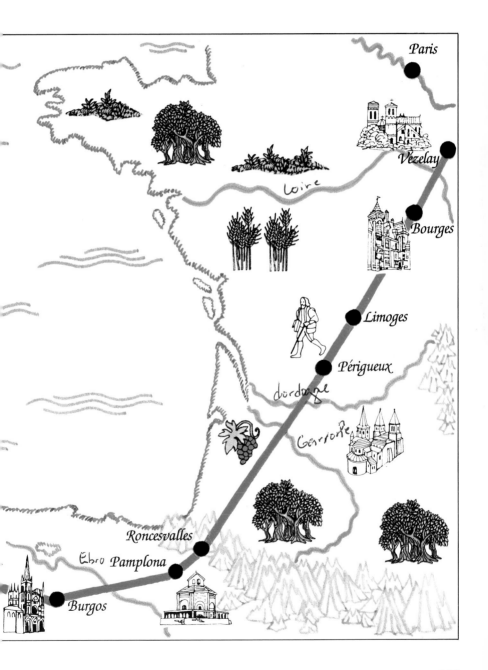

Did pilgrims travel on foot? Not all of them, and not always. Fatigue being very meritorious, the more fervid or fanatical went barefoot or even on their knees, but the cheerful pilgrims in Chaucer's *Canterbury Tales* make their way easily on horseback. Then there is the lady pilgrim in one of Cervantes' novels—actually, she is disguised as a pilgrim, but the disguise would have been useless had it not been based on reality—who arrives at the Inn of the Sevillian in Toledo "in a litter, accompanied by four servants on horseback and by two gentlewomen and a maiden in a carriage."

Nor were pilgrims all poor people. Hieronimus Monetarius (or Münzer), a doctor from Nuremberg, traveled in 1494 to Compostela in the company of three rich men. He wrote about it in his *Itinerarium*.

St. James the Greater—apostle, brother of and fellow fisherman with St. John, the brothers known as the "Sons of Thunder"—was an evangelist, the first of the apostles to be martyred, and was the patron saint of Spain (*Santiago* is Spanish for St. James). The period of greatest fervor for pilgrimages to his tomb was during the 11th and 12th centuries, but the practice continued, bringing crowds into Galicia from all over Europe, some moved by faith, some by curiosity, by a desire to visit distant lands, or merely by the three things that, according to a well-known proverb, made a man yearn to leave home: a smoky chimney, a leaky roof, and a nagging wife. It must be added that during this period women also went on pilgrimages to Santiago; Isabella d'Este was one who made the journey.

Among the pilgrims who visited Compostela were the painter Jan van Eyck and the French diplomat Philippe de Comines, though the latter probably went as a pleasant detour while on a political mission. Ferdinand and Isabella went in 1486, and without doubt they went not only for questions of state, but for religious reasons as well. In spite of all this, the religious sensibility of the period was not always favorable to pilgrimages. In his *Praise of Folly*, Erasmus includes among "madmen" those who "go on pilgrimages to Jerusalem, to Rome, to the Sanctuary of St. James, where they have absolutely nothing to do, and in the meantime they abandon their wives and families." What's more, doubts had been raised as to the veracity of the claim that the apostle's body was actually to be found in Santiago. In Toulouse it was said to be preserved in Saint-Servin. Münzer states that he certainly did not see it and that the king of Castile had not either. "Only faith, which saves men, believes" was the German pilgrim's conclusion. Later, life in Spain was made unbearable by scoundrels, cutpurses, vagabonds, beggars, and penniless wretches who roamed the land with knapsack and staff, taking advantage of the free hospitality offered by hospices for pilgrims. In 1590, Philip II was forced to forbid the pilgrim's robe and to oblige foreigners to carry on their persons suitable documents.

Santiago de Compostela, in Galicia—*finis terrae* ("the end of the earth")—was not exactly easy to reach. Spaniards arrived there from the south and east; Portuguese, English, and other peoples from those parts of Europe giving onto the Atlantic traveled by sea. Many, perhaps the majority, had to cross France, and in that land four itineraries had traditionally been established, each with variations. These were described as early as the 12th century by a holy man of Poitiers, Aimery Picaud, in a Latin text that forms the final part of a compilation in honor of St. James, conserved in a codex

Opposite: The pilgrim, a wooden carving by the Master DS, 1506. Opinions differ on the assistance given pilgrims; the diary of an anonymous Milanese merchant records that in the Hostal de los Reyes Catolicos, founded by Ferdinand and Isabella in 1492, close to the Cathedral of Santiago de Compostela, poor pilgrims who were not sick could find only a place to eat, firewood, salt, and certain other "trivialities."

from the capitular archives of the cathedral of Santiago: the *Liber Sancti Jacobi*. Each of the four roads began in a place that was itself a goal of pilgrims: Tours for St. Martin, Vézelay for Mary Magdalene, Le Puy for the Virgin Mary, and Saint-Gilles-du-Garde for St. Giles. The first three converged at the Pyrenean pass of Port-de-Cize (Roncesvalles); the fourth passed over the mountains at Puerto de Somport. From Puente la Reina in Navarre one went on, via the *camino francés*, the road through Spain taken by the French pilgrims, through Burgos and León (although there were also those who followed a route close to the coast of the Bay of Biscay). The road starting from Vézelay, which Aimery calls the *via lemovicensis*, or "alms road," gathered those coming from northern France, from Lorraine, Burgundy, and even farther afield. It was a journey full of abbeys, churches, sanctuaries, hospices, and relics.

Vézelay is in Burgundy. In 1486—the year pilgrims had the opportunity of mixing their prayers on the apostle's tomb with those of the royalty of Aragon and Castile—the state of Burgundy no longer existed, Charles the Bold having met his death in 1477 under the walls of Nancy during yet another battle against Lorraine and the Swiss. The province of French Burgundy had been united to France, which had been under the reign of Charles VIII for three years; in 1486 he was just 16. Ferdinand and Isabella had managed to grab a portion of Granada by taking Loja; and at the start of the year, in Córdoba, a Genoese going by the name of Christopher Columbus had been presented at court.

In Vézelay's church one could venerate the remains of Mary Magdalene—Mary of Magdala—which had been in Provence, where the saint had arrived in her flight

from the Holy Land, but had been brought to Vézelay for safety when Saracens had infested those Mediterranean shores. No one had any doubts concerning the poetic tales written in the *Legenda aurea (Golden Legend)*, by Jacobus da Varagine, a work greatly appreciated by all those of religious sentiments. But the saint, dressed in red to symbolize her fervid love, and with long blonde hair, the patron of penitents and perfumers—her emblem is an ointment jar—does not play a large role in scriptures.

In any case, the Church of the Magdalene is one of the most important monuments of French Romanesque. It formed part of an abbey founded in the 9th century by one of the feudatory knights of Burgundy, Girart de Roussillon, who is also a leading character of the chivalric age, appearing in a *chanson de gest* that was revived around the middle of the 15th century by Jean Vauquelin at the Burgundy court. The church is on top of the hill on which the town stands and has a wide view all around. The knight and his wife, Bertha, had themselves piously hauled the stones and mortar up the slope.

At the crossing of the Loire River, when starting along the road to Spain, hospitality could be found at the Cluniac abbey of Charité-sur-Loire. Bourges, where the Yevre and the Auron meet, was the capital of Berry. De Beatis, who visited it alongside the cardinal of Aragon, says it was very large and grand with many streets and statues and notes that many types of woolen cloth were worked there. He also lists the relics in the gothic cathedral of Saint-Etienne (among these the head of St. Lucy, part of that of St. Stephen, and the hand of St. Andrew "in flesh and bone"), as well as those in the Sainte Chapelle (destroyed in the 1700s), which stood close to the cathedral. This cathedral was larger than that of

The four routes of the Jacobins which, coming across France, converge at the passes over the western Pyrenees—that including Vézelay is one of them—were not the only roads taken by pilgrims heading for Galicia; they were perhaps those which offered the most frequent stimulus for faith and the most occasions for pious visits to sanctuaries and relics. But one also encountered the "profane" life of the French cities, which this miniature from the Regime des Princes *illustrates.*

Witnesses of the times and places:
The Cardinal of Aragon and De Beatis

When venerating relics, beware; many are duplicates, but must be tolerated "because many cities, lands, and peoples who possess several devotions and ancient relics, will allow themselves to be ruined and abused a thousand times" rather than renounce them. Such was the disenchanted opinion of the canon of Molfetta Antonio de Beatis, secretary and chaplin to the cardinal of Aragon, on whose behalf he wrote a travel diary. A Neapolitan prince (Ferdinando I, or Ferrante, the king of Naples, was his grandfather), Louis of Aragon had been made a cardinal at the age of 20. His journey, which started in May 1517, lasted twenty months and is recounted in detail in the diary. It describes, for example, that having left Bourges after lunch they went on to supper "at Dunroy, which is seven leagues distant and a goodly place." The itinerary was as follows: upon departing Ferrara, the cardinal passed over the Alps and arrived in Nuremberg. He then returned south to Constanz and descended the Rhine as far as Cologne. Next, he visited Flanders. At Middleburg he was received by Charles of Hapsburg, who was not yet emperor; this audience appears to have been the principal objective of the journey. He subsequently crossed France, traversing Paris, Mont-Saint-Michel, Nantes, the Loire, Chabéry, the Rhone from Valence to Avignon and Arles, Marseilles, the Riviera as far as Genoa. He then returned to Ferrara via Milan. He covered in all almost 5,500 kilometers.

Paris, but less ornate, and had been built by the duke Jean de Berry, who was in fact buried in the center of the choir. Other visitors noted that, in one of the porticoes outside the church, there were to be found a leg bone, rib, and single tooth all from a giant "infidel." De Beatis, however, makes no mention of the duke's castle, by then completed, or of the palace of Jacques Coeur, a splendid 15th-century abode with two figures sculpted in its false windows.

Limoges was reached by descending from Saint-Leonard-de-Noblat. St. Leonard, the hermit believed to have founded a monastery at Noblat, was a patron saint and liberator of prisoners: thus, shackles, pillories, and chains hung from the beams of his church. Limoges already had its two-centered structure: the chateau around the abbey (no longer in existence) of Saint-Martial, the converter of the area, and the Bourg around the cathedral of Saint-Etienne. During the 7th century, under the guidance of St. Eligius—himself apprenticed to the master of the mint at Limoges and the patron of smiths and all metalworkers—the local people had started making a kind of enameled goldwork. The city was on the route to Compostela, and wealthy pilgrims bought these colorful and costly religious objects (coffers, reliquaries, and ciboriums).

At Périgueux, in Dordogne—which also consists of two centers, the city on the site of the Gallic-Roman Vesone and Puy-Saint-Front, which was formed around an abbey—one could visit the tomb of St. Front, who was consecrated bishop by Peter in Rome and sent to preach in Limoges. The Romanesque cathedral dedicated to the saint, built in the form of a Greek cross with five large cupolas, is still, even today—in its 19th-century reconstruction—one of France's most original religious buildings. At

*For Jacobins making their way on foot, an ample cloak was of
great use during nights passed in the open between one city
and the next. Below: Jacobin pilgrims with cloak, knapsack,
and staff near a church, an engraving from the 1400s from the*
Chronica mundi *by Schedel. Opposite: The homes of laborers
in the country, in a detail from the* Flight into Egypt *by
Joachim Patenier.*

Ostabat, where the road from Limoges
joined those from Tours and Le Puy, and at
Saint-Jean-Pied-de-Port, the pilgrims
formed groups before taking on the crossing
of the Pyrenees, which loomed over the
countryside ahead. This was Navarre, a
small kingdom that extended along the two
sides of the mountain chain and was ruled
at that time by the house of Albret.

The word *port* here means "pass," and
the pass in question was that of Port-de-
Cize and Roncesvalles. Janis wrote that one
"climbed and descended mountains along a
long and narrow vale." This road, like all
those traveled by pilgrims, was marked
with cairns of piled stones. At Roncescalles
there was an abbey and hospice in which the
pilgrims could find lodging for the regula-
tion three days. From the beams of the
church ceiling hung the ivory horns of the
heroic knight Roland and his companion-
in-arms, Oliver, along with their iron-tipped

maces (the great paladin's sword, called
Durandal, was no longer to be seen, although it was said it had once been there,
too). The story of the brave Roland had
been well described by Charlemagne's bio-
grapher, Einhard: in their perfidy, the
Basques had organized an ambush for the
Frankish army as it moved in long lines
through the mountains in an area that
"seemed created on purpose for a snare,
thick as it was with dark forests." The epic
of the *chansons de gest* mixed into this
encounter the Arabs of Spain, who had
arrived in Galicia four decades earlier. The
time of the formation of the Carolingian
epic is the same as that of the consolidation
of the Christian kingdoms in northern Spain
and the encouragement of pilgrims by the
religious orders.

Along roads dotted with monasteries,
churches, and hospices moved not just pilgrims but warriors en route to do battle
with the servants of Islam. Charlemagne's
expedition into Spain had been changed
into an attempt to free the holy sepulcher of
the apostle. Even so, an air of notoriety
remained attached to the Basques. "The
inhabitants of Navarre and the Basques,"
wrote Aimery Picaud, "make it a practice
not only to rob pilgrims traveling to Santiago but also to ride them like mules and
then kill them." By 1486, stories such as
these were out of date, but the air of
heroism and chivalry of the paladins and of
St. James' *metamoros*—which in 844 had
appeared on a white horse, his sword un-
sheathed, while Ramiro I, first king of
Aragon, fought the Saracens at Clavijo—
was still very much up to date. Granada still
had to be won back.

Descending into Spanish Navarre "by a
most vile path, mountainous, stony, and
muddy" (F. Janis again), one passed Pam-

plona and Puente la Reina, where one might meet the pilgrims who had passed over the mountains at Puerto de Somport, arriving finally in the Ebro valley and the Logroño plain in the wine region of La Rioja. This entire distance was fully "equipped": there were hospices, churches recalling those of France, and monasteries. For some time now bridges had been built and roads were open in the more difficult areas. Santo Domingo de la Calzada, on the banks of the Oja River, for example, was named for the hardworking hermit who built the bridge next to which the town was founded (11th century), repaired the streets, and made a hospice of his hermitage. In the church, a white cock and hen were always kept in a cage in memory of a miracle performed by St. James, in which punishment was meted out to an innkeeper who had caused the son of a German pilgrim to be hanged by hiding a silver goblet in his knapsack and then accusing him of theft. Passing on his return, the bereft German father saw that his hanged son was still alive and rushed to inform the local magistrate. "He's no more alive than those birds roasting on the fire," responded the magistrate, but at that moment the birds hopped off the spit and began to crow. This miracle was read as a warning to pilgrims to beware of innkeepers.

Once south of the Cantabrian Mountains, the route proceeded from east to west, through Old Castile. From the *castella* erected in defense of the Christians who had been driven back northward by the advance of Islam, the name Castile spread to the regions that were gradually recovered. The historic heart of Spain beat in a luminous countryside, full of bare expanses crossed by slow flocks of sheep. Two large cities were encountered, Burgos and León, both the capitals of kingdoms.

In Burgos rose one of the most beautiful gothic cathedrals in the peninsula. The German Hans von Koln—otherwise known as Juan de Colonia—had erected the gracefully pierced towers of the facade and was then—in 1486—starting work at the far end of the apse on the Capilla del Condestable.

On the outskirts of the city the pilgrims found the Hospital del Rey (12th century). In the monastery of St. Augustine they venerated the famous crucifix (now in the cathedral) that had miraculously arrived there from Jerusalem. In the Royal Monastery of la Huelgas (12th century), on the site of the royal playing field (*huelgas*), a statue of the apostle, with a mobile right arm, was used to give the kings of Castile the *espaldazo*, the touch of sword on shoulder that dubbed them knights of the Order of

Burgos was the capital city of the kingdom of Castile, and remained so until the start of the 16th century. Below: The city in a 16th-century view (from Civitates Orbis Terrarum*); it is possible to distinguish the cathedral and, on the hill, the castle residence of the princes of Castile, destroyed by fire in the 1700s. Opposite: Drawing showing the cathedral, a splendid gothic edifice, consecrated only nine years after its foundation (1230); but work continued on it for another three hundred years.*

St. James, since no mortal was worthy of performing such an action. The merchants of Burgos had control of the export of wool from the enormous migrating flocks. They bought it in the market of Castile, gathered it together in the city, and then sent it off on caravans to Bilbao, where fleets of ships made the crossing of the Bay of Biscay to bring it into Flanders.

In their passage through Burgos, Lev z Rozmitalu and his companions were honored with a *corrida* of thirteen bulls in the market square. The animals, freed one at a time into a ring, were attacked by dogs in such a way as to allow a man to tie a hempen rope to their horns and drag them away to be killed.

At León, the body of Isidore of Seville, the learned saint who in his work, *Etymologies*, had explained the world to Visigothic Spain, lay in the Romanesque collegiate church. In the sepulchural crypt, beneath the vault with its hallucinatory 12th-century frescoes, were the tombs of

127

Right: The labors of the month of September in a detail from the Romanesque frescoes (end of the 12th century) in the chapel of Santa Catalina in San Isidoro. The chapel is known as the Pantheon Real because eleven kings, twelve queens, and twenty-one princes are buried there (including the 11th-century Ferdinand, who united the crowns of Castile and León).

Witnesses of the times and places: Baron Lev z Rozmitalu

Among the pilgrims traveling to Santiago de Compostela in 1466 was the Bohemian Baron Lev z Rozmitalu (or Leo von Rosenthal, according to the German name of the city his ancestral castle overlooked). He was accompanied by an entourage of about forty persons. He found himself at the tomb of the Apostle James at a most inopportune moment. The archbishop Alonso Fonseca had been imprisoned by the powerful lord Bernardo Yañez de Moscoso. The arch-bishop's mother, along with another of her sons, had taken refuge in the cathedral, accompanied by their soldiers, horses, and cattle, and Moscoso had laid siege to them. The fighting was hard, but a one-day truce was held permitting foreigners to visit the venerable site. The noble pilgrim was the brother-in-law of George Podebrady, king-elect of Bohemia, excommunicated by the pope because of his Hussite sympathies. It is possible that the baron's long European tour of 1465-67 had diplomatic motives. Visiting relics at every site with devout curiosity, partaking of the hospitality offered by the nobles of the land, and ever ready to participate in tournaments, Leo and his followers crossed Germany and Flanders and sailed the Channel to England. They then toured France, Castille, and Portugal and returned to Prague via Catalonia, Provence, Milan, Venice, and Vienna. There remain two extremely interesting accounts of the long journey, which was not without dramatic moments. Both give a sense of what caught the eye of a traveler.

eleven kings, twelve queens, and twenty-one princes of Castile and León, laid out in rows. The gothic cathedral, in the plan of which could be recognized the cathedral of Rheims—and in its elevation that of Amiens—was known as *pulchra leonina.* Inside, the light rained myriad colors through its famous stained-glass windows.

In Galicia, in the valley of Triacastela, it was a custom for every pilgrim to gather a stone from a quarry and carry it as far as Castaneda, where the furnaces that prepared mortar for the construction of Santiago de Compostela's cathedral were located. At Mount Joy, one went forward quickly, even barefoot. From its summit the goal could be seen—"rich with pomp and faith," to use one of Cervantes' expressions—with one entire side of the ramparts aflower with yellow violets. The city had seven gates; the pilgrims whose itineraries we have followed would have entered through the one known as the Francigena Gate.

According to the Acts of the Apostles, James died a martyr (in A.D. 44) by the order of Herod Agrippa, king of Palestine ("Herod the king stretched forth his hand to vex certain of the church. And he killed

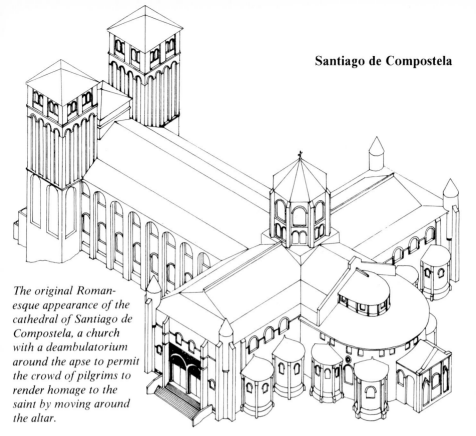

The original Romanesque appearance of the cathedral of Santiago de Compostela, a church with a deambulatorium around the apse to permit the crowd of pilgrims to render homage to the saint by moving around the altar.

James, the brother of John, with the sword"). Then came the legends: seven disciples carried the saint's body by sea as far as Galicia, disembarking at the same place where James himself had previously arrived to start the conversion of the Iberian peninsula. Their arrival disturbed a nearby marriage procession, perhaps because their ship was being guided by an angel. The bridegroom's horse bolted and charged into the sea; when horse and rider reappeared—unharmed and also completely dry—they were encrusted with scallop shells, a miracle attributed to the presence of the saint's body. The disciples buried the body secretly at a point not far from the coast. In 813, almost eight centuries later—when it was needed to sustain the small kingdom of Asturias and León against the triumphant advance of Islam—the tomb was rediscovered by a hermit named Pelayo, in an oak grove, thanks to visions given him of mysterious lights and angelic singing, or even thanks to stars (*Compostela* is thus said to derive from *campus stellae*, "field of stars," but there are doubts regarding this poetic etymology). A church was soon built on the spot. When the Moslem leader Al-Mansur

destroyed Santiago de Compostela in 997 and had the church bells carried off to Córdoba on the shoulders of Christian prisoners to make lamps for the mosque, the tomb of the saint remained inviolate. The present church was begun in the 11th century by a certain Master Bernard, a Frenchman, and built according to a plan adapted to the needs of the flow of pilgrims, whose number may have reached from two hundred thousand to half a million each year.

The Romanesque church had nine crenellated towers and dominated the city's skyline. The royal hospital founded by Ferdinand and Isabella in 1492 had, of course, not yet been constructed in the square in front of the church; nor was there the present Baroque facade between the two towers known as the *Obradoiro*, or "work of gold." One entered through the marvelous Glory Gate, the narthex teeming with sculptures by the master Mateo (finished 1188), in which the artist had even left his own kneeling image. It is called the saint *de los croques*, that is, of the propitiatory butting, because owing to some strange custom it is traditional for people to knock their heads against it (students do so on exam days). In

Before the baroque, or Obradoiro, facade was built (1738), one entered the cathedral of Santiago de Compostela through the Portico de la Gloria, a Romanesque masterpiece by Master Mateo, chief mason for the building after 1168. Opposite: The central doorway, with Christ in glory among angels and the evangelists and, in the archivolt, the twenty-four ancients of the Apocalypse. Below: The Apostle James, from the divisory pillar.

the lateral square of the Azabacheria (*azabache* is the fine gravel with which religious objects and amulets were made), it was possible to buy shoes, deerskin knapsacks, medical herbs, and the scallop-shell badge of the pilgrimage. Aimery Picaud wrote of this, describing also the tavern-keepers, money lenders, and merchants of all kinds who could be found in France Street—the inevitable noisy world of commerce that moves around crowds united by faith. On the principal altar of the cathedral was the statue of the saint, the axe with which he had been beheaded, and the staff used on his travels. It had been necessary to cover the latter with lead in order to avoid its total destruction, since each pilgrim tried to take home a splinter. The pilgrim went up behind the altar, placed on his own head the silver crown hanging above the sacred image, covered the saint's head with his own hat, and embraced the saint, pronouncing the formula "Friend, recommend me unto God."

The pilgrimage was completed by traveling to Finis Terrae and El Padron. At Finis Terrae, which northern pilgrims who did not understand Latin took to mean *finster Stern*, "dark star," nothing could be seen but water and sky.

In the fjord of Arosa, at El Padron (the *padron*, or pillar of stone, to which the boat bearing the mortal remains of James had been tied, was in the parish), one contemplated at night the vague pallor of the Milky Way. It was the road the saint had indicated to Charlemagne for the liberation of his sepulcher. On the beach, the long waves of the Atlantic—an ocean for a short time yet to remain unexplored—rolled in to die on the beach, turning over in the sand the shells with which one proved one had reached the point where the world ends.

The armor merchant

From Milan to Mont-Saint-Michel

In Brittany, during one of the rebellions of the princes against the king of France (1488), traveling merchants from Milan furnished the battling knights with armor. This is the itinerary they may have followed across the plains of Lombardy, through Savoy, and along the course of the Loire.

**Milan ● Turin ● Susa
Mont Cenis ● Chambéry
Lyon ● Roanne ● Orléans ● Blois
Amboise ● Tours ● Langeais
Angers ● Mont-Saint-Michel**

Images of Milan. Below: The plan of the Ca' Grande (the Ospedale Maggiore), founded by Duke Francesco Sforza, from Filarete's treatise on architecture, ca. 1464. Opposite: *The Castle of Porta Giovia (Sforza Castle), from the* Cosmographia universalis *by Sebastian Münster, Basel, 1588. On the page opposite the title: Men at arms in the countryside, detail from* Crucifixion with Virgin and St. John the Evangelist, *by Antonello da Messina, 1475.*

Saint-Aubin-du-Cormier is in the Breton countryside, at this time close to the border between the duchy and the kingdom of France. A powerful castle—now little but ruins—then rose between a marsh and a deep ravine. The rocky cliffs of Mont-Saint-Michel, with its shifting sands and sudden tides, were less than fifty kilometers away.

On July 27, 1488, a bitter battle was fought around Saint-Aubin-du-Cormier. On one side were the men of the king of France, under the command of the less than 30-year-old Louis de la Tremoille, future *chevalier sans reproche* of the Italian Wars, destined to be killed in the disastrous tussle at Pavia in 1515. On the other side were the men-at-arms of the duke of Brittany and of other great rebel lords who had joined in the *guerre folle.* The victory of the young royalist general had political consequences of varying importance: the brilliant period of substantial independence seen by Brittany under the De Monfort dukes—who had given only formal feudal homage to the king of France—went into rapid decline; a future king of France, the duke d'Orléans (later Louis XII), taken prisoner on the battlefield, began a three-year period of reclusion, princely but strict; a treaty made it impossible for the 12-year-old daughter of the duke of Brittany, Anne, the most

desired heiress in France, to marry without the king's permission, leading (not surprisingly) to her marriage to the monarch himself three years later; and the great French historian Philippe de Comines, clever diplomat and expert political navigator—who had nevertheless unwisely backed the losing Orleanist party—ended locked in an iron cage for five months.

Another small but surprising detail can be found among all this news of the Breton campaign of 1488: among the tents of the camped army were Milanese merchants selling their highly prized steel armor, which was produced in workshops a short distance from Milan's great cathedral (eternally in construction), in the streets of the Broletto, toward San Satiro. With their wares in caravans of mules, on carts, or perhaps upon barges on rivers, these men had made a journey into the heart and history of France.

The ruler in Milan was one of the sons of Francesco Sforza, Ludovico, known as "the Moor" (his complexion was swarthy), who had been educated in humanistic culture by Francesco Filefo and who for four or five years had used cunning, deceit, arrogance, and intrigue to make his way toward a power that by right was not his.

In its center, the city of Milan had cobbled streets, the ambitious gothic cathedral (un-

134

der construction since 1387), and a system of *navigli*, or waterways, that included the useful coordination of natural water courses (the Seveso, Nirone, and Olona, which left the city as the Vettabia) and canals, such as the Naviglio Grande, a derivation of the Ticino River, the Naviglio Pavese, whose waters returned to the Ticino, and the Martesana, which derived from the Adda and had been dug out beginning in 1457. Connected to the ring of water encircling the city center, this network, gradually perfected, was rendered navigable; the various levels of water were made passable by means of the *conche*, or basins, beginning in the second half of the 15th century (the first built was the Via Conca del Naviglio). It furnished water for the activity of the tanners and dyers, who had their workshops in the southern part of the city, and energy for the mills and fulling plants as well as for the paper and saw mills grouped along the branches lower down. The boats that traveled the canals bearing loads embarked and disembarked at docks: there was one at St. Eustorgio, and at another, situated by

Milanese Tales

Ludovico Maria Sforza, known as il Moro ("the Moor"), was not destined for power. He was the younger son of the skillful Francesco Sforza. His elder brother, Galeazzo Maria, through his birthright became duke, but revealed himself to be viciously tryannical, extravagant, cruel—and imprudent. Two noble youths, Gerolamo Olgiati and Giovanni Andrea Lampugnani, assassinated him (1476) in the church of St. Stephen in conspiracy with Carlo Visconti. They were politically inspired by the classical models of tyrannicide, but also held personal grudges: a sister had been seduced, a farm usurped. Condemned to be drawn and quartered, during his torment Olgiati managed to say, "Be strong Girolamo; the memory of what you have done will last forever." The new regent was Galeazzo's widow, Bona of Savoy, who reigned on behalf of her eight-year-old son, Gian Galeazzo. The parvenu Francesco Sforza had been extremely proud of his son's marriage, as Bona was a sister-in-law of the king of France. The widow amused herself with a favorite, the young Antonio Tassino of Ferrara. Comines tells us that he accompanied her about the town and that "all was mirth and merriment, but it did not last; perhaps a half-year." Ludovico proclaimed himself the guardian of Gian Galeazzo (1480), thus usurping power. When Charles VIII arrived in Italy (1494) he was to find Gian Galeazzo and his wife, Isabella of Aragon, exiled to Pavia. Ludovico, then titular duke, was ill and died later that year, perhaps poisoned.

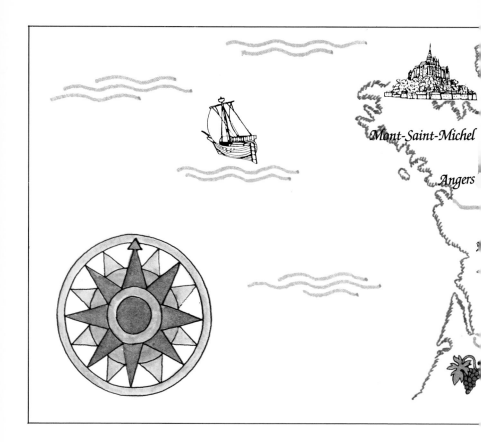

Mont-Saint-Michel

Angers

the little lake of Santo Stefano, the endless stream of Candoglia marble with which the cathedral was being built arrived along the Ticino from Lake Maggiore.

Milan was perhaps the richest city in all of Italy, which was itself then the richest country in Europe. There was the agriculture of the fertile, well-watered countryside; the dynamic manufacture of silk and other articles that were exported over the Alps as far afield as Catalonia and Castile; and there were also the lands to the north, then dotted with mulberry trees. As a chronicler then wrote, "Attention is paid to nothing but the accumulation of riches, to which all ways are opened."

From 1480 to the end of the century—the years of Ludovico the Moor—court life in the castle of Porta Giovia (forever in the course of construction) was sumptuous and cultured. Learned men and artists found hospitality and fortune in Milan. Around the Sforza family the many threads of Italian culture seemed to weave together and in a certain measure to blend. Above all, two artistic geniuses were then living and working in Milan for the Sforzas.

First and foremost of these was Leonardo da Vinci, who owned a suburban vineyard between the Grazie and San Vittore al Corpo, a present from Ludovico. He had started by presenting the duke with a lyre that, according to Vasari, "he had fashioned in silver for the greater part in the form of a horse's head, a thing both bizarre and new." He did a bit of everything: he painted several artistic masterpieces, including a portait of the duke's mistress, Cecilia Gallerani (*Woman in Ermine*, now at Krakow), he consulted on engineering and hydraulic works, and he directed celebrations, such as those for the wedding of Gian Galeazzo, still nominally duke, to Isabella of Aragon in 1490. He meditated, studied, wrote, fantasized, perhaps really saw in the stains on the walls "the semblances of diverse lands, decorated with mountains, rivers, rocks, trees, plains, great valleys, and hills, strange appearances of faces and clothes and infinite things."

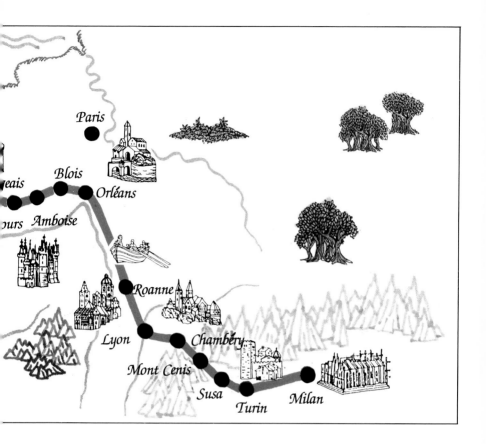

The other great mind was that of Donato Bramante of Monte Asdrualdo (today Fermignano), in the duchy of Urbino. He had already constructed Santa Maria, near San Satiro, with its cunning perspective choir and, in 1488, had begun construction, following his own plans, of the cathedral of Pavia. One of Bramante's sonnets, biting and bitter, draws a picture of the conditions of a court artist: "In truth, courts are like priests, giving water and words and illusions and vanities: those who wish for more go against the rules."

Among all these people in Milan were the city's armorers. The merchant armorers of Milan could have hauled their loads of curaisses, gorgets, cuisses (armor for the front of the thigh), helms, and all the other parts that went to form fighting armor— more sober and less refined than that used in tournaments, but no less mechanically ingenious—in boats along the towpath of the Naviglio Grande as far as the Ticino River, taking the route to Turin from there.

Turin was the capital of the lands in Piedmont belonging to the duchy of the Savoy family. The Savoys had not yet determined their destiny in Italy, in spite of the fact that one of them had already attempted to take Milan. In reality, they wrangled just to keep their composite holdings together, a job at times rendered complicated because of the number of children: Ludovico, the father of Bona, once regent of Milan, had eighteen by his first wife, Anne de Lusignan. The king of France tended to consider the Savoy family his vassals; the state had recently been guided by Jolanda, sister to King Louis XI of France, in her role as wife and then widow of the epileptic Amadeus IX, who gained beatification thanks to his charity. Now the duke was one of Jolanda's sons, Charles I, known as a warrior, and France had broken off some of its foolish aims at expansion.

Turin gazed beyond its red-brick walls toward the green hills descending to the Po River. The mountains appeared close at hand on the horizon. The city itself was tiny; with the exception of one or two

suburbs along the roads outside town, it was completely enclosed within the seventy-two *insulae* of the original Roman colony (less than 800 meters along the longest side). The ancient walls had been repaired and still served as a defensive perimeter. The castle of the Acaia had been built on the site of the principal gate, on the northeastern side of the city. At the start of the century, two poligonal towers had been added to it, and these can still be seen in the rear facade of Palazzo Madama. The city had nothing of the calm, baroque atmosphere that distinguishes it today, but in Via Doria Grossa (now Via Garibaldi), the commercial street, three-story houses stood in ordered rows, their façades already made with arched porticoes.

The Alps were crossed at Mont Cenis, 2,084 meters high, the easiest pass between Piedmont and the capital of the duchy of Savoy. It is reached by following the course of the Dora Riparia upstream along the Susa Valley, guarded at its entrance, called the Lock, by the Sagra of San Michele, an abbey built into the summit of the mountain. Along the way, in the little town of Avigliana, just before the start of the valley, at the Sagra, and in Susa, it is possible to experience the presence of the ancient in the landscape and architecture. At Susa, the noble quarter just outside the Roman walls had come into being because the court of the count of Savoy had found no lodgings within the township during the period (12th to 13th centuries) he had one of his headquarters there.

Before making the ascent to the pass, a stop was made at Novalesa, where pack mules were kept. Novalesa is the name of an ancient and, at that time, powerful abbey a short distance away. Immediately beyond the pass was a small group of houses called

the Ramasse, in memory of the sleds made of branches with which young men of the mountains used to slide travelers downhill. This saved them unnecessary fatigue, although perhaps added one or two extra risks. From the pass, one descended into Savoy through thick fir woods (perhaps there is reason behind the etymology that connects the name Savoy to a root, *sap*, from which the French *sapin*, "fir," also derives). Ahead, the glaciers of the Vanoise glittered white. The valley of the Arc, or Maurienne, is like a wound in the face of the mountain, wild and grand; from below, among the enormous slopes of forest cut by rushing streams, the snows lying above cannot even be imagined. Close to where the Arc joins the Isère, the formidable castle of Miolans rises on its rock. A short distance beyond stands Chambery, the Savoyard capital, on the wide saddle between the Isère and Lake Bourget. A labyrinth of narrow alleys surrounded the castle, which had been enlarged and rendered, if not less sullen in appearance, at least more comfortable a few decades before. In 1452, after a series of bequests and donations, the Holy Shroud had arrived there, but at the time of the Milanese armorers' journey, the Sainte Chapelle, in which the relic was to be conserved until its transfer to Turin (1578), had not yet been completed. The cardinal of Aragon was to have the privilege of kissing the shroud, and the canon who wrote a diary about the journey (1517) states that at first the dukes of Savoy carried it with them at all times, "but with the greatest veneration, wheresoever they did ride." Two Savoyard brothers had once wanted to divide it in two, but the tailor who attempted to set scissors to it was miraculously blinded. In any case, after the relic had been placed in the chapel, the city only rarely suffered

From Milan, heading toward Savoy and Lyon, the Alpine pass most often used was that of Mont Cenis, 2,084 m, which was reached from Susa. Below: Traveling a mountain road, detail from the Adoration of the Magi, *painting by Ambrogio da Fossano, known as the Bergognone, in the church of the Incoronata at Lodi. Opposite: An imaginary Alpine landscape, a carving from* All the Proprytees of Thynges *by Bartholomew of England, Westminster, 1495.*

plague, whereas before "not a year did pass without it."

The last holding of the duke of Savoy on the road to Lyon was Aiguebelette, which the canon described as "a village of few houses but good inns," being an obligatory stopping place for those coming from and going to France.

At Lyon, the Rhone and Saône run almost parallel for a certain distance, leaving between them a strip of land about 500 meters wide, before they finally join. At that time, the city was almost entirely on the right bank of the Saône, at the foot of the hill of Fourvière (which stands for "Forum Vetus"), where the Roman colony had been. The cathedral of Saint-Jean was being completed during those years, after almost three centuries of work. In the left-hand transept one could already stand, nose in the air, before the marvel of the astronomical clock, complete with figures and automatons, of which the baroque version can now be seen.

The Romanesque Manecanterie (the building of the choristers; the name derives from Latin: *mane cantare*) was on the right of the cathedral, while on the left began Rue Saint-Jean, the principal street of the city, with the beautiful façades of its gothic houses and the governor's palace.

The silk industry had been introduced by Italians in the very century that was now coming to a close. It was to become extremely important during the 17th and 18th centuries, but the city had already begun growing during the 16th, with the start of the formation of a quarter between the Saône and the Rhone where churches, such as that of Saint-Nizier, and abbeys had already been built. Louis XI had granted Lyon four trade fairs in 1463, and this had been an important factor in the development of the city. In fact, the trade fairs of nearby Geneva—in their prosperous days such fairs were a kind of economic engine for Europe—had gone into rapid decline, and the

139

As the anonymous Milanese merchant of the manuscript in the British Library recalls with precision, in ancient times Lyon was built upon a hill, where "the relics and foundations of the city can still be seen" (the ruins of the Roman city on the hill of Fourvière); later it was rebuilt lower down "for greater ease," at the point in which the Rhone and the Saône join. In this 16th-century view (from Braun and Hogenberg), the Saône is in the foreground.

Medicis had hastened to move their local branch from Lake Leman to the Saône. From that point, it was only a few years before Lyon had a stock exchange (1506), the first in France.

De Beatis was to see the city as "not very large, but neither small, well-ordered as to streets, with houses generally in stone, of skilled workers and many goods, all perfection." Due to the intensity of commerce, men and women—"of great beauty," notes the ever attentive canon—and surroundings seemed to him to have something of "beautiful Italy," and this made him judge the place the most lovely of all French cities. The Milanese armor merchants must also have felt themselves at home here.

One of the fundamental geographic and economic roles of the area was its function as a center for the commerce that took place between the Mediterranean and central France along the Rhone and Loire. The land between the two river routes was the one stretch of overland travel between Lyon and Roanne, where the Loire became navigable. The majority of the inhabitants of the latter city were the owners of riverboats, drivers, carpenters, sailors, oarsmen, porters; with varying financial and social rewards, they all had interests in the Loire, living off the transfer of merchandise from one river to the other. At Roanne, the Milanese merchants were able either to load their packs onto a *sapinière* (a raft of fir trunks that descended the river bearing goods and was undone at the end of the voyage) or onto one of the oak longboats in which the richer people traveled and which were provided with a cabin.

France's longest river (1,020 kilometers), the Loire descends from the Massif Central, flowing toward the north. A good deal below Roanne, at Nevers, it is joined by its

main tributary, the Allier; then for a distance of over 500 kilometers, washing Berry, Orléans, and Anjou, it makes a wide bend to the west, with its northernmost point at Orléans, before finally widening out into its estuary on the Atlantic coast.

The stretch of river from Gien to Angers, and the adjacent regions on both banks—the "land of the Loire," which Rabelais so loved (he was from Chinon)—is considered the garden of France, the most "French" area of all France. Such was probably already the case when the Milanese merchants were descending the river: vineyards on the edges of the hills, poplars and willows in the wide valley of the province of Orléans, the slow flow of blue waters between banks of golden sand in the light of Touraine. This was a landscape loved by French kings, and during this period they made their homes

along the Loire: Charles VII at Chinon; Louis IX at Plessis-les-Tours; Charles VIII at Amboise; and all the others, during the 16th century, until the reign of Henry III, last of the house of Valois. These kings and princes loved dogs and hunting, falconry and exotic birds. They kept monkeys and lions in the moats around their castles, parrots in their bed chambers. They renovated their gloomy residences with the most graceful gothic and began to create pleasant gardens with pergolas, splashing fountains, and carpets of flowers, even before the pious Neapolitan Don Pacello di Mercogliano, brought by Charles VIII from his Mediterranean kingdom, reordered the gardens of Amboise and Blois "in the Italian style." The opulent flower beds that gladdened the heart of Duke Jean de Berry and King René d'Anjou passed into the tur-

The Loire, "garden of France." Below: Grape picking in the vineyards of the castle of Saumur, a miniature from Les très riches heures *of the duke of Berry, 15th century. Opposite below: Drawing of the castle of Langeais. Opposite above and following pages: Two famous French tapestries from the times in which kings and princes held court in the castles of the Loire:* Concert by the Fountain *and* Lady with Unicorn *with the device* A mon seul désir, *product of the Loire, early 16th century.*

quoise and rose backgrounds of the tapestries manufactured in the Loire—and known as *millefleurs*—in which the idyllic scenes of courtly or pastoral life take place on a carpet of flowers interspersed with squirrels, peacocks, partridges, and young hares.

To recapture the picture of the "garden of France" in those final years of the 15th century, it is necessary to remember that the

Renaissance had not yet begun. The region of the Loire was full of castles, but the most famous of the *Chateaux de la Loire*—an expression in which the word *castle* had a special meaning—did not yet exist. Chenonceaux of Dianne de Poitiers, which is on the Cher River and stretches across the bridge from one side of the river to the other, had not yet been begun. Azay-le-Rideau was called Azay-le-Brulé, because the dauphin (later Charles VII), who passed that way in 1418, had been insulted by the garrison and had therefore attacked the place, executed the captain and all his 350 men, and burned the village. In the forest a few miles from Blois, where Francis I was to later build the fantastic castle of Chambord—with its white walls and phantasmagorical terrace with innumerable pinnacles, chimney-tops, and shafts around the lantern—there was only a small hunting lodge for the lords of Blois. If one wishes for a structure truly representative of the time, perhaps the best is that of the castle of Langeais, built without second thoughts or stoppages over a period of four or five years (beginning in 1465), with its high outer walls of severe gray stone, its round towers,

143

Walled cities on rivers, such as those of the Loire, characterize this imaginary landscape of the kingdom of France by the engravers of the Chronica mundi *(1493) by Hartmann Schedel: Michael Wolgemut and Wilhelm Pleydenwurff (the latter stepson of the former, who was the master of Albrecht Dürer).*

and its sharply pointed roofs.

There were dangerous sandbars and floods, and disturbances caused by water-wheels and tolls, but all in all navigation on the Loire was well organized and speedy. One could get from Orléans to Nantes in six days, and between fifteen and twenty could be sufficient, with luck, to return upstream against the current. Regular Atlantic winds filled the sails (and turned the sails of the windmills on the crests of hills). From the 14th century onward, a *communaute des marchands*, with its base in Orléans, took care of certain necessary maintenance work along the waterway and, to this end, received offerings, which had to be placed in boxes.

The rivermen were robust fellows with exaggerated habits (at one time they wore gold rings in their ears) who displayed all manner of unruly conduct at inns. They called on St. Nicholas (the same saint who later became Santa Claus) for protection and indulged in strong language, from which comes the story of the parrot (and we all know how well parrots learn and repeat words) sent by river from certain nuns in Nevers to their holy sisters in Nantes.

The castle of Blois, on a cliff dominating the city, was very different from the present one, which is one of the classics of the Renaissance. The poet Charles d'Orléans had already embellished it, however, and held his court there after his return from twenty-five years of imprisonment in England (having been taken prisoner at Agincourt) up to his death in 1465, passing his time among elegant ladies and well-read men with a keen taste for allegory and poetical contests. In 1457, François Villon took part in one of these poetical tournaments and won with the ballad *Je meurs de soif auprès de la fontaine.*

Already twice a widower, Prince Charles had married again at the age of 50 a bride only 14. At age 71 he had a son, the very rebel who was to be defeated in the war during which the Milanese sold their armor—the next king, Louis XII. For his part, Villon had ended up for a time in prison, at Meung-sur-Loire, in the castle of the bishop of Orléans.

The castle of Amboise had only its position above the roofs of the town in common with the magnificent royal residence built in succession by Charles VII, on his return from Italy, by Louis XII, and by Francis I. Francis I held fights with wild boar, mastifs, and lions on the terrace, while Charles VIII died after banging his head in one of the new galleries he was having built. His father, Louis XI, had housed his wife there, remaining faithful to her, at least from a certain date onward, but visiting her only rarely. Charles VIII had been born and bred at Amboise and had become child king there, under the regency of his sister Anne of Beaujeu, and it was there that he became betrothed to Margaret of Austria (daughter of Maximilian of Hapsburg and Mary of Burgundy)—who, however, he was never to marry. At the time of ceremony, which took place with great pomp, he was 13, his betrothed three. In the church of St. Denis a wooden cage was shown in which madmen were locked: after eleven days they came out sane. The Clos-Luce had also been built at Amboise, the graceful gothic residence in which Leonardo da Vinci was to spend his final years. The cardinal of Aragon, who was to visit the old artist in his house two years before his death, saw, among the other paintings, the "completely perfect" portrait of a certain "woman of Florence, done in the size of life." He was speaking of the *Mona Lisa.*

At Tours, overlooking the Loire and not

far from the Cher River, draperies of silk interwoven with gold were worked. Along with the unfinished cathedral of Saint-Gatien, with its marvelous windows, the basilica of Saint-Martin could still be seen. It was later sacked by the Huguenots and left in a state of abandon until the roof finally fell in during the French Revolution. It housed the tomb of Martin of Tours, the soldier who had divided his cloak with a naked beggar (in whom he recognized Christ) and later had become bishop of Gaul.

Lower down the river one passed Langeais. Louis XI had had the castle built in order to place a formidable obstacle on the road to Touraine, should the subjects of the duke of Brittany ever decide to invade it. It was in this very castle that, in 1491, Charles VIII married Anne of Brittany, the heiress of the precious duchy, whose power had been humbled in the battle of Saint-Aubin-du-Cormier.

The merchant armorers probably left their vessels at the point where the Maine joins the Loire, making for nearby Angers before heading toward Brittany. They followed the Mayenne Valley, in which the river runs between steep slopes covered with chestnuts and broom. In Angers, which they were leaving behind, the renovated castle of St. Louis, adorned in bands of slate and white stone, had its seventeen crenellated towers with their embrasures and conical roofs (these were destroyed during the religious wars). A malicious proverb circulated in the city: *Basse ville, hauts clochers, riches putains, pauvres escholiers...* " The last duke of Anjou, the "good king René" (king of Sicily, but in name only), learned in modern and ancient languages, wrote romances in verse and treatises on chivalry, composed music, and,

---

Memories of Joan

Although not yet a saint, she had already been pardoned the sin of heresy, for which she had burned at the stake in Rouen on May 29, 1431. The pardon had been issued by Calixtus III in 1456, after Charles VII on conquering Rouen had ordered an enquiry into the trial and execution. In Orléans no one had yet forgotten the spring of 1429. At that time, the siege had been underway since October of the previous year. The Orleanists were defending themselves successfully with their artillery. Seventeen-year-old Jeanne Darc (her name was written thus; "d'Arc" started to be used later, after her family, originally of farming stock, was ennobled) had gained entry to the castle of Chinon on the evening of February 25, 1429. There she had recognized the dauphin (later Charles VII), who had disguised himself and mingled with a group of three hundred men at arms, princes, lords, and courtiers. She had given him the message of the "voices" of St. Michael, St. Catherine, and St. Margaret to vanquish the English and be crowned at Rheims. With the army assigned to her, the girl from Domrémy appeared before Orléans at the end of April. She found herself on the left bank, and was surprised to see the city on the opposite side of the river. The war lords, tired of being hampered by a woman interfering with strategy, had intentionally confused her, for she had only rough topographic knowledge. Her army was forced to return to Blois. But the English were forced to break the siege, starting the legend of the warrior-maid.

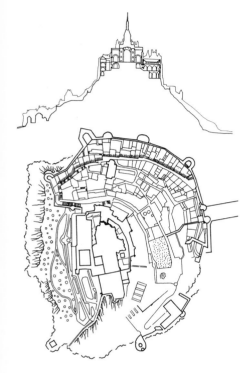

perhaps, painted when he moved from Angers to Aix, in Provence, of which he was count. He donated to the cathedral of Saint-Maurice the famous "Apocalypse Tapestries," woven in Paris (1375-80) to a design of Hennequin of Bruges (incomplete today, they can be seen in the castle). Lev z Rozmitalu visited there and was amazed by the tapestries (he was amazed to learn that the one on his bed had a value of over 40,000 crowns) and the menagerie: two lions, two leopards, two ostriches, and goats.

In the city a great event two years past was still remembered with emotion: a doctor of the town, Master Jean Michel, had arranged and produced—triumphantly and sumptuously—a mystery play of the Passion, the most famous of the century, that of Arnoul Greban. His corrections and additions, however, underlined its profane character, insisting, for example, on scenes of the worldly life of the sinner Mary Magdalene. All together, from the various stages on which the scenes were acted for the delight and benefit of the crowds of onlookers, as many as 65,000 verses had been recited.

It is possible and even probable that, having sold their merchandise to the knights of the *guerre folle* in their camps along the road to Brittany, and finding the route cleared by the victory of the valiant Louis de la Tremoille, the Milanese armor merchants traveled on as far as Mont-Saint-Michel. Perhaps they joined the pilgrims who risked drowning to cross the bay to the rocky mount and venerate the saint *au peril de la mer*; perhaps they too bought as souvenirs lead jars to be filled with sand on the beach. These things are possible because even arms merchants then believed in archangels.

Below: Mont-Saint-Michel in a miniature from Les très riches heures *of the duke of Berry. Opposite: Drawing of the ground plan and section of the tiny island. Only one road runs through the walled village, climbing to the steps of the abbey, which had arisen for a pilgrimage in honor of St. Michael and of which there is mention as far back as the 8th century. The village was not connected to the shore by the dam, as it is today, and it was totally surrounded by water during the high tides at the full and new moon.*

Gothic: the final season

In Europe at the end of the 15th century gothic architecture, already three centuries old, continued to shape cities. The embodiment of the gothic sense of space—the cathedral—is admirably interpreted by Jan van Eyck in *The Madonna in a Church*, painted about 1425 and now in Berlin (opposite). The birth of gothic architecture is usually dated as 1140, the year in which the first stones were laid for the new choir of the abbey of Saint-Denis, near Paris. The style thus was already antiquated by the end of the 15th century and had evolved sufficiently to leave its mark throughout the cities of Europe. A new style of architecture, inspired by ruins of antiquity, had begun during the 15th century, but had not yet become established, and

At the end of the 15th century, gothic was still the style of Europe's cities

construction continued in the gothic style until well into the 16th century. The final phase of gothic architecture had various names: flamboyant in France, so-named because of the flaming forms of the window traceries, "perpendicular" in England (see 4, where traceries are used in a perpendicular

window), and, elsewhere, "decorated." The drawings here display some of the significant gothic buildings of the period: the house of Jacques Coeur at Bourges, built during the years 1443-51 and considered one of the best examples of gothic civil architecture (1); the chapel of King's College, Cambridge, begun in 1446 and completed in 1515 (2); the choir of the church of St. Lawrence in Nuremberg, erected between 1445 and 1472 (3).

151

From Nuremberg
to Venice

German businessmen, particularly those from
Nuremberg, had a *fondaco*—a warehouse and chamber
of commerce—in Venice for their trade. Goods, men,
and information flowed between the two cities, across
the Tyrol, over the Brenner Pass, and along the valley of
the Adige River. The same road was taken in 1494 by
the young Albrecht Dürer.

**Nuremberg ● Augsburg ● Innsbruck
Brenner Pass ● Bolzano
Trent ● Verona ● Padua ● Venice**

In October 1494, Albrecht Dürer, 23 years old, left his home town of Nuremberg and set off for Venice. He traveled on foot and on horseback, avoiding competition with the swift couriers who maintained business connections between the two cities. In fact, he moved rather slowly, always ready to loiter and paint watercolors of what he saw along the way. He was from a rich and cultured city, open to humanistic interests, and having completed his artistic formation he was perhaps seeking in Italy the "form" of the new culture that his colleagues from south of the Alps gained from the study of ancient sources. News of this had reached Germany, as the subject of talk and tales, and even by means of a few printed sheets of engravings, a technique that was at that time still fairly new. De Beatis, who, in the company of the cardinal of Aragon, made almost the same journey as Dürer (though in the opposite direction, going from Verona to Nuremberg), but one generation later, describes Nuremberg as "most copious with

merchandise and various artifacts, mostly those of iron," a city of ingenious mechanics. In fact, the cardinal ordered clocks and other objects in iron and brass to the tune of a good many ducats. He also observed the rich arsenal of arms and artillery, the grain warehouses, and "a long and large house" filled with coal so that it would be possible to continue the iron works even in the event of a siege.

The city's economic power had been increased when the activities regarding the extraction and working of metals had been joined to the exchange of goods between Italy and northern Germany. The iron foundries were numerous upstream of the city along the Pegnitz River, whose waterwheels gave energy to the wire-drawing machines; these foundries were considered the best in Germany. Printing houses also flourished, a new form of manufacture closely connected to the new metallurgic techniques for the preparation of movable type. The city was in the vanguard and predominated in the printing of illustrated books (books with the main body in movable type and with inserted engraved illustrations).

One book of this kind was the *Neue Weltchronik*, or *Chronica mundi*, in its Latin edition, by the Nuremberg doctor Hartmann Schedel, published in 1493 by Anthony Koberger, Dürer's godfather, with woodcuts by Michael Wolgemut and his stepson, Wilhelm Pleydenwurff. In that work one could read that since Nuremberg was built on sterile sands, the inhabitants had developed industriousness and respect for obligations. Indeed, historians identify this period as one during which the eco-

nomic and social panorama of Germany changed, with importance moving from the traditional commercial cities such as Lübeck and Cologne to cities in which a new form of "modern capitalism" was being developed—that is to say, Nuremberg and the nearby Augsburg.

Situated in the Pegnitz Valley, in a belt of thick woods, at the intersection of various great travel routes, the city had had more than one foundation. During the 11th century, on a hill to the right of the marshy river, an emperor had built a castle with a small village at its feet; the Burg, the castle itself, can still be seen, and Dürer was to buy a house along the road leading up to it in 1509. Another built-up area had been founded by Frederick Barbarossa in the 12th century on the opposite bank of the river, around the church of St. Lawrence. Each of these two cities had its own circle of walls. A single, quadrilateral wall on both sides of the river had then enfolded both centers and their relative suburbs, and the layout of the roads respects this historical logic.

Separated by the river, the city contained important monuments, among them the most illustrious of German gothic, which had taken centuries to build and which would continue to be enriched. On the right-hand side rose the Romanesque and gothic church of St. Sebaldus (Sebalduskirche), and the Rathaus (townhall), at that time bearing its stony 14th-century appearance, with an enormous meeting hall with its ingenious high wooden roof on the first floor and a long line of cells for prisoners on the ground floor. Nearby was the mar-

ketplace (Hauptmarkt), created during the 14th century by the razing of older cottages. Here rose the Frauenkirche (St. Mary's), which was to house a clock (from which, at midday, seven electorate princes marched out in line to revere the Emperor Charles IV), the gothic spire twenty meters high bearing forty statues of the *Schonen Brunnen*, and the beautiful fountain by Heinrich Parler from the end of the 14th century.

On the other side of the river, in the church of St. Lawrence (Lorenzkirche), work had recently been completed (1477) on the new choir, with its fluid, uninterrupted, rigidly vertical gothic lines. Adam Kraft was also finishing the extravagant, incredibly tall case of the Holy Sacrament. The church of St. Martha was the headquarters of the *Meistersinger* ("master singers"), but the most famous of these, the great Hans Sachs, would only be born a few weeks after Dürer's departure.

The Heilig Geist Spital, the Hospital of the Holy Ghost, was built across the river. Since 1424, its church had guarded the imperial treasure, which King Sigismund

155

Nuremberg was a city of skilled metalworkers; the work was carried out in iron-foundries situated along the banks of the Pegnitz, the river that also crossed the city. The energy of its current moved the drawing-mills, which were set up according to local technical innovations. One of these mills, which stood to the west of the city, was reproduced in this watercolor by Dürer, in 1494, on his return from a walk.

had entrusted to the free and faithful city when it was transferred from Bohemia. This treasure included the crown and orb of Charlemagne, the tip of the lance with which the centurion had inflicted the wound in Christ's side, and the sword given to St. Maurice by the angel. De Beatis, careful of every detail, relates he had been told that the lance head had been compared with the holy lance, kept at St. Peter's in Rome and from which the head was, of course, missing, but nobody in that city of metallurgists could say of what metal the sword of St. Maurice, of angelic manufacture, was made. Outside the gates, it was possible to stroll on the grass of a "merry" green, planted with five rows of trees. De Beatis calls them *lindi* (from the German *Linden*). In Germany they were extremely common, in Italy unknown, and "they give pleasant

shade" and their white flowers give off an intense perfume; indeed, the canon could not imagine trees giving better views, pleasure, and "amenities."

From the large city of the Franconian region, the route to Venice crossed the Alb hills, one of the primary sources for the minerals necessary for the iron foundries of Nuremberg. The route then descended into the valley of the Danube and crossed the

river, which flowed sluggishly between fields, then followed the Lech upstream until arriving at Augsburg, where it then continued across the Swabo-Bavarian highlands. In the background the rocks and snows of the Bavarian Alps began to appear: Mittenwald, Innsbruck, and Tyrol on the two sides of the Brenner Pass, then Italy. Philippe de Comines, who started his career at the Burgundian court, where he learned

From Nuremberg, the classical route to Venice crossed the Tyrol, hunting ground and land of mineral resources for the Hapsburgs. Below: Watercolor with a view of Innsbruck mirrored in the Inn River, painted by Dürer in 1495 during his first visit to Italy. Opposite: Maximilian of Hapsburg at a hunting party in Tyrol, an illustration by Jörg Kölderer from the Tiroler Jagdbuch, *1500.*

the best of the *douceur de vivre* of Europe, expressed a rather dry opinion of the Germans: "They are crude and live crudely." The canon from Molfetta who kept a diary of his journey with the cardinal of Aragon recorded a greater variety of impressions. He appreciated the inevitable trout kept by every innkeeper in the running water of a fish preserve in front of the inn "made of wood and locked with keys," the maid servants at the inns, who were young and pretty, accepted drinks and chatted with the clients (who did not miss the opportunity of setting hands on them, "but only above cloth"), and the men and women who went to church regularly and did not talk there "of goods, neither do they make merry" as in Italy, but prayed on their knees. However, many torture wheels and gallows could be seen, with hanged men, and even women, a sign to the canon that "great justice is done, as is without doubt most necessary in such countries." In the small castles owned by the lesser nobility, which were scattered about the country, the rogues and scoundrels gathered. The "people of wealth" who governed the free cities—those subject to no master but the empire—had a heavy

hand when it came to protecting property and order.

One such city was Augsburg. When the cardinal of Aragon passed through, he found it a moving experience, with its beautiful fountains fed in a technologically advanced manner by a raised tank, from which the water, which was poured into it "by strength of wheels," was carried underground to be released in high jets. But even more impressive were the riches and splendor of the Fugger family. The houses of the Fuggers, with their gabled fronts, can still be seen today. The 106 apartments there were rented out for one florin per year to destitute but respectable and certainly not wretched paupers. Such was the "social work" of the fabulously rich head of the Fugger family, Jacob Fugger II, called Jacob the Rich, who in 1519 secured the election of Charles V as Holy Roman emperor by providing over half a million florins with which to bribe the electors. It was also in 1519 that Jacob began his charitable work. At the time of Dürer's journey the family had not yet reached the zenith of its power. Jacob the Rich, then about 35, was industriously building up his

fortunes through international commerce, banking, and mines in the Tyrol and Carinthia. The economic development of the city had begun during the first half of the 14th century, with the production and commerce of fustian, the low-priced cloth with its weft of Egyptian cotton, imported from Venice, and its warp of German linen. The merchant families who had thus began to enrich themselves were looking for safety through

159

the investment of funds. Hans Fugger, four
generations before Jacob the Rich, had
been a weaver from Graben who moved to
Augsburg in 1367. Halfway through the
15th century, the city housed the headquarters of the principal foreign trading societies,
those to whom distance was no limit.
Transferring its resources from the commerce
of products to that of money, Augsburg soon
became a world economic power. Over a
period of eighty years, the Fugger family was
to multiply its capital fifty, perhaps seventy
times. The Welsers were another Augsburg
family with a great future. Among the inhabitants of Augsburg was also the painter Hans
Holbein. In a house on the Lech, shortly after
1497-98, a son was born to him, Hans
Holbein the Younger, the magnificent portrait
painter of English society and court during
the times of Henry VIII.

The Tyrol was both the hunting ground
and mining land of the Hapsburgs. Innsbruck, the "bridge over the Inn," is por-
trayed by Dürer in one of his watercolors as
a throng of sharp roofs that are mirrored in
the river against a background of mountains. Here suits of armor were made that
would resist the bolts of a crossbow and the
projectiles of portable firearms. Another
watercolor shows the courtyard of the Hofburg (castle) that was later altered by Maria
Theresa. Maximilian had not yet ordered
the start of work for the casting, at a place
not far from the left bank of the inn, of the
statues of his ancestors to decorate his tomb
in the imperial chapel of Weiner Neustadt.
This megalomanic enterprise was interrupted by the death of the emperor, and the
statues, by then numbering twenty-eight,
remained in Innsbruck around the empty
tomb of the Hofkirche (castle church). The
cardinal of Aragon began his journey
abroad upon entering the Tyrol, and the

first impressions he put down in the diary
of his travels make one think of the habitual
surprises to be encountered in the German
alpine world: wooden crucifixes along the
roads, projections with two or three windows from which to look onto the street,
roofs in shining or colored tiles, and "tall
and sharply pointed" belltowers.

The Brenner (1,375 meters high) is the
lowest of the passes by which it is possible
to cross the Alps. Even then it was used by
large and heavy carts, and the goods that
traveled back and forth over the pass sum
up the international economic relationships
that had their centers at Nuremberg and
Venice: traveling north were Oriental spices,
cotton, silk, fruit, alum, dying materials,
glass from Murano, and barrels of wine; on
their way south were mineral salt, copper,
lead, linen, wool, metal utensils, and arms.

From the pass the land slopes downward
toward the Isarco (according to De Beatis,
this German name comes from "sack of
snow"; the river rises when the snows melt).
Bolzano was then a walled city belonging to
the bishop of Trent. Here, and even more so

in Trent itself, an imperial episcopal principate, one feels that the sky, the air, the very colors have changed—one is no longer in northern Europe, but in Italy, another land. Goethe noticed the change; Dürer stopped there to paint more watercolors.

At that time Rovereto was the first of the Venetian lands. Evidence of this could be seen not only in the lion of St. Mark carved above the town gate but in a certain style of urban construction. In the Lagarina valley, along the Adige River, mulberry trees had been planted. The Veneto was firmly in the hands of the "most serene" Venice. In the cities—Verona, Vicenza, Padua—the transposition onto dry land of the architectural style used on the lagoon was just beginning. The patricians of Venice had begun to invest in land; in Venice itself one or two of the older people lamented this new tendency, looking back sadly to the times when money and fortune were risked adventurously by sea and in the warehouses overseas. Now eyes were turned to the fields, where hydraulic and drainage works were being devised and the transformation of crops

was underway. Future generations would give themselves heart and soul to the construction of villas with classical columns from which they could look out over the green countryside dotted with buildings where they housed hay and crops.

Schasek, the knight who left an account of his journey with Lev z Rozmitalu, describes the Veronese Arena, the city's enormous Roman amphitheater—which he mistook for Theodoric's palace—abandoned and in ruins. During the day there were *faeminae nobiles* (actually prostitutes) around the Arena; these were chased off with nightfall. At the center of the amphitheater the Bohemian saw a gallows, reserved, he was told, for the execution of local malefactors, thus saving them the shame of being hanged alongside foreigners.

In Padua, Mantegna (the frescoes in the chapel of the Ovetari agli Eremitani) and Donatello (the bronze equestrian statue of the condottiere Erasmo da Narni, bestknown as *Gattamelata*, and the bronzes on the altar of St. Antonio) accentuated the powerful breath of the Italian Renaissance.

Descending from the Brenner one enters "beautiful, sweet, pleasant, gentle, and sober Italy" (Antonio De Beatis). Dürer went there to complete his artistic education; his companions were heading for Venice to do business. Below: The Venetian countryside, detail from the Madonna del Prato *by Giovanni Bellini, 1505. Opposite: Venetian architecture, detail from the* Miracle of the Relic of the True Cross, *by Gentile Bellini.*

The university, famous and of great prestige, attracted many foreigners. Young men from Nuremberg went there too. It had recently been host to the humanist Willibald Pirkheimer, a friend of Dürer's. In this city one took a boat to descend the Brenta canal; this is what Philippe de Comines did on his diplomatic mission to Venice during the very months the young artist from Nuremberg was in the city. The Frenchman wrote that at Fusina one left the ship on board which the journey from Padua had been made along the river canal and got into very clean, small boats, which were lined with tapestries and had velvet carpets on their seats. These were gondolas, used to cross the calm water of the lagoon, which was the color of pearl at dusk.

Perhaps in Venice, as in no other city in the world, does one have the impression of being able to turn back time. On its ephemeral islands, in the autumn of 1494—the doge then was Agostino Barbarigo—the city had a configuration not very different from that which can be seen today. Its own particular architecture, which seems an iridescent coagulation of color between water and sky, already exerted its fascination. On closer examination, however, there are more differences than one would first think; the preponderant image of the present-day city, in fact, shows the classical taste of the 16th-century revival, the first mover of which was the Florentine Iacopo Sansovino.

The basilica of St. Mark looked then almost exactly as it does today, standing before the enormous square. Petrarch, who had seen it with its brick pavement, asked himself "if earth contains another like it." But around the square then there was almost nothing of what can be seen now. Even the continuous porticoes of the old Procuratie, the oldest part of the architectural frame,

were different from the present ones, which were rebuilt at the start of the 16th century. The belltower, which did not yet have its cuspid, was joined to the Hospital of Pietro Orseolo, no longer existent.

On the façades of the doge's palace the sun illuminated the precious interweaving of pink and white lozenges set above the open galleries in Istrian stone, already streaked with salt, but on the side giving onto the small square the large central window did not yet exist. When the *trottiera* called the council from the top of the belltower, the patricians entered through the Porta della Carta, through which visitors pass today, but they saw the side facing onto the courtyard of the wing facing toward Rio del Palazzo and the Giant's Stairway, both of which were under construction after a fire that had taken place in 1483. Directing the construction works was the Veronese Antonio Rizzo, who had already sculpted *Adam and Eve* for the Foscari Arch, but who would in 1498 be accused of peculation to the tune of 12,000 scudi and would escape to Cesena. In the immense hall of the Great Council, the patricians lifted their eyes not to the swirling *Paradise* by Tintoretto but to a fresco full of haloed angels by the Paduan Guariento.

On the Grand Canal there was much boat traffic but only one bridge, the Rialto, which was built of wood, was covered, and whose central portion worked as a draw bridge. Philippe de Comines described the great canal with much enthusiasm, with galleys passing along it and ships of over four hundred barrels moored alongside the houses: "I think it is the most beautiful road that can be seen in the whole world." Some of the houses were painted, and all had façades in the "white marble that comes from Istria," with inserts in porphyry and serpentine. Inside there were usually at least two rooms with gilded ceilings, fireplaces in sculpted marble, gilded beds, floors both

This is the facade of the Basilica of St. Mark's and the Venetian square as Albrecht Dürer and Philippe de Comines saw them. The painting is The Procession of the Relic of the True Cross in St. Mark's Square, *by Gentile Bellini, 1496. It is easy to see several differences in the well-known urban scene: on the left the clocktower above the entrance to the Mercerie has not yet been built, while on the right, in line with the belltower, the now vanished Ospizio Orseolo can be seen.*

Philippe de Comines, sent by Charles VIII, received by the Signoria, was stupefied by the palace, "fair and rich in its contents, all in well-cut marble." Below: Corner of the doge's palace and the Paglia bridge on Rio del Palazzo, detail of a woodcut from the Fasciculus temporum *by Werner Rolewinck, 1480. Opposite: Women at windows in Campo San Lio, detail from the* Miracle of the Relic at St. Lio *by Giovanni Mansueti, 1496.*

gilded and painted, and a great quantity of furniture. Among the roofs was a forest of fantastic chimney-tops, and there were roof terraces where gentlewomen went to bleach their hair in the sun. The prevailing fashion for the façades was that of the "flowered gothic," with various entertwined floral patterns. The most beautiful house was Palazzo Contarini, known as the Ca' d'Oro ("house of gold"), but close to the Punta della Dogana the little palace of Giovanni Dario already stood, its sharp Renaissance forms dissolved, in the version by Pietro Lombardo, by the polychromy of its marble encrustations. Furthermore, under the direction of Mauro Condussi of Bergamo, construction had started, using the lexicon of the classical orders, on the palaces of the Corner-Spinelli and Vendramin-Calergi.

Pietro Lombardo and Mauro Condussi were the most popular architects. The former had just finished—in its guise of a precious casket—the tiny church of Santa Maria of the Miracles. Benedictine nuns had summoned the latter to work on the façade of St. Zacharias. Painting was draw-ing near its magic moment. About twenty years earlier (1465-76), Antonello da Messina had passed through Venice and had painted his *St. Sebastian*, perhaps for the church of St. Julian (the painting is now in Dresden), along with the altarpiece for the church of St. Cassiano (divided, what remains of it is now in Vienna). Of the latter work, the chronicler Marin Sanudo had written that "the figures are so good as to seem living, and nothing do they lack save a soul." Everybody had learned from these works. Now Carpaccio was working on his canvases showing the story of St. Ursula. Onto these he lavished, somewhat incongruously, all the elegance of Venetian life. The *Two Courtesans* had already been painted, but no one gave this name to the painting, which probably represented two ladies of the patrician class. Courtesans were numerous in Venice, but they were still confined to one quarter; in a few years, they were to begin wandering about the city, well dressed, wearing extremely high heels, making all well brought up women blush— but indistinguishable to the eyes of foreigners—and scandalizing all good folk.

The most important painter in the city was Giovanni Bellini, who was perhaps already nearly 70. A decade or so later, at the time of his second journey to Italy, Dürer, who had received courteous praise from Bellini, wrote to Pirkheimer, "Everyone told me that he was a great man, and he is so... although now very old, he is still the best painter of them all."

In the gossip in the squares or at the Rialto one question had for some time regularly come under discussion, both artistic and otherwise: the equestrian statue of the great condottiere Bartolomeo Colleoni. The greatest tactician of his time and commander of the Venetian armies, Colleoni

Opposite: The Grand Canal and Rialto bridge—built of wood with a central part that could be opened to allow the passage of commercial galleys going up to moor before the homes of merchants—in a detail from the plan of Venice by Jacopo de' Barbari, 1500. Below: Facade of the Ca' d'Oro, then the most beautiful of the houses along the Grand Canal, built in the gothic style, between 1422 and 1440, for the attorney Marino Contarini.

had bequeathed the republic 216,000 ducats in gold and silver and more than twice that value in land and property—with the single condition that a monument in his honor be built in St. Mark's Square. The senators balked at the notion of honoring a warrior in front of the doge's church and moved the site to the front of the "school" of St. Mark, an astute move. The Florentine Verrocchio had modeled both horse and rider and had had some tempestuous exchanges with the senate; at a certain point the senators sent to tell him that if he were ever again to set foot in Venice they would have his head cut off—in the same way that he, engraged because he thought the commission was going to be given to someone else, had torn the head off a model he had prepared. All this was now in the past. Verrocchio was dead, his marvelous horseman was finally being cast by Alessandro Leopardi, and everyone was impatient to go and see it, as they would all do on its unveiling.

By then, Dürer and Comines had departed Venice. The Frenchman had been staying there to further the interests of his king, Charles VIII, busy with his conquest of Naples, but in the meantime, among the ambassadors in Venice, the so-called Holy League (Ferdinand of Aragon, the emperor, the pope, the Milanese, and the Venetians) was closing its ranks against the king of France. Comines, growing more and more worried, was kept at bay with soft words, but on the day when the agreement was ratified, all the ambassadors of the league passed under his windows in boats, at least forty gondolas accompanied by minstrels. That night there were celebrative lights on the belltowers, bonfires on the homes of diplomats, and the thunder of artillery. The Frenchman ventured out in a closed gondola to see the festivities and slid, embittered,

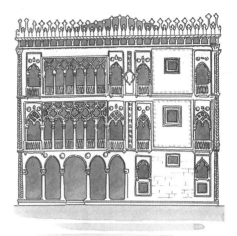

along the canals in front of the homes of the foreign plenipotentiaries, "full of banqueting and great cheer." On a preestablished date, the wooden trestle bridge in St. Mark's Square was put up "as is the usage on the day of Corpus Christi" (Marin Sanudo), and, on emerging from mass, the senators and ambassadors (the Germans dressed in velvet at the expense of the Venetians) paraded along it with great pomp.

Waves gently rocked the galleys tied up at the dock in front of the doge's palace. Here were ships destined for all Mediterranean ports, for the passage to Flanders, perhaps even those that carried pilgrims to the Holy Land. Foreigners came from all over Europe for the voyage to the Holy Land: it was a journey toward the marvelous, and Venice was the magnificent preface. In his account of the pilgrimage made by the landgrave of Axia (1491), Dietrich von Schachten wrote of Venice, "It is situated in the middle of the sea and is built neither on a hill nor on land, but only on piles of wood, a thing which, for those who have never seen it, is incredible to hear."

Jubilee

From Trondheim to Rome

A year of Jubilee was celebrated in Rome in 1500.
Guides gathered on the thresholds of the basilicas
to welcome pilgrims of every European language.
This is an account of the long journey to Rome
from one of the most distant dioceses. Pilgrims
journeyed by sea from the Norwegian coasts to the
estuary of the Elbe, then across Germany along
the Rhine to the Alps and entered a rich but
troubled Italy.

**Trondheim ● Bergen ● Hamburg ● Cologne
Coblenz ● Mainz ● Strasbourg ● Basel
Lucerne ● St. Gotthard Pass ● Milan
Florence ● Rome**

On the page opposite the title: At the start of his pontificate Nicholas V commissioned (1447) Beato Angelico to fresco his private chapel in the Vatican Palace. The Dominican painter depicted episodes of the lives of St. Stephen and St. Lawrence; the two soldiers who, in this detail, are breaking open the walled Holy Door, are an allusion to the pope's intention to proclaim a Jubilee for the year 1450, as he did in fact do.

During Advent, about halfway through December of the year 1499, His Holiness Alexander VI visited the Veronica Chapel in the Basilica of St. Peter to identify the site of the "Porta Aurea" to be reopened for the Jubliee. The pontiff made disposition for a suitable marble cornice, gave orders to the datary to set down the details of the bull giving plenary indulgence to those foreigners who visited the four basilicas of St. Peter, St. Paul, St. John Lateran, and St. Mary the Elder fifteen times (thirty times for inhabitants of Rome), and ordered that four religious men, two by day and two by night, remain to keep watch over the Basilica of St. Peter so that nothing untoward should occur during the upcoming ceremonial o-pening. It was found that there had never been a door at the point indicated by canons, but so as not to contradict tradition orders were given that the Master Mason Tommaso Matarazzo should reduce the thickness of the wall so that the pope, at the hour of the Christmas Vespers, would be able to knock it down with the pressure of his hand.

Many pilgrims bound for Rome had already started their journey, some from the most faraway places. Not from Green-land this time; that Scandinavian colony, whose pastor had been the bishop of Gardar, had dwindled and finally been abandoned due to malnutrition, sickness, and probably the worsening climatic conditions. In better days these Christians had made small offer-ings in the form of whalebones, which were sold at Bruges in benefit of the Apostolic Camera.

The archbishop of Trondheim, as it had recently been renamed (it first had been called Nidaros, then Trondhjem), was the head of the most remote Catholic ecclesias-tical province in the whole continent. In terms of latitude it was situated only slightly to the south of the coast of Iceland; the nights there are white in the summer, the days extremely brief in the winter, but the sea is eternally free of ice. The tiny city stood on a meander of the Nidelva River, slightly above its outflow into the sea at the fjord, but then there were over one hundred additional kilometers of water before reach-ing the open sea, outside the fjord and beyond the coastal islands.

They were not friendly waters, but all the same they were frequently navigated, though not always by direct confrontation with the high seas: as far as possible boats went via channels between the islands, along routes indicated by stone beacons. In May the little boats bound for Bergen from the islands much farther north of Nidaros—where great gulls wheeled and screamed continuously in the solitude—transported the products of their fishing: stockfish "dried in the wind and sun without salt," which had become "as hard as wood," and large flounder, cut into pieces and salted. About seventy years earlier, a handful of sailors, surviving shipwreck in a Venetian cog from Candia in those islands—probably the Lof-otens—were astonished by the "honest men of pleasing appearance" and the "simplicity" of the women, who "take no care to close any of their things" and come out naked to go to the sauna, carrying in their right hands "a tuft of grass as a brush, they say to wipe off their sweat," and then go to church on Sunday "in long and most honest garments," with head and face covered (from the reports of Pietro Querini and of Cristoforo Fioravanti and Nicolò di Mi-chiel).

The days of the wooden Viking churches, which withstood the wind and snow, built as they were with nautical carpentry tech-niques and carved like the prows of boats,

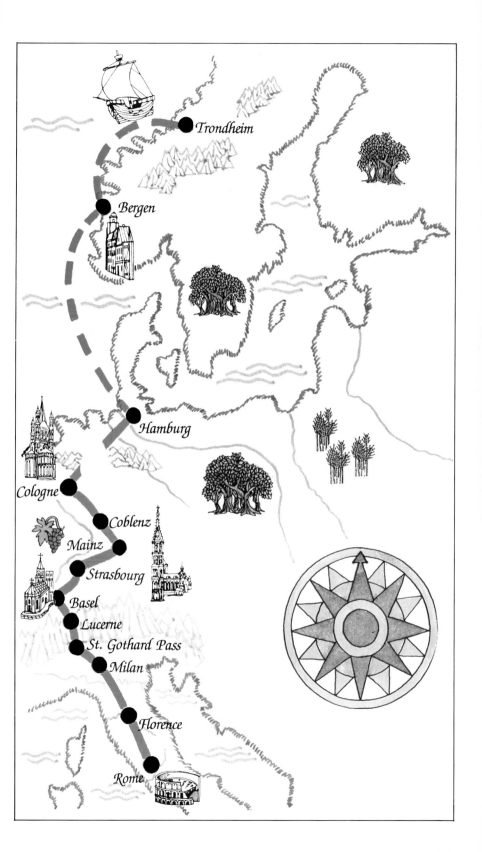

Trondheim

Bergen

Hamburg

Cologne

Coblenz

Mainz

Strasbourg

Basel

Lucerne

St. Gothard Pass

Milan

Florence

Rome

173

*Northern Europe. Below: Herring fishing in the northern seas,
from the* Historia de gentibus septentrionalibus *by Olaf
Magno, Rome, 1558. Opposite: The fisherman, an illustration
by Jost Amman for Hans Sachs'* Ständebuch *(1568).
Following pages: Sunset on the snow and the ice-bound river,
detail from* The Census at Bethlehem, *or* The Payment of
Tithes, *by Pieter Brueghel, 1568.*

had passed, but it was probable that at
Trondheim the only stone buildings were
the gloomy archbishop's palace and the
Domkirke, the unexpectedly enormous
cathedral that is the most important medieval monument of all Scandinavia. Was and
is, thanks to its partly Romanic-Norman,
partly gothic forms, which recall Lincoln
Cathedral. Here, in a precious silver case,
were preserved (until the Reformation) the
remains of St. Olav (King Olav II Haralds-
son, who died in battle in 1030), who had
first been buried secretly on the banks of
the river exactly where the church was later
to rise.

Although not very populous, Norway
was short of cereals. In Bergen, one hundred
dried fish could be exchanged for fifty kilos
of the grain brought by German merchants
from the Baltic. The city of Bergen, a
necessary stage in the long journey of the

pilgrim to Rome, was one of the fundamental centers of Hanseatic commerce; the
flourishing *kontor* had many privileges,
which the Norwegians suffered rather than
accepted. But Norwegian exports and im-
ports were then in German hands: fish and
furs traded for cereals, wine, and cloths.

In the inner part of the Byfjord, protected
by a dusting of bare, flat islands and islets,
Bergen emerged among rounded mountains
of rock smoothed by glaciers. The climate
is mild in comparison with the latitude, but
the rain brought by the swollen clouds from
the Atlantic falls for two hundred days a
year. In the Gulf of Vagen, at a point
illuminated by the sun during its rare appearances, was a fort that once had been a
royal residence—at this moment Norway
was united with Denmark and Sweden
under the scepter of John I, the son of
Christian, first of the Oldenburgs on these

174

thrones—as well as the wooden houses of German merchants, aligned on the jetty of the port. The place was called Tyskebryggen, Port of the Germans; it was here that the Roman pilgrims from Trondheim, leaving the boats that had carried them through narrow straits between islands, fjords and halts in remote villages, could find a ship on which to continue their journey south.

At the end of the 15th century, the "round" boats had become relatively homogeneous in aspect, or at least so it appears from the various illustrations that can still be seen: bloated lines, the sides of the ship well above sea level, width approximately one third of the length, large fore- and aftcastles, a great rudder hinged upon the sternpost. Of the three masts—this was the most recent technical improvement—the central one (the mainmast) carried an enormous square sail, the front one (foremast) another square sail, but of smaller dimensions, the third, to the rear (the mizzen-mast), a lateen sail. In the prow, some ships had a fourth, almost horizontal mast (bowsprit), beneath which a further square sail, the spritsail, could be spread. With greater mobility (thanks to the division of the sails) than the northern, single-masted cogs from which they derive, these ships, though of greatly varying size, took care of most of the traffic in the Atlantic, the Baltic, and the North Sea, and even partially in the Mediterranean. The *Santa Maria*, by now foundered in the shallows off Cuba, had been one of these, constructed in Galicia, a region connected by trade to Flanders and the north.

The journey from Bergen to the Hanseatic city of Hamburg was a voyage of over five hundred nautical miles. One followed the Norwegian coast, with fir trees above rock faces swarming with seabirds, a gleam of white on the rounded hills behind the firs.

Cutting across the mouth of the Skagerrak into the North Sea, one followed the almost invisible shores of Jutland and the northern islands of Friesland. It was an uncertain landscape, with lowlands and shallow waters, and navigation here could frequently be treacherous due to tides and storms, as well as dams built, destroyed, and rebuilt: "God created the land and the sea," says a proverb of Friesland, "the Frisians made the coast."

The most delicate point in the voyage was probably that of recognizing the Elbe estuary. On a little island of sandy dunes the people of Hamburg had already built, in the early 14th century, the lighthouse of Neuwerk, the oldest on the German coasts. During the middle of the 15th century, the lower course of the Elbe, which spanned about one hundred kilometers from the sea to the port of Hamburg, had been suitably marked with beacons. The city was growing. A lot of water had passed down the Elbe since Barbarossa had granted it customs rights for all the navigation and commerce along the river, which crossed the whole of northern Germany. It was spoken of in the marketplaces as the "city of beer," which it exported. Pirates, inevitable brigands of the sea, were afraid of ending up hanged on the Grosse Grasbrook, a region of recurrent floods a short distance beyond the city walls.

The wide plain, which extends away from the northern coast of Germany under a dull sky, was a country of marshes, pine forests, and peat-moors; here and there rye was grown, though potatoes had not yet arrived from the New World.

From Hamburg the journey proceeded, just touching the Lüneburger Heide, the moors of Lüneburg, and crossing many rivers (the principal of which was the

Below: Woods in northern Europe, detail from St. John the Baptist in the Desert, *by Geertgen tot Sint Jans (perhaps born at Leids between 1460 and 1465; died at Haarlem before 1495). Opposite:* Arrival of St. Ursula in Cologne, *a panel from the "Reliquary of Saint Ursula" by Hans Memling. Of the city of Cologne, faithfully reproduced, it is possible to recognize among other buildings the cathedral, still under construction.*

Weser). Between Osnabrück and Münster, in Westphalia, the highlands and dark woods of the Teutoburger Wald, the Teutoburg Forest, were crossed; humanists recalled the ghosts of Arminius and the Roman legions of Varus. Before reaching the Rhine one touched Solingen; its master ironworkers were already famous, above all for their swords.

In order to enter Cologne it was necessary to cross the Rhine. The city was the largest in Germany. In its river port the two fleets of the river could be met, that of the upper course and that of the lower; the farmers from the surrounding countryside came in through the gates in the walls at dawn, bringing bread and vegetables to sell to the burghers just waking in their beautiful stone houses. A grand prince, the archbishop was one of the seven imperial electors, although the city itself did not form part of the electorate, having won its liberty, by arms, at the end of the 13th century. Its economic prosperity had been both a premise and a consequence of this victory.

All in all, religious emotions were intense for the passing Roman pilgrims. "There are displayed the heads of the three kings Caspar, Balthasar, and Melchior," the canon accompanying the cardinal of Aragon was to state, "which we saw through railings in an iron coffer." The relics of the Magi had been taken from the church of St. Eustorgio in Milan by Bishop Reinhard von Dassel, who had accompanied Barbarossa. The cathedral had been begun in 1248 in order to give them fit housing; the light, impregnated with the colors of the 12th-century

stained-glass windows, was broken and re-flected by the precious stones and gold of the glistening reliquary; the altarpiece, called the *Dombild*, with its central panel repre-senting the *Adoration of the Kings*, which the German religious painter Stephan Lochner of Meersuburg had painted in 1444, was to be admired by Dürer. Comple-tion of the cathedral, with its fifty-six pillars, however, was going ahead slowly; the two towers of the facade would not point their

pinnacles to the sky until the 1800s.

Cologne was also the site of the martyr-dom of Ursula and her eleven thousand companions, massacred as they returned from a pilgrimage to Rome by Huns who were besieging the city. A description of this slaughter—"and upon sighting them, that barbaric people with great noise set upon them and, like hungry wolves among sheep, killed all that multitude"—can be read with emotion in the *Legenda aurea* (*The Golden Legend*). The body of the saint lay in the church bearing her name, and the relics of the virgins, especially their heads, were scattered in different churches through-out the city, as well as to various sites throughout the Christian world. The un-happy journey, the moving and tragic story of the wanderings of Ursula and her pious virgins, was an extremely popular religious theme. The complicated legend both en-thralled the believer with exotic sensations and romantic fantasies and induced a mov-ing and heartfelt experience of faith. In a similar manner religious emotion, in the meditation on the fifteen mysteries of Re-demption, was fed by the hypnotic repetition of prayers in the "rosary." It was in fact in Cologne, at the start of the 15th century, that a Carthusian monk had invented (or renovated) the rosary, inserting one "Pater noster" for every ten "Ave Marias"; while a confraternity, founded in Cologne in 1474, had promoted the universal spread of the practice. Luther was a youth of only 16 and had not yet started his university studies at Erfurt.

Following the Rhine upstream, vineyards began to appear above Cologne. The course of the river from Cologne to Mainz fired De Beatis with enthusiasm; he saw vines on both banks, followed by more hills covered with vineyards, and every half mile small

The heads of the three kings Caspar, Melchior, and Balthasar were shown, as we are told by De Beatis, who saw them "through railings in an iron coffer, where it is said that their bodies also lie." Below: A detail of the Reliquary of the Magi from Cologne Cathedral, the work of the goldsmith Nicolas de Verdun (12th century). Opposite top: Outline of the city from the Fasciculus temporum, *Cologne 1474. Opposite bottom: Drawing of one of the city's ancient churches, St. Martin the Greater, 12th-13th century.*

Stained-glass windows in much greater numbers than today rendered the light within churches softly colored. Opposite: Detail of a stained-glass window showing the Adoration of the Magi from the Strasbourg workshop of Peter Hemmel, 1480-90. An Alsatian from Andlau, Hemmel is a prime example of the art of the stained-glass window during the second half of the 15th century; he became a master in the art and a citizen of Strasbourg by marrying the widow of a glass painter and taking over his workshop.

towns or "walled lands," with castles on the hillocks that, as was characteristic of Germany, were the possession "of private gentlemen."

The Frenchman Comines analyzed this aspect of the social structure with his usual realism. He marveled at the number of strongholds and the number of people inclined toward evil deeds, violence for the smallest reason. A knight who could count on no one but his squire and himself was capable of challenging a large city or a duke, as long as he had a safe refuge in some little castle, where he could hide with twenty or thirty armed riders. It was rare for the princes to punish these marauding knights; on the contrary, they made use of them. The cities, however, fought them, keeping paid men at arms, and often besieged and destroyed their castles.

On the whole the countryside along the Rhine must have been fascinating. On both banks were cities, castles, and so much beauty that it was impossible to describe everything that could be seen; infinite images crowded the eyes, and the towers were decorated with crosses and weathercocks in gilded metal. These were the impressions of Pero Tafur (1435-39).

The cities follow one another along the Rhine. Coblenz (its name comes from the Latin for "confluence") stood on the banks of the slow and sinuous Moselle, at the point where it joined the Rhine. On the thin tongue of land between the two rivers, there is a castle. Farther upstream, at Kaub, an imperial castle stands in the middle of the waters. Close by, a terrible threatening rock constituted a danger for navigation. From its summit, Lorelei, the enchantress, bewitched mariners with her song.

At Mainz, another electoral episcopate, one could see "infinite boats and ships of a certain shape with one deck, and so large as to carry 200 *bucte* each" (De Beatis). Made a noble and provided with a pension by the archbishop, Johannes Gensfleisch (whose nickname was Gutenberg) had already been dead for about thirty years.

Strasbourg could be seen in the distance amid the green of the Rhine valley, thanks to the red stone spire of its cathedral. It was not on the banks of the Rhine, but close to it, shut in by the two branches of the river Ill, which surrounded it. An imperial city (it became French in the period of Louis XIV), it had only recently established a tolerable institutional balance between patricians and guilds. Here also the atmosphere was cultured. The Strasbourgian Sebastian Brant, a well-read humanist and poet, was at that moment teaching at Basel University. He had recently (1494) published *Das Narrenschiff (The Ship of Fools)*, perhaps the most celebrated book of those times. Unlike many others, the gothic cathedral there was complete, the pinnacle of its spire rising to a height of 142 meters (it had been completed in 1439). The canon from Molfetta was to note that it was even higher than the dome in Florence, the Asinelli tower in Bologna, the belltower of St. Mark's in Venice, "or any other building in Italy of which I have seen or heard tell." The summit could be reached by climbing over eight hundred steps, each one palm high.

Basel was already a fundamental center of European trade. Having traveled over the Alpine passes, caravans of mules arrived at the warehouses of the commercial associations (a single company could own and mobilize over one thousand). Large, four-wheeled wagons, which were estimated to carry four times the load of their fellows in Lombardy, "come and go in infinite number and continuously," each drawn by many

The city of Basel as shown in the Chronica mundi *by Hartmann Schedel. With the exception of the fantastic shapes of the mountains, the town is faithfully represented. In the foreground is Lesser Basel, the suburb on the right bank of the Rhine. A wooden bridge, with a chapel halfway across it, passes over the river and leads to the gates of the city. On the cliff overhanging the water, one of the towers of the facade of the Münster is still under construction.*

Typography

Was typography invented at Mainz? It was partly by convention that the first anonymous examples of printing in Europe using movable type were attributed to the goldsmith from Mainz Johan Gutenberg. Gutenberg had worked in Strasbourg between 1439 and 1444 and in Mainz from 1448. The printing works he operated in partnership with the burgher Johann Fust is known to have been active in 1450. The new art, which should have remained a secret (the workmen of Mainz had sworn themselves to secrecy), had boomed within a period of less than fifty years. The earliest printers included Albert Pfister in Bamberg, Johann Mentelin in Strasbourg, Heinrich Quentell in Cologne, and Anton Koberger (Dürer's godfather) in Nuremberg. Soon printers patiently set line after line of lead characters, one letter at a time, in as many as two hundred and fifty cities, as far afield as Portugal, Montenegro, and Scandinavia. In 1484 in Mainz, Peter Schoeffer published his popular Herbarius Latinus, *containing delicate woodcut illustrations of plants that were described with medieval fables. Like Gutenberg (but with greater financial success), Schoeffer had also been a partner of Johann Fust, who had died in Paris of the plague. Fust's money had enabled Gutenberg to set up his printing press. In 1455, the year in which the master completed his "42-line" Bible — the first book printed using movable type — Fuchs initiated legal procedings against him for the return of his investment and even ordered the confiscation of his printing presses and type.*

horses. Boats were loaded along the wharves of the port. One could make the journey to Strasbourg between dawn and dusk.

The city, prosperous and well-served, stood tightly around the high land, on the left of the Rhine and overhanging the river itself, on which rose the Münster, the stone cathedral of a warm rosy color. It was in this church that a council was held (1431-49) that had vigorously opposed the pope and had refused the orders of Eugene IV to dissolve; on the contrary, it had deposed him as a heretic and had elected to the papal seat, in a conclave held in the Haus zur Mucke (House of the Mosquito), in a nearby late gothic sidestreet, the pious Amadeus VIII of Savoy (last of the antipopes as Felix V). From the center of the town, under the shadow of the cathedral, at the Marktplatz, where the Rathaus (townhall) was still a 14th-century building, one could visit, by way of a wooden bridge on the site of the modern-day Mittlere Brucke, the houses on the right bank (Lesser Basel), where, however, "life is not lived as civily as in the city." Basel, an ancient imperial city, was allied with the Swiss, but did not yet form part of the confederation. On September 22, 1499, to crown the diplomacy of the duke of Milan and his ambassador Galeazzo Visconti, the treaty between Maximilian I and the league of cantons had been concluded, thus putting an end to the Swabian war and in fact consecrating the independence of Switzerland. Basel, eleventh of the cantons, was to join the confederation in the summer of 1501.

The priests and Norwegian pilgrims bound for the Roman Jubilee crossed Europe at a time when their journey could easily carry them into the midst of a war. The conflict in Swabia, in 1499, which had seen the inhabitants of opposite sides of the

Rhine above Basel set against each other, was, as has been said, over. At the battle of Dornach, Imperialists and the Swabian League had been overcome. It is said that the war cost twenty-six thousand lives, together with the destruction of two hundred castles and villages. To the south of the St. Gothard Pass another war was in progress: Louis XII of France wished to gain possession of the duchy of Milan. His grandmother had been called Valentina Visconti and had been the daughter of Grand Duke Gian Galeazzo.

The Swiss were involved, directly or indirectly, in both wars. The Eidgenossenschaft ("confederation") was undermined by suspicious mistrust between the rural cantons and the city ones and by rivalry among the three principal cities, Bern, Zürich, and Lucerne. It was nevertheless held solidly together by its mutual hatred of the house of Hapsburg and by its taste for independence. The Swiss were "horrid and uncultured" people, states Guicciardini,

"men by nature ferocious, rustic, thanks to the sterility of the land more often shepherds than farmers." In point of fact the Swiss lived by stockbreeding, taking their animals up into the Alps to the pastures which in spring were covered with flowers; by trading in goods, since businessmen could not avoid passing through their country; and by the manufactures based in Zürich and Bern. But above all they made war for money, with discipline, pertinacity, and razor-sharp halberds. Their traditional employer was the king of France. With the proceeds of war—both pay and booty—the cities of the Mittelland, the highlands between the Rhine and the Alps, had renovated their walls, built monumental gates, municipal buildings, arsenals, granaries, and city fountains topped by vivaciously colored statues; they built beautiful houses decorated with graffitti work and with warm, wood-lined interiors and painted glass at their windows.

From Basel, the route to Italy passed over the hilly undulations of the Mittelland,

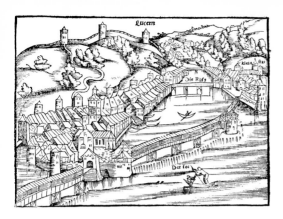

a tree-covered expanse dotted with lakes, and crossed by the Aare before reaching Lucerne, which was situated on the Reuss, at the end of the Lake of Lucerne, where the tranquil waters mirrored the mountains. The city owed a good part of its prosperity to the travelers using the nearby St. Gotthard Pass, a use that had begun after the 13th century.

The natural surroundings were savage and splendid. There were brown bears, chamoix, and roe deer in the forests (along with the stags whose horns were used to make chandeliers). On the south-facing slopes the marmots dug their holes, and in the Alpine pastures the capercaillie danced; in the sky high above flew eagles and peregrine falcons. On clear days the Alps provided a constant vista for the traveler but gave a sense of imminent dread rather than joy. Nobody from Lucerne climbed the Pilatus, as they would do later, to admire the horizon filled with snow-capped mountaintops; the name of the mountain recalled the legend according to which the corpse of Pontius Pilate had been thrown into a small lake on the mountain.

Larches and firs grew thickly on the slopes of the valleys, reaching as high as the St. Gotthard Pass, at 2,114 meters. The Swiss pine stood solitary on the rockiest and most windswept slopes. The upper Reuss valley was bitter and frightening; and no less terrifying, beyond the pass, were the Leventina gorges. Then one was suddenly in Italy. The Canton of Ticino was only later taken by the Swiss, when they attacked from the Gotthard Pass in 1503.

Italy was the richest, most beautiful, most sought-after of countries? Certainly it was the most interesting. If one looks at its politics, the situation was dangerously dynamic and changeable; it was not yet evident

that a tragic sixty-year period had begun that was to end with the dreary mastery of Spain in the enfeebled Italian peninsula. For the moment there were troubles enough with the French, the Swiss, and the Turks, as well as the lively ambitions and intrigues of native Italians.

After a couple of decades of peace, the Turks had once again attacked the Venetians in 1499, and the fine ships of the republic, inefficiently commanded by Antonio Grimani, had been defeated at Zonchio, a sinister first; in Friuli, a fulminating devastator—cavalry bearing the arms of the half moon—had reappeared. At the beginning of September in that year the French had taken Milan—the first city through which the Roman pilgrims had to pass—but Ludovico Sforza, having enlisted eight thousand Swiss soldiers, had regained his hold over the duchy (February 5, 1500). The king of France, Louis XII, had a much greater number of Swiss than Sforza, and when the two armies came face to face, at Novara (April 10), they avoided the slaughter of compatriots. Sforza, taken prisoner, was to await his death in the castle of Loches, on the Loire.

Florence, the second stage on the route to Rome, had changed greatly from the time of Cosimo. There were new buildings and an even greater number of works of art with which to amaze visitors. The most important artist of the moment was the aged Sandro Botticelli, who was tormented by the prophecies of Savonarola. The son of Lorenzo the Magnificent had been driven away because of his heedless actions (1494), when Charles VIII, lance on hip, was wandering around Italy; Savonarola had ended hanged and burned in Piazza della Signoria on June 23, 1499. The hesitant republic then gave itself Soderini as gonfalonier for life

Opposite: A view of the city of Lucerne drawn in the 1400s: the Kapellbrücke on the Reuss is clearly visible, today the oldest wooden bridge in the whole of Europe. Below: The Campidoglio, the Forum Romanum, and the Colosseum, in a detail of the map of Rome by Antonio Tempesta, 1593. Following pages: Rome in an anonymous canvas from the Hall of Cities in the Ducal Palace of Mantua; painted after 1530, it shows the city as it appeared around 1490.

(1502). In the meantime (1500) Machiavelli, 31 years of age, secretary to the chancery competent for international relations and military affairs, was on a mission in France. Cesare Borgia, younger son of Pope Alexander VI, with his brand-new title of duke of Valentinois given to him as a gift by the king of France along with a French wife, was taking possession one by one of the cities of Romagna, as though he were eating the leaves of an artichoke. Later (summer, 1502), Leonardo da Vinci was to enter his service, as "architect and general engineer," especially to draw plans of cities and design fortresses. On reflection, this last development alone is the epitome of the Italian situation.

Proceding from Florence toward Rome in that year of 1500, the Roman pilgrims' journey suggested a more symbolic shift that brought the arts, at the turn of the century, from the 15th-century world of Florence (as well as Milan, Mantua, Ferrara, Padua, Urbino) to the 16th-century fullness of Rome. One only has to look at the migration of geniuses. Leonardo and Bramante had left Milan just in time to avoid the disgrace of Ludovico Sforza. Before leaving for Mantua to work for Isabella d'Este, and then traveling on to Venice and finally Florence (he arrived in Rome before the Medici Pope, Leo X, in 1513), the 48-year-old Leonardo had completed the *Last Supper* (French archers furiously attacked his model of the equestrian statue of Francesco Sforza, in the courtyard of the Milanese castle). The 56-year-old Bramante was working in Rome on the cloister of Santa Maria della Pace, but, above all, "solitary and meditative," he occupied himself with "comfortably measuring all the ancient constructions" of the city (Vasari). Even Michelangelo was in

Rome and, at 25, had given proof that his talent was comparable to that of the ancient artists. Having carved "a marble Cupid and, after having kept it buried for a certain time and then bringing it to light, so that the rust and other small defects, inflicted to that purpose, would simulate antiquity, he sold it at a great price, through an intermediary, to Cardinal Riario" (Paolo Giovio). Raphael was only 17 but, alongside his master Perugino, he had already painted his first enchanting pictures, *The Three Graces* (Chantilly) and *The Knight's Dream* (London). In a few years time he too would take the road to Rome and glory.

Along the Tiber and in the hills, in the marshy and sinister Roman countryside, the red walls bearing the name of Aurelian, still strong and secure in places, while crumbling in others, marked off an extremely vast area, totally incongruous with the city's

limited number of inhabitants. In the ancient monuments, which had been decaying for a thousand years and of which none, with the exception of the Constantinian churches, had maintained its original function, the nobles had taken up defensive positions from medieval times onward. This can still be seen in the house of the Savelli family in the Theater of Marcellus. Every building was comprised of varying amounts of plundered ancient materials; in the portico of Santa Maria in Cosmedin, a Roman drain had become the menacing "bocca della Verità."

The fields of ruins were extensive. In the Forum Romanun, which was known as Campo Vaccino, among stones and under-brush, beneath the umbrella pines, skinny cattle trod history and the shadows of heroes under their hooves. Under the crumbling vaults of the Basilica of Maxentius and the Temple of Venus and Rome, in Santa Maria Nuova, the noble Francesca, example of piety, had founded the order of Oblates; after her death (1440) her body lay in state for three days within the church (which is now known as Santa Francesca Romana). Time had felled arches, columns, vaults, and had caused the level of the ground to rise. The "cunicolari" disappeared into the pipes of disused drains in order to strip the buried buildings of the treasures that could sometimes be found there. There were popes who loved to collect ancient

coins, small pagan bronzes, and marble sculptures. The "calcarari" produced lime mortar from cornices, drums, capitals. Pope Nicholas V had established a policy on the use of ancient remains as material for new buildings, for most of the ruins were the property of the church. The pieces of fallen marble were the first to be used, but Romans later moved on to the demolition of much that was still standing, and for two centuries Rome renewed itself by devouring its own remains.

Many of the hills (Esquiline, Viminal, Pincio, Quirinal, Coelian, Aventine) were uninhabited; there was countryside there, areas of rural freshness with shepherds and their flocks. On the Quirinal stood the

statue of the *Dioscuri* with their horses (the horses of Monte Cavallo), and guidebooks compiled to amaze pilgrims attributed the statue to the arrival in Rome, in the times of Tiberius, of two *philosophi iuvenes, Praxitelis et Fidia* [Praxiteles and Phidias]. On the Lateran, where the popes no longer had their residence, stood the statue of Marcus Aurelius, *quidam caballus ereus qui dicitur Constatini*, with between its ears the nonexistent prophetic "cocovaia," the owl that waited to announce the Last Judgment. The Capitol, to which the horse was to be brought in the 1500s, was already the seat of the Roman commune. The medieval tangle of the inhabited city occupied three zones: Campo Marzio, Trastevere, and the

189

Below: The loggia on the first floor of the Cloister of Santa Maria della Pace (from Edifices de Rome moderne, *by Paul-Marie Letarouilly, Paris 1840-47). This is the work with which Donato Bramante began his activity in Rome. Later, under the pontificate of Julius II, he was to set his hand to the demolition of the Constantinian St. Peter's, and begin (April 18, 1506) the long and complex construction work on the present-day basilica.*

suburbs between Castel Sant'Angelo and the Vatican. In Campo Marzio, shaped by the great loop of the Tiber, more or less from the Mausoleum of Augustus to the Theater of Marcellus, there rose majestic from among the smaller houses Santa Maria ad Martire, or rather the Pantheon, still sporting the bronze framework of its pronaos, which Urban VIII was to have removed to make the Berninian canopy over the pulpit of St. Peter's and the cannons of Castel Sant'Angelo. Sixtus IV had already had the market, which was held at the feet of the Capitol, moved to Piazza Navona (1477).

The popes, who had returned to Rome only thirty years earlier, had taken real control over the city only halfway through the century. The humanist Tommaso Pa-rentucelli of Sarzana, who served as pope as Nicholas V (1447-55), had been the initiator of the construction plan that was to render Castel Sant'Angelo (the indestructable Mausoleum of Hadrian, on the summit of which Gregorius Magnus had seen the angel sheathe its sword, having ended the punishment of plague), the "Suburbs," and the Vatican the seat of the Curia and fortress of the pope. On his death the conclave was held in the Vatican for the first time. The Venetian Paul II (1464-71) had preferred, as did some of his successors, to reside in the city palace, which he had built while still a cardinal and which was later donated to the republic of Venice (Palazzo Venezia). The architectural forms of the Renaissance, in fact, began to enter the city in the palaces of the princes of the church (the names are those of the families that were traditionally masters of Rome, such as Colonna and Orsini, and those of the "cousins," Borgia, Della Rovere, Cybo). Such, for example, is the palace built by Pietro Riario, nephew of Sextus IV, with money that he is said to have won at games of chance (later Palazzo della Cancellaria).

The pontiffs took a greater and greater interest in the city, which they felt to be ever more theirs, but the urban aspect of Rome was built slowly. Sextus IV (Francesco della Rovere, 1471-84) built the Sistine Chapel and employed the best painters (Botticelli, Ghirlandaio, Perugino, Signorelli) to fresco it, though these men chose not to remain in Rome. The building works proceeded in the midst of others left half-finished; the palaces of the Vatican were still fragmentary. Innocent VIII (Giovan Battista Cybo, 1484-92) chose an isolated spot on the hill for the pleasant and salubrious Belvedere villa.

The pope of the Jubilee in the year of 1500, Alexander VI Borgia, had celebrated the wedding of his daughter Lucrezia to Giovanni Sforza in the Belvedere (1493), had his apartments in the Vatican frescoed by Pinturicchio, and, together with his cardinals, had sought refuge in Castel Sant' Angelo when Charles VIII had installed himself in the Palazzo Venezia. His soldiers, realizing that the pope opposed their leader, sacked the palaces of the prelates and even that of one of the pope's lovers, Vannozza de Cataneis (the French also gave chase to

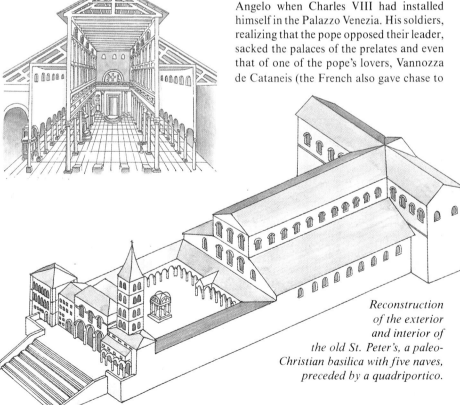

Reconstruction of the exterior and interior of the old St. Peter's, a paleo-Christian basilica with five naves, preceded by a quadriportico.

In spite of the thickly built-up area within the bend of the Tiber River, Rome also had enormous undeveloped areas, containing vineyards, gardens, and vast ancient ruins, within the wide circle of the Aurelian walls. This is evident even in the details of Antonio Tempesta's map shown on these pages. Opposite: The Isola Tiberina, Santa Maria in Cosmedin, the Palatine and Aventine hills. Below: A fragment of the Trastevere area.

the Jews, who were not yet closed within the Ghetto—founded in 1555—strangling many and destroying the synagogue).

The bad times appeared to be over as the pilgrims, with their money and the profits that could be made by their movements, were eagerly awaited. Together with the Holy Year, on December 24, 1499, the Holy Father had inaugurated the new access road to St. Peter's, the Via Alexandrina, completed in less than a year; the demolitions it had caused had been the first "clearance" in the urban history of modern Rome.

Before the Holy Door in St. Peter's, crowds of "porticani" or "duces" awaited the pilgrims (guides, in other words), ready to illustrate the marvels of the most important church in Christendom, which was no longer exactly the Constantinian basilica, with five naves, preceded by the quadriporticoed atrium of Paradise, but was not yet that which can be seen today. Noting the dilapidated state of the illustrious temple,

Nicholas V had entrusted its restoration to Bernardo Rossellino (1452), who had proceeded with care, doing his best to save every sacred memory. Three years later, on the death of the pontiff, work had been suspended; it would be taken up again only when Julian II gave the task over to Bramante.

In St. Peter's, the most venerated relic was the Veronica, but the lance that had wounded the side of Our Saviour was also preserved there. It had been sent to His Holiness by the Grand Turk (1492) and delivered by an ambassador who traveled to Ancona solely for that purpose (in the Curia there was discussion on how the relic should be received; there was embarrassment regarding the gift giver and doubts about its authenticity, as there was already one Holy Lance in Nuremberg and another in Paris; however, in the end it was decided to accept the offer with due solemnity). In the atrium one could admire the mosaic

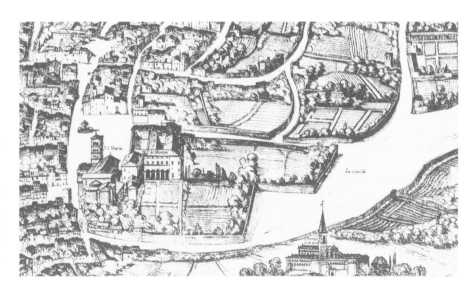

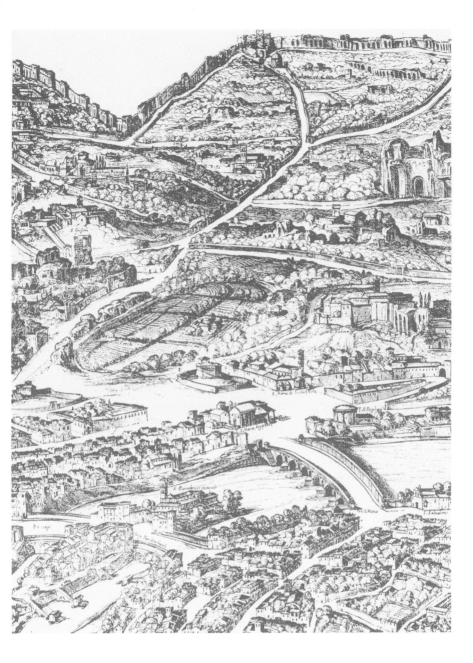

showing the Apostles aboard a boat, symbolizing the Church, and Jesus who, walking on the waters, invites Peter to join him, reproving him for his lack of faith (this is Giotto's "Navicella"). At the main entrance were the bronze doors by Filarete. Michelangelo's *Pietà* had just been placed in the St. Petronilla Chapel, frequented by the kings of France. Jean Bilheres de Langranles, cardinal of Santa Sabina, who commis-

sioned the work, had paid the artist an amount equal to approximately one and a half kilos of gold. It is not known what the "porticani" said to visitors about this work, but the artist "did gain great fame therefrom" (Vasari).

In the city there rampaged a rich lifestyle, thought by some to be excessive and obviously sinful. It is known that prostitutes rented houses that were the property of the

The Tiber, the floating mills, the bridges, the Roman remains, the great fortified mass of Castel Sant'Angelo; sketches of Rome from the Libro di Giuliano da Sangallo, *or* Barberini Codex. *The young Florentine had been in Rome for at least seven years, studying and drawing antiquities; he was to return again later and, at the end of his life, after the death of Bramante, was to direct, alongside Raphael and Fra' Giocondo, the work on the new St. Peter's.*

Witnesses of the times and places: Johann Burckard

He moved to Rome in 1481 when he was about 30 years of age. Sitting on Peter's throne was a greedy and violent exhibitionist: Pope Sixtus IV. Johann Burckard was originally from Haslach, near Strasbourg, and his native language was German. In 1483, shortly after his arrival in Rome, he purchased a letter of investiture to the office of master of ceremonies in the papal chapel. In this capacity, he directed processions, organized banquets and receptions, and selected furnishings, decorations, and ceremonial robes for five popes: Sixtus IV (who died in 1484); Innocent VIII (1484-92); Alexander VI (1492-1503); Pius III (who survived the conclave by little more than a month); and Julius II (elected in 1503). Late in life (1506), he bought another important appointment in the chancery but, immobilized by gout, was unable to take it up. He died later that year. His noted Liber notarum *was begun at the end of 1483 and was intended as an aid for the performance of his duties: "I shall take note of those things that have taken place in my time in the field of ceremony, and perhaps somewhat else." Year after year until 1506, this observer of the papal court recorded virtually everything: liturgy, carnival festivities, marriages, the arrival of new cardinals, intrigues, visits of potentates, homicides, scandalous behavior of priests, floods, tidings of war and peace, trials in the city, and capital executions. As a chronicle of the times it can be read with relish. It offers few opinions or judgments, except on etiquette and taste.*

Vatican. Since her mother and stepfather had started to invest in real estate in 1499, it is thought that Lucretia, who was later to be called Imperia, the most famous of all courtesans, had started her career. She posed as model, allegedly for Raphael, was under the protection of the rich banker Agostino Chigi, and died of poison, perhaps taking her own life in despair over an unrequited love in 1512.

Chronicles record other interesting facts during that year which further our sense of the time and place. On the fourth Sunday of Lent His Holiness offered the golden rose to his son, the Valentine; at the start of September the not unusual flooding of the Tiber occurred; due to a summer storm, a chimney had fallen down in the Vatican, breaking through the roof; the pontiff's throne had been tragically buried by the rubble but, protected by a beam, the pope himself had survived with only a few insignificant injuries; during August, in front of the house of the Massimo family, a man from Rieti had mortally wounded and castrated a cardinal's servant, who had taken his wife as a concubine; on the same day Lucretia Borgia had been widowed, when the prince of Salerno, after being wounded during an attempt on his life, was strangled in his bed. A doctor and surgeon at the hospital of San Giovanni in Lateran had made a name for himself by leaving the hospice every morning at an early hour armed with a crossbow, in order to kill "comfortably all those he could" and rob them of their money. He had ended like one of the eighteen hanged men who the cardinals, returning from the Vatican Palace in the city, could see dangling from their gibbets on the eve of Ascension Day "at about the mid-point of the bridge: nine on the right and nine on the left" (Burckard).

The future based on the "ancient" style

The painting below, displaying palaces and a symmetrical central edifice in beautiful perspective, is a 15th-century artist's conception of an ideal Renaissance city. There is no purely "Renaissance" city, however. New buildings that astonished foreign visitors to Italy

1

between the second and third decade of the 15th century. The portico of the Spedale degli Innocenti by Filippo Brunelleschi, dated 1419, is innovative yet connected to Florentine tradition. The "antique" features of the Baptistry of San Giovanni or San Miniato al Monte contain

were erected in a medieval setting. (The painting, which is at Urbino, has been attributed to various artists: Piero della Francesca, Luciano Laurana, and Francesco di Giorgio Martini. The latter, who was from Siena, was an architect, sculptor, painter, and also the author of an architectural treatise.) This new, formal style introduced the rounded arch and capitals, columns, and parastrades using designs from antiquity. It was first seen in Florence

3

Born in Italy, Renaissance architecture had not yet spread to the rest of Europe

purer designs than monuments and ruins from the Roman period. Roman antiquities soon became subjects of habitual study and scrupulous measurement (Brunelleschi probably went to Rome in 1433). The drawings shown here serve as visual references of the first phase

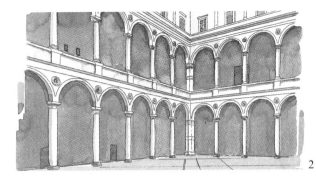

2

of the new architectural language: a Corinthian capital from Brunelleschi's San Lorenzo (1); a two-paned mullion window from the ducal palace of Urbino (3, left); the facade of Palazzo Rucellai by Leon Battista Alberti, divided by cornices and parastrades (3, right); the loggia from the courtyard of Palazzo della Cancelleria in Rome, an example of spreading Florentine influence (2); the ground plan and elevation of Santa Maria degli Angeli by

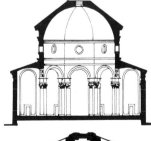

4

Brunelleschi, a building of Roman inspiration (4; the central plan was the theme on which the architectural ambitions of the Renaissance were to be measured). Architects such as Luciano Laurana, Michelozzo, the Sangallos, Bramante, Raphael, and Michelangelo enlarged on and varied the new style. Political forces and the widespread distribution of printed architectural treatises contributed to the spread of the style throughout Europe.

197

The archer of the king of France

From Edinburgh
to Paris

Scottish soldiers of fortune frequently journeyed to
countries where they could earn money. One of the
Scotsmen who served under the banner of the king of
France may have followed this itinerary across England
to the area of his enlistment. The marriage of the
daughter of the king of England to the king of Scotland
began a brief peace between the two kingdoms.

**Edinburgh ● Newcastle-upon-Tyne
Durham ● York ● Lincoln ● Boston
Cambridge ● London ● Canterbury
Calais ● Amiens**

Below: A view of Edinburgh drawn in the 1500s. Surrounded by walls, the city extends at the foot of the basalt rock crag on which the castle rises (from Braun and Hogenberg). Opposite: A house in the woods mirrored in a lake, from the Portinari Triptych *by Hugo van der Goes. On the page opposite the title: Mill with water wheel; swans swimming in the millpond. From the* Madonna Enthroned with Two Angels *by Hans Memling.*

Scottish men-at-arms at the side of the king of France were a tradition perpetuated from monarch to monarch. Before Liège (1468), fighting beside Louis XI, they had shown themselves to be *"bien bonnes gens,"* shooting their arrows at the enemy without retreating a single pace (Philippe de Comines). At Fornovo (1495), Charles VIII had one hundred Scottish archers with him. Later, on a diplomatic mission to the France of Louis XII, Machiavelli was to note that, of the four hundred archers "charged with the protection of the king's person," one hundred were Scots, and that "they receive three hundred francs a year per man," along with a tunic in the colors of the royal livery. These Scottish mercenaries on the continent were men from the Highlands, where the authority of the king of Scotland was inferior to that of the heads of clans. The men wore multicolored kilts and were unyelding fighters, both for money and for spoils.

Their green and rainswept country was in a backward condition, enemy of the English and in a state of unease. There were those who considered it a border country, barely civilized. In the *Memoires* of Philippe de Comines one can read of the "king of Scotland and his son, in battle one against the other. The son and those taking his part won the day and said king departed his life there." The reigning house was that of the Stuarts, or "Stewart," as it was written in the Scotland of that time.

During the 12th century a Norman had been made stewart, or seneschal, by the king of Scotland for his services, and presented with goods. The function, which was hereditary, had become a surname, and one of his descendents (Robert II, 1371) had gained the throne. In the early years of the 16th century, Margaret Tudor, the 13-year-old daughter of Henry VII, king of England, had been married to James IV Stuart (it was this marriage that, one century later, on the death of the great Elizabeth I, allowed a Stuart to receive the crown of England, James VI of Scotland and I of England). The wedding had been the cause of a brief period of peace between the Scots and the English. It is possible to imagine during these years the journey of an archer from

Scotland to France, crossing England, on his way to enlist with the royal guards.

Close to the sea, at the foot of the bare hills on the southern coasts of the Firth of Forth—one of those deep inlets that characterize the geography of the British Isles—Edinburgh was still a long way from being the beautiful, classically styled city we know today. It had become the residence of the court, in place of Perth, about seventy years earlier, and at that time the modestly built-up area at the foot of the castle hill had been protected by walls. The elements of greatest importance on the site were three: the castle, on its sheer cliff of basaltic rock; the 13th-century Dominican monastery (Blackfriars); and the Augustinian abbey of Holyrood. The appearance of the castle at the time of James IV can today be guessed from the remains: the tiny Romanesque oratory (St. Margaret's Chapel), built in the 12th century in honor of St. Margaret of Scotland by her son, King David I; the remains of David's Tower, which now form part of a 16th-century bastion, part of the 14th-century strengthening works carried out by King David II; the banqueting hall, which was also used for celebrations and for the meetings of the Scottish Parliament (Old Parliament Hall), in one wing of the palace, the foundations of which are from the 15th century, but which was modified on a large scale between the second half of that century and the start of the next. Among the Regalis, the Scottish Royal State insignia, which are today conserved in a special wing of the palace, are the scepter with figures of the Virgin, St. James, and St. Andrew, patron saint of Scotland, which had arrived in 1494 as a gift from Pope Alexander VI to King James IV. Nothing remains today of Holyrood Abbey but ruins beside the royal palace of Holyrood-house. The latter is built in the style favored for French homes during the Renaissance, but it was begun by James IV, and retains from that period the square tower to the left of its facade. As today, south of the palace rose the volcanic peak that bears the name of Arthur's Seat.

On the road to France, the archer soon left behind the soaring, screaming gulls flying over the gray waters of the bay and, on horseback, ventured inland to the south. He crossed the Tweed and Teviot rivers, climbed the hills up to the ridge of the Cheviots, at the pass of Carter Bar, 418 meters high. On the other side of the crest, England began.

Imaginary England, from Chronica mundi by Hartmann Schedel.

On the fields of Otterburn his pride as a Scottish soldier stirred as he recalled their legendary victory over the English, a century earlier in 1388. He then crossed Northumberland, before reaching Newcastle-upon-Tyne, on the left bank of the river, once again close to the sea. It was a port from which some were already sailing to Scandinavia. The "new" castle was the 11th-century Norman one, several portions of which, divided by the railway, survive to this day: the Black Gate, the 13th-century fortified entrance; and the older Keep, the great tower of Henry II. The site was originally a stronghold along Hadrian's wall, which had been built by the Romans to protect Britannia from the Picts inhabiting Scotland. The mysterious wall extended like a long grassy snake across the green hills of the Tyne Valley.

Immediately beyond, one entered County Durham. The capital, Durham, nestled on a rocky promontory, was entirely surrounded by a loop of the Wear River. The Scottish archer, a man destined to suffer the uncertainties of war, and for that reason certainly predisposed to faithfulness, was here able to admire the first of the great cathedrals of England that he would encounter along his route. Norman-Romanesque, built over a period of little more than thirty years (1093-1128), it contained the tombs of St. Cuthbert and the Venerable Bede, a writer of astronomy, physics, mathematics, music, rhetoric, and grammar and the first historian of the English (7th-8th century). At a later date the Galilee (12th century) had been built before the entrance, which in the abbey churches, such as that of Durham, served as a chapel in which corpses could be laid before burial. Also added on, at the end of the nave, was the Nine Altars Chapel, built in the early gothic style. At the start of the 15th century the cathedral had been restored by the prior John of Wessington. The Scottish archer could hardly suspect that one of his descendents was to cause a large amount of trouble to Great Britain: his name was to be George Washington.

The country and its people were the cause of curiosity and surprise among foreigners, Philippe de Comines judged the English to be *"fort collericques"* and for this reason ill adapted to the astute diplomatic dissimulation used on the continent. He considered this a characteristic of temper that was inevitable for all "nations of cold lands." The anonymous Milanese merchant who traveled around Europe (1517-19) and left a diary of his travels underlines the xenophobia of the English: "They are great enemies of all nations and speak ill of all" (for their northern neighbors the least malicious appelative was that of "lousy Scots"); generally speaking they think every place other than their own country "most sad" and that others, not having enough "to eat in their own homes," come to England and thus deprive the English of "the gains they would have made, had they not come there."

The two counties encountered by the Scot as he proceded on his journey were Yorkshire and Lincolnshire. The former was thick with looms installed in homes. Pack horses came bearing bales of wool to the weavers and carried away lengths of finished cloth.

The latter was one of the regions in which flocks of sheep could be found, a greater part of which was the property of the abbeys. Gabriele Tetzl, the man from Nuremberg who accompanied the Bohemian baron Lev z Rozmitalu and kept the diary of his journey, did not miss this scenic and economic feature: there is an abundance of

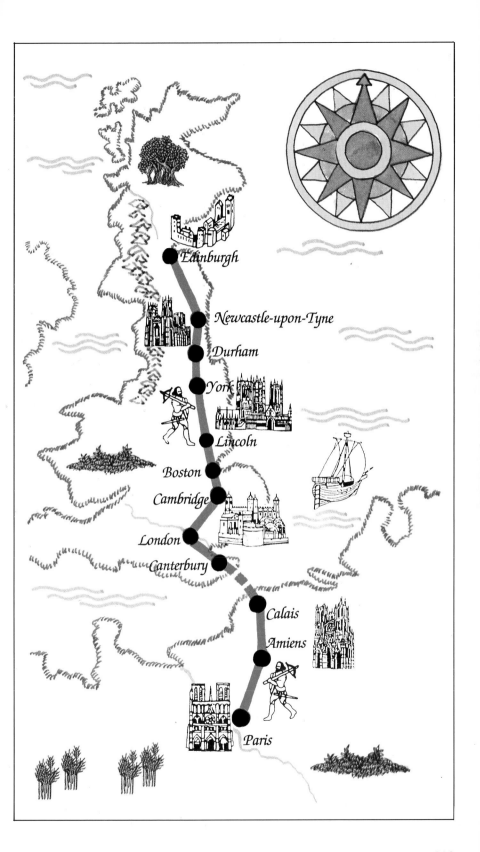

Edinburgh

Newcastle-upon-Tyne

Durham

York

Lincoln

Boston

Cambridge

London

Canterbury

Calais

Amiens

Paris

villages, cities, castles, forests, and cultivated land, he tells us, but there are also vast uncultivated areas that provide pasture land; the greatest profit from the land is that deriving from sheep. Even the Milanese merchant is appreciative of the pastures, which have a grass "very minute, shining and short, which seems just like green velvet"; English wools are greatly prized because of the quality of the pastures and because the sheep are kept particularly clean, never in stalls but "in the air of the country, both by day and night."

Schaseck, another of the Bohemian baron's companions, notes another significant aspect of the English agricultural and economic geography: each forested area is surrounded by dikes. In the same way, farmers—but we know that these "farmers" were very often in reality audacious and unscrupulous "precapitalist" agricultural entrepreneurs—dig dikes around their fields and grasslands, thus giving them boundaries so that nobody can pass through the countryside, either on foot or on horseback, except on the roads. This hints at the well-known theme of enclosures that has caused controversy among historians. Uncultivated lands were being closed in and destined for pasture, but even the common fields in the villages (open fields) were undergoing the same process, certainly increasing the productivity of the land, but at the same time dislodging many peasants, who ended up swelling the ranks of the poor. Hugh Latimer, a Reform theologian (who was to die at the stake during the reign of Bloody Mary), was at that time a little boy. He was later to preach against the grabbing landowners, who were the cause of the misery of small farmers. The phenomenon was complex, producing at the same time poverty and well-being. Latimer himself was the son of a small landowner holding closed pastures for one hundred sheep and thirty cows, which his mother milked.

Ending on a sandy coast, the long Humber estuary separated Yorkshire from Lincolnshire. The capital cities of both these counties were gathered around a famous cathedral.

York is at the center of the wide depression of the Vale of York, where, amid slight undulations in the ground, the Fosse flows into the Ouse (this is the river that farther south joins the Humber). It was a site where the river was easy to cross, and the city occupies both banks, surrounded by walls built in the time of Edward III (14th century), which had in part made use of their Roman predecessors. From Bootham Bar, a Norman gate built upon one built in Roman times (a gate is called a bar in York), one entered a city full of tortuously winding streets, along which were lined the unusual black-and-white houses: black framework thick with beams, white mortar used as a filling, the spaces between forming the walls

Below: An English village among trees depicted in a miniature from De proprietatibus rebus *by Bartholomew of England, ca. 1410. Of England the anonymous Milanese of the British Library manuscript recalls among other things the many parks, with their great quantities of fallow deer and even red deer. He noted that it was seldom possible to hunt them without royal license "sub pena capitis." Opposite: An example of English wood-frame architecture.*

Opposite: Lincoln Cathedral and the plan for same, with its double transept, the Angel Choir at the extremity of the nave, the cloister, and octagonal capitular chamber in which various kings held council before beginning military expeditions into Scotland. Below: Haymaking and the family at table, woodcuts of English society during the Tudor age, from the Roxburghe Collection.

in the grid of planking (this is the typical construction of the master carpenters, widespread throughout the regions to the north of the Alpine chain, which the English call timber-framing).

Above the roofs, not far from Bootham Bar, in the northern angle of the encircling walls, there lifted, as they still do today, the three towers of the Minster, the Cathedral of St. Peter, largest among the English medieval cathedrals (163 meters long; two of the towers are at the sides of the facade and the third, the lantern tower, is more or less halfway down the church, where the arms of the cross intersect). The final touches had been given to the building only in 1474, after two and a half centuries of work that ended by exemplifying all the phases of English gothic: the first (early English) in the transept, the decorated in the naves, perpendicular in the choir and towers. The famous stained-glass windows that speckle the linear, almost unadorned interior with colored light were all in place:

"The Heart of Yorkshire" (1388), for example, in the great front window, and the "Five Sisters" (13th century) in grisaille, in the left transept.

At Lincoln, the cathedral of St. Mary dominated the outline of the city, which stood thickly around a hillock. It is difficult to say whether or not it was already considered the most beautiful of English cathedrals at the time in which the Scottish archer passed through the city; today, it is considered so. In the form of a cross with straight heads to its arms, as can usually be seen in English cathedrals, it has three towers, like York Minster, but there is a second transept before the terminal wall of the choir. Part of the facade belongs to the Romanesque building dated 1075-85, which was destroyed one century later by an earthquake; the rest of the church (1186-1200) is mainly the work of the bishop, and later saint, Hugh of Avalon, and displays in its design the transition from Romanesque to gothic.

A frieze on the facade that illustrates stories from the Old and New Testaments has reminded some critics of the cathedral of Modena. Did Italian Romanesque masters venture this far north to practice their art? The terminal section is one of the earliest English gothic constructions (begun in 1192) and is the work of the master Geoffrey of Noiers, probably French. This kind of probable foreign contribution only serves to underline the unity of medieval European Christianity. Inside, passing alongside the whole nave one reaches the Angel Choir, with its thirty figures of angels decorating the pennons of the triforium. There are those who consider this a masterpiece within a masterpiece. If we imagine our Scottish archer wandering among the pillars and beneath the vaults we have to think

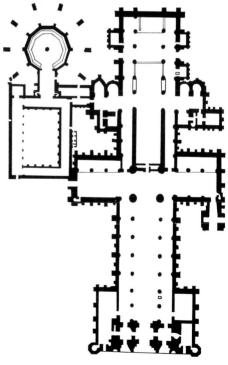

Wine merchants, an engraving from Les Ordonnances de la Prévosté des Marchands et Echevinage de la Ville de Paris, *1500-1. On the island, all wine was imported, the local drink being beer; during the Tudor age hops were introduced from Flanders, thus giving rise to the saying (somewhat simplifying history) "Hops, Reform, bays and beer, all came to England in just one year." The bays also came from Flanders.*

The colleges of Cambridge

Many of the famous colleges of Cambridge were already in existence. Peterhouse was the oldest college (1284), its statutes having been set down by Simon Montague, bishop of the nearby Ely, based of those of Merton College, Oxford. Michaelhouse and King's Hall later merged into Trinity College, founded by Henry VIII. Clare College was established in 1326, and Pembroke College in 1346. Corpus Christi College was founded immediately after the great plague of the mid-1300s to augment the number of priests, who had been decimated by sickness. King's College was founded in 1441 by Henry VI and enrolled only students from Eton. The exquisite King's College chapel, a masterpiece of perpendicular gothic, had been under construction since 1446 and would be completed in 1515. Other colleges of the period included Queen's College, St. Catherine College (1473), and Jesus College (1496). A beautiful period was about to begin for the university. The cultured Lady Margaret Beaufort, countess of Richmond and mother of King Henry VII, was soon to found Christ's College (1505) and to transform the ancient hospital of St. John's into a college (1509). Bishop Fischer, a friend of Erasmus's, would become provost of the university in 1504, and Erasmus himself was to become a professor there in 1511. "I find here a healthy and pleasing climate," he wrote from England, "a culture and doctrine indeed not replete with subtleties and trivialities, but a culture that is profound, precise, and classical."

that, as was customary in those days, the guide accompanying him would have indicated above all the relics (the urn, for example, containing the head of Hugh the Holy), the names of the important personages buried in the church, perhaps the supposed statues of King Edward I with his wives Eleonor and Margaret. But appreciation of architecture occurs in a manner too mysterious for us to be able to imagine its effects upon the people who lived half a millennium ago. Among other things, some people did not like medieval English churches. "In Anglia the churches are without proportion," writes the Milanese merchant, "they are all long and narrow."

Lincoln is on the Witham River, which flows into the North Sea in that vast gulf called The Wash, between Lincolnshire and Norfolk. On the lower course of the river, about four miles from the sea, at the farthest inland point, where the effect of the tides can still be felt, stands Boston. In those times it was the second largest port in the kingdom. The parochial church of St. Botolph, a building in decorated gothic style, was already dominated by the Stump (15th century, height 91 meters), the tower on whose summit stood a lantern that served as a lighthouse for sailors.

Another port reachable from The Wash was King's Lynn, on the right bank of the Great Ouse River, close to its mouth. From this port the road leading to London passed through Cambridge. The expanse to the back of King's Lynn was the low, marshy Fenland. A large part of its land had been cultivated in the past, but then came the great flood of 1236. Only in the 1600s would the work finish that would once again allow the cultivation of those lands. The drainage had been done according to the plans of a Dutch engineer.

At Cambridge, however, the archer whose footsteps we are following would arrive from the direction of Boston, probably via Peterborough. Here there also stood a famous cathedral, an imposing edifice of Romanesque-Norman fashion. It was exactly at this time that the construction of the New Building was underway, featuring the rear choir (1496-1508) with its beautiful fan vaults, one of the genial decorative elements of insular gothic.

At Cambridge the placid Cam River makes an wide bend. The landscape blends into the highlands bearing the curious name of Gog Magog Hills, which form the highest point in the county (68 meters). Then as now, colleges lined the city street that follows the concave curve of the river bend.

The city was the seat of one of the only two universities in England. The other, as is well known, is Oxford; across the whole island only one other university was to be found: St. Andrews in Scotland, founded in 1411. Oxford and Cambridge were much older and, as is the case with all the earliest European universities, it is impossible to identify a date corresponding to a specific foundation. They were active and considered themselves authorized *ex consuetudine.*

Oxford came into being as the result of the migration of English students from Paris during the second half of the 12th century. Cambridge owed its origins to another migration, this time of teachers from Oxford, at the start of the following century. Within the first forty years of the 13th century it had been recognized as a *studium generale* (an expression understood to mean a place of study open to all).

Even the system of colleges, which characterized the universities of the English-speaking world, is of Parisian origin. Initially they were inns, established by patrons in order to ensure food and lodging for those students who would otherwise have been without means. During the years of the journey of the Scottish man-at-arms, Paris numbered some seventy-eight colleges, among them the one founded by Robert de Sorbonne (1257), from which the name of Sorbonne derived. In France, the Revolution abolished these institutions as obscure holdovers from the Middle Ages, for they were corporations exactly as the universitites were; in England they continued.

Our Scot probably entered the walls of London by Bishopgate, along the road which headed straight for the only bridge over the Thames, London Bridge. The city had many things with which to impress foreigners. The two personages who set down the travel diary of the Bohemian baron have left us significant notes. For Schaseck, London is "grand and magnificent." He is particularly impressed by the stone bridge, on which, all across its length, houses are built, and by the abundance of kites. There are more than he had ever seen elsewhere, and it is a capital crime to hurt them in any way. For Tetzel, the city is powerful and busy, maintaining an intense trade with all other countries; a large number of people live there, among them many artisans, mainly goldsmiths and tailors. He also notes that food is expensive and that there are many beautiful women. At that time in England there was nothing scandalous in an honest woman going alone to drink and exchange gossip in taverns, but custom did allow a husband the right to beat his wife: "the wife has to bear this, leaving her husband the last word and allowing him to be the master," states an extremely fashionable manual of living (which was, in fact, translated from the French).

The walls of the "City" defined a strip of land on the left bank of the Thames, from the Tower of London to the mouth of the Fleet River. The Milanese merchant mentioned previously compares the extent of the circle of walls with those of Pavia, but immediately adds that outside said wall there are suburbs which extend as far again. During the Wars of the Roses the nobility had reduced its own numbers in fighting for the crown, but London had lived in peace, working, doing business, growing. All the same it was still a medieval walled city, immersed in a green hilly countryside with numerous villages all around.

The famous Tower of London appears to the Milanese merchant as not particularly large, not beautiful, and not even very strong. At that moment it was in need of repairs, which were to be carried out by Henry VIII. Within its perimeter were the mint and "a tower of great size in which the King keeps the most part of his treasure and of his vestments and wardrobe in brocade and silk." This treasure is carefully guarded—the present-day Yeomen warders (members of the Royal Guard) wear a costume that may date to the period of Henry VII, first of the Tudor kings, who reigned in the years of which we are speaking—and nobody, with the exception of a few foreigners, is allowed to see it. The visit was granted to Lev z Rozmitalu and his band.

The principal church of the city was St. Paul's. This is not the structure that can be seen today, built by Christopher Wren, but its predecessor, destroyed during the "great fire" of 1666: a gothic church, completed in 1222, which the Milanese merchant sees as "all covered in lead and plaster." Outside Ludgate, the nearest gate, there was a long line of taverns and inns for pilgrims on their way to venerate the precious relics in the cathedral: the crystal phial containing drops of the Virgin's milk, the hand of John the Evangelist, the hairs of Mary Magdalene, and, in a famous reliquary, the blood of St. Paul.

Inside the church many lawyers also walked, in discussion with their clients. After the formation of Oxford University, the teaching of law had been prohibited in the city (there had once been a school next to the cathedral), and the lawyers had moved themselves outside the walls, to a point halfway between the city tribunals and the royal ones of Westminster. One of these places was the group of buildings that had belonged to the Templar Knights, disbanded in 1312, known as the Temple.

According to the always helpful Milanese merchant, within the city only three or four streets are "fair and spacious, the others are ugly." In point of fact there is a maze of disorderly back streets within the walls, sometimes so narrow that one could stretch out one's arms and touch the houses on both sides of the road. Signs hung everywhere: they festooned the hostelries, the booths, and every other place in which business was done, even private houses. If a noble happened to stay for a short time in a house that was not his usual residence he would hang his coat of arms at the window. Even the brothels in Southwark, Cock Lane, and Smithfield had signs of their own.

The houses were made with a skeleton of wooden beams filled in with bricks; the latter came from the furnaces of Whitechapel and Limehouse, while the carpentry work was, in a certain sense, prefabricated at Maldon, in Essex, and transported to the city in boats. These houses could be three, four, or even five stories high, each story jutting out above the one below. This added

Below: The Thames, the White Tower, and London Bridge are easily identifiable in this miniature showing the capital of England during the 15th century; from the poems of Charles of Orléans, who is depicted in the Tower, where he was held as a prisoner of war for twenty-five years. Opposite: The pillory, a not infrequent detail in the Europe of half a millennium ago; woodcut of a biblical subject from the Speculum Humanae Salvationis.

London Bridge was the only bridge over the Thames; like others of its kind elsewhere it was thick with buildings. Below: The bridge in a detail of a drawing by Anton van der Wyngaerde, 1543-44. Opposite: A plan of London, from the Speculum Britanniae *by Norden, 1593. Closed from the sea, on the left bank of the Thames, the city reached from the Tower to the Fleet River. Farther away (on the left), around the bend in the river, lay Westminster.*

living space, but took away light and air from the street below, not to mention from those living there. Sometimes the roofs extended so far they touched those of the houses on the opposite side of the street.

The great churchmen and nobles, *"ces grands Mylords/Accorts, beaux et courtois, magnanimes et forts,"* as Ronsard was to say a few decades later, lived in a very different manner. Their homes extended around the four sides of a courtyard. Beside the entrance and in the side wings were lodged squires, domestics, kitchen maids, scullery boys, servants and valets; the residence of the master of the house occupied the wing at the end of the courtyard. The family met for dinner in the great hall, which formed the heart of the house. There were carpets on the floors, tapestries on the walls, and gracious bow windows looking out onto well-ordered gardens. Well-to-do

merchants were able to build themselves similar mansions.

The mercantile and industrial development of the city had caused the concentration, in the suburb of Southwark, on the right bank of the Thames just beyond the bridge, of many families of workers, glassblowers, smiths, tanners, and weavers with their laboratories. But Southwark was universally known for the taverns and brothels along its banks; the prostitutes there were known as "the geese of Winchester," and the houses in which they worked did, in fact, belong to the bishop of Winchester.

Outside the walls, toward the east, two bridges crossed the Fleet River. Via one, leaving through Newgate, one crossed present-day Holborn; via the other, leaving through Ludgate, along the Strand, following the curve of the river, one arrived at Westminster. The Strand was a country road on both sides of which were spread the residences and gardens of the nobility. It seems that in the streets of Westminster Flemish merchants selling hats and reading glasses were frequently to be seen.

The court resided at Westminster Palace. It was Henry VIII who was to transfer it to Whitehall (1529), under sequester from Cardinal Wolsey, and later Westminster was to become the seat of Parliament (1547). Westminster Hall, the great hall begun at the end of the 11th century by the son of William the Conqueror, is a remnant of the ancient royal palace, and it is there that the Milanese merchant says the king's chancellor presided at the court of justice four times a year.

At Westminster Abbey, "where are buried for the most part the kings," the great restoration works had just been finished, and construction was starting (1503) behind the apse on the Henry VII chapel in the best perpendicular gothic style.

212

What can the impression of the Scottish man-at-arms have been in this, the first metropolis along his route? The English habit of eating in complete silence surprised continental travelers; a Venetian who took part in a banquet in the city during this period was unable to refrain from reference to ancient history: it seemed to him that he was taking part in a Spartan meal. Southerners even came to appreciate the difference between two kinds of beer (beer and ale); someone states that they cease to be unpleasant after one tries them four or five times, and that in any case they are pleasing to the palate when one is, for any reason, hot. If he arrived there at the right time of year, the Scot would be entertained by the illuminations "in certain streets down toward the Thames," by the nighttime processions, and

the streets strewn with flowers for the feast-days of St. John and St. Peter, feasts to which foreign merchants often made their own contribution. He would certainly have seen cockfights. This is a spectacle that our friend the Milanese merchant describes in sufficient detail. The spectators sit on benches around an arena about eight arms in width. He who wishes to start the game throws a cock into this arena "with clipped wings," somebody else quickly throws in another, and the two birds immediately fall to, sometimes even killing each other. Round about the bookmakers are at work.

At night the gates of London were closed. Those wishing to set out on a journey at the crack of dawn, as was the common practice, passed the night in the suburb of Southwark, on the southern bank of the Thames, where

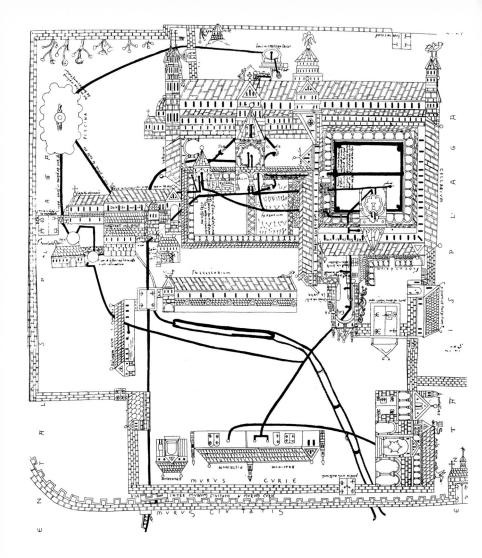

the road to Canterbury and Dover began. This is what the thirty pilgrims in Geoffrey Chaucer's *Canterbury Tales* had done, meeting "at this gentil hostelrye / That highte the Tabard, faste by the Belle."

Crossing Kent, one passed Rochester. A strange story circulated regarding this place. It was said that babies here were born with a tail, so that women giving birth preferred to do so on the other bank of the Thames. In fact, the reply to the sarcastic expressions of the English regarding people of other nations was usually "inglis tayled," Englishmen with a tail. Rochester's troubles had to do with the malediction of St. Thomas Becket. A traveler relating the legend assures us that it is a thing of the past, nobody is now born with a tail, not even in Rochester.

Becket had been assassinated on December 29, 1170, in the northwest transept of Canterbury Cathedral by the four knights Brito, Moreville, FitzUrse, and Tracy, who thought that they were carrying out the wishes of Henry II. While a violent storm blew up, a mourning crowd immediately gathered on the spot. Two days later the miracles began.

Pilgrims could now read of the deeds and miracles of the saint in the red and turquoise windows of Trinity Chapel. The reconstruction of Canterbury Cathedral, after the fire of 1174, by the French master Guillaume, builder of Sens Cathedral, had marked the introduction of gothic architecture to the island. In the tower above the transept, Bell Harry had just been finished (1503), and the saint rested in a coffin all of gold, long enough and wide enough to contain an average-sized man, and so richly ornamented with pearls and precious stones as to

Opposite: In a medieval drawing, Canterbury Cathedral and Abbey (the black lines indicate the level of the conduits for the distribution and drainage of water). The first monastery was founded by Augustine, converter of the Angles, who arrived on the island along with forty monks in 597. Below: Dover, the "white cliffs," ships under sail on the waters of the Channel, in an English drawing, ca. 1520-30.

make one think that none richer existed in the whole of Christendom (Tetzel). It was to be plundered shortly afterwards (1528), and Henry VIII had the Régale de France, the ruby that the king from the other side of the Channel, Louis VII, had sent in homage to the memory of the saint, mounted on a thumb ring.

The Channel crossing, in the memories of travelers, is not without its adventurous moments and unpleasant details. The most sober of those who speak of it is the by now well-known Milanese merchant: it is "necessary to await the wind, as in calm weather it is not possible to depart." Leaving the English coast, one can see high mountains covered with chalk (Schaseck); these are the "white cliffs" of Dover.

Calais at that time was the last fragment of French land still in the hands of the English, who sent the wool to be exported to France there; the sovereign leavied a tax of many scudi from this, as many as one hundred and ten thousand. The Merchants of the Staple, the company of wool exporters, had there a "most beautiful palace" in which they resided, almost always in a number of over one hundred. The city was considered to be impregnable, because of the walls, the moats, and the ability to flood the surrounding countryside for four miles in half an hour. It appears that there was a garrison: the canon of Molfetta who accompanied the cardinal of Aragon (he was

The beautiful countryside of France. Below: A miniature from Les Heures d'Etienne Chevalier by Jean Fouquet, ca. 1450, showing St. Margaret taking sheep to pasture. Opposite: The city of Paris in the background of a miniature from Chroniques *of Jean Froissart (the episode shows the arrival in Paris, in 1385, of the king of Naples, Louis II of Anjou, then still a youth).*

in Calais in order to cross over to the island, but decided against it) states that the soldiers "are so tall, strong, and fair men as ever were seen; from which it is easy to make conjectures on most Englishmen."

One then had to cross Picardy, "a fair land with several goodly woods," and fertile. There were cattle of the same variety as the German ones, "red swine," and many sheep. Wine grapes were not cultivated, but in all the inns along the road red wines could de bought, "good but costly." The women, alas—it is again the canon who tells us this—were ugly.

The Scottish archer was on French soil at last. In how many hostelries along the way would somebody have alluded to the *Franc-Archer de Bagnolet?* This is a theatrical monologue (1468) with a grotesque hero, the personification of a cowardly and boastful soldier. It is a satire on a militia of archers founded by Charles VII in the vain hope of imitating the efficiency of the English archers; Louis XI had disbanded the corps. The archer of Bangnolet mistakes scarecrows for warriors, and his greatest pride is that of wrecking havoc "*en poulaille.*"

Having passed over the Somme, one reaches Amiens, which stands on the left bank of the river. The Milanese merchant, whose negative appraisal of English churches has been set down above, did not hesitate to affirm that Notre-Dame, the gothic cathedral of Amiens, built over a period of fifty year during the 13th century,

is the most beautiful church in the realm. In the morning, the front part of the head of St. John was shown "to all good men" (the rest of the head was conserved in Rome). The charm and artistic value of the *Beau Dieu*, the celebrated statue of Christ in the central portal, and of the *Vierge Dorée* with her singular smile in the pillar of the transept door, had not yet, perhaps, been evaluated. The one hundred and ten meter spire standing high above the transept had not yet been constructed.

Finally, Paris. According to the practice of the time, visitors did not miss the opportunity to view the city from the top of the towers of Notre-Dame (and there were three hundred and twenty steps). As De Beatis tells us, the city is situated on flat land "in a most beautiful countryside," surrounded by many villages and vineyards providing excellent wine—"the most graceful that I have ever tasted." Wandering around the city, one found streets that were narrow and, for the most part, "extremely muddy," in which so many carts passed that riding there was more dangerous than navigation among the Syrtes. There are also a great number of people all around (the experience of large crowds was not frequent in those times). As the ambassador Marino Giustiniano (1535) was shortly to write, "in general all men and women, old and young, masters and servants, pass their time in the shops, on the doorsteps, or in the street." It appears, in fact, that the city already suffered from overcrowding at the start of the 15th

Images of Paris. Below: The Ile de la Cité, in a miniature by Jean Fouquet for the Chroniques de Saint-Denis. *When Labienus, Caesar's general, arrived there in 52 B.C., there was a fishing village of the Celtic tribe of the Parisii. Opposite: The Sainte-Chapelle and the towers of the Conciergerie (the* concierge *was a lord with the right to administer low and middle justice) from* Les très riches heures *of the duke of Berry.*

century. One must remember that each family was squeezed into one or two rooms; the wooden houses, which the canon of Molfetta sees as "large and commodious and well planned," often had to be divided among a number of tenants on each floor, while the courtyards were filled with hovels and lean-to sheds.

Our friend the Milanese merchant notes that in this crowd half the people are foreigners; very few are gentlemen, but there are many merchants, artisans, priests, and students. Even then, it was probably possible to eat at prices suited to every pocket. Later

(1577), another Venetian ambassador, Girolamo Lippomano, was amazed by this: the landlords serve you "for one testone, for two, for a scudo, for four, for ten"; for twenty-five they would create for you a broth of biblical manna or a roast of mythical phoenix. The supply of foodstuffs was provided even then by the "belly of Paris," the *halles*, which existed as a covered market from the time of Philip Augustus (13th century).

In reality, Paris meant three different cities: the *ville*, the *cité*, and the university. The Milanese merchant calculates that each of these corresponds respectively to half, one-sixth, and one-third of the entire surface of the city. The *ville* was the part on the right bank of the Seine; it was bounded by the walls built by Charles V (1370), whose path can be imagined: from their river end at the Canal St. Martin, they formed a curve that returned to the Seine lower down, at the level of the most ancient part of the Louvre, after having touched, in succession, Place de la Bastille, the Porte St. Denis, and the Palais Royal.

Below: The Ile de la Cité and the cathedral of Notre-Dame, the Pont Saint-Michel, and the Petit-Pont, both flanked by buildings, and the quarters on the left bank, in a plan dating from the time of Henry II (16th century); in a small square on the Rive Gauche a man can be seen hanging on a gallows.
Opposite: The Louvre as it appeared in the 15th century, in the miniature for the month of October from Les très riches heures *of the duke of Berry.*

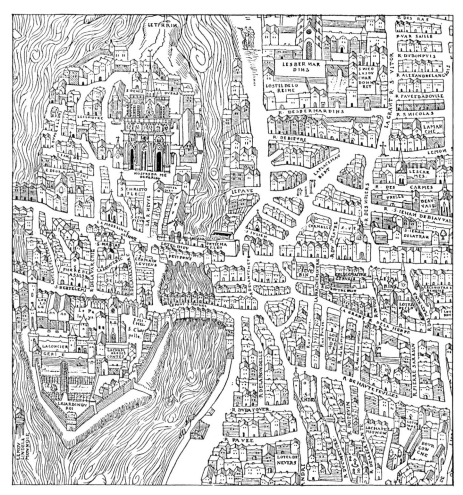

The king lived by preference in the castles of the Loire. When in Paris he resided at the castle "des Tournelles," so-called because of its numerous little towers (the site is that of the present-day Place des Vosges). It had belonged to the dukes of Orléans; when Louis XII, who was of the family of Orléans, came to the throne, it had received the name of Hotel Royal. Catherine de' Medici was to have it demolished in 1565, saddened by the fact that her husband, Henry II, had died by accident in a tournament in the nearby Rue Saint-Antoine. There were five bridges over the Seine: Pont Notre-Dame, Pont Saint-Michel, Pont au Change, Petit-Pont—names that can still be found in Parisian topography—and Pont aux Meuniers, which was formed by mills floating on

Opposite: The Hôtel de Cluny (in the reconstruction by Viollet-le-Duc). The building was commissioned by the abbot Jacques d'Amboise, at the time of Charles VIII, in "flamboyant" gothic. It is an illustrious example of 15th-century civil architecture. Below: Plan of the Parisian city walls, with those of Philip Augustus (12th century) on both banks of the Seine, and those of Charles V, 1370, protecting the "ville" on the right bank.

The Parisian university

From a document dating from the year 1200: following a fight that left a number of students dead, King Philip II formed special courts of justice for students. Some aspects of the university were already in existence. It had originated in the cathedral school in the cloisters of Notre-Dame on its island in the Seine. Here students could obtain the licentiae *indicating they had received the necessary preparation to teach. These teachers gave lessons wherever they could, gathering students around them on street corners, or lecturing from windows. The school overflowed onto the left bank, where it became a* universitas magistrorum, *or corporation of teachers. At the end of the 15th century the University of Paris was no longer the cultural authority at which Thomas Aquinas had taught. The famous Sorbonne was a newer institution. Robert de Sorbon (Sorbon was the name of his birthplace, situated near Rethel in the Ardennes), a Thomist theologian, canon of Cambrai, and chaplain to Louis IX (St. Louis), was the founder (1253) of a* collegium pauperum magistrorum, *of which he was also the first superintendent. There masters of theology and poor students alike were recipients of hospitality and learning, thanks mainly to the generosity of the sovereign. The college was situated close to the Roman baths on the left bank. After the first half of the 16th century it became the site where the faculty of theology met to deliberate. The name Sorbonne thus came to indicate the faculty and, later, the whole university.*

the river and which, after a number of fires, was not rebuilt. Pont Notre-Dame was made of stone; during those years the Italian Fra Giocondo was working on it. Petit-Pont had two stone arches, but the rest of the structure was wood; the other bridges were made entirely of wood. On these bridges one passed among houses and booths, rendering the river almost invisible. The island, the *Cité*, was the site of the monuments that stood out in the memories of visitors: Notre Dame—which De Beatis considers "large, but not particularly beautiful," showing an early Italian judgment against gothic—the Palais de Justice, and the Sainte Chapelle. In the Palais it was possible to admire the Grand-Salle (which corresponds to the Salle de Pas-Perdus, in its present shape; the whole palace was rearranged and enlarged after the fires of the 17th and 18th centuries). It was embellished by the statues of all the kings of France—fifty-five, counting Louis XII, who reigned at that moment—the warlike with their swords raised on high, the pacifists with the blade down. The hall was destined for the administration of justice, but in it, along with the benches of the judges, De

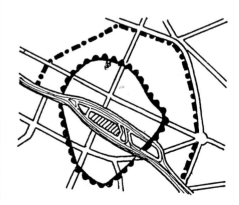

Beatis was to see, as in the adjacent halls, and even on the staircase, "many little booths" in which goods of all kinds—gold, enamels, jewels, laces and other trimmings—were sold. The Sainte Chapelle, constructed by St. Louis, was resplendent with precious tabernacles, jewels, crosses bearing pearls and rubies, and relics. The crown of thorns borne by Jesus, "entire, but without thorns," was allegedly there as well. The colored light of the marvelous stained-glass windows drenched the entire interior. On the left bank of the Seine, at Montagne Sainte-Geneviève, was the university: here it was possible to study every form of science, with the exception of necromancy, which was prohibited (De Beatis). There were as many as three thousand students. However, there is a scarcity of rooms; according to the Milanese merchant the students are "sometimes seven or eight in one room, a most dirty thing." Thanks to

scholarship provided by the bishop of Cambrai, Erasmus had studied there at the College Montaigu, which stood more or less on the site of the Pantheon today. He was to remember with a shudder the chilly dormitories, which were too close to the latrines; the insects, which tormented his sleep; the stale food; and the wine, which had turned to vinegar. The life of the student was not all fun and sport.

Perhaps the journey of our Scottish archer ended in Paris, perhaps, in order to take up his service with the guards of Louis XII, he had to travel as far as the Loire, to the castle of Blois, of which the king was particularly fond. In the future he would have to nock arrows in his bow of yew during famous battles: Agnadello (1509), Ravenna (1512), Guinegatte (1513). Perhaps he would even do so during the youthful, ardent, and fortunate campaigns of Francis I, who at that time was only nine years old.

223

From Genoa to Istanbul

The peace of 1503 gave Christian merchants new access to the ancient city once called Constantinople. Here is a sea voyage across the Mediterranean, from Genoa to that teeming metropolis on the Bosporus, Istanbul, now in Turkish hands for a half century.

**Genoa ● Naples ● Strait of Messina
Modone ● Malvasia ● Chios
Dardanelles ● Istanbul**

"The surprising beauty" of Genoa was praised by Cervantes (*Novelas ejemplares*); it "seems to have its houses set in the folds of the hills like diamonds in gold." This image would have seemed fitting even in the early years of the 1500s, in spite of the large-scale urban renewal that had taken place in the decades before it was seen by the Spaniard. At the start of the 16th century the appearance of the city was still entirely medieval. A lot of time was to pass before construction work started (commencing at the site of a brothel close under the walls) on the New Road, with its noble palaces (Via Garibaldi), from which "not only utility but also the beauty of the city" was expected (as was stated without hesitation in the official documents). But there were immediately those who suspected—as can be read in a petition—that rather than worrying about the aesthetic appearance of the city there was a prevailing desire among the developers to "please five or six citizens," without taking into account the "damage and inconvenience" to the landowners. There are always conflicting interests in the urban enterprises of Genoa, for it had been a city of fractious nobility, perhaps more so than any other.

In any case, beauty seemed to be a natural part of its destiny, and not only because of the favorable situation. Those inhabiting the city and those merely passing through it were aware of this fact. Petrarch asked himself "who would not look down in stupor at towers and palaces, nature subdued by man, the bitter hills covered with cedars, vines, and olive trees, the marble buildings in the hollows of the hills." The picture was still exactly the same.

The city was at that time entirely on the eastern side of the anchorage, surrounded by a ring of medieval walls and dominated by the fortress of Castelletto, which Galeazzo Sforza had strengthened. The network of the city was thick with churches, extremely tall houses, towers, narrow streets, and little squares that the social structure divided into *alberghi* (noble alliances that were reflected in the coordination of the adjacent properties) reserved for the exclusive use of the given consortium. The houses often had loggias or colonnades giving onto the street, doorways with carvings cut into the slate, facades in black-and-white stripes, as can still be seen in the cathedral of San Lorenzo, which at that time displayed its antique "nolar" tower, replaced by Galeazzo Alessi's cupola.

The port was protected by a single jetty, which had recently been made longer, and upon which stood a large lighthouse in the shape of a battlemented tower (it came by its current name, the "Molo Vecchio"—the Old Jetty—when construction of a new one began in 1638) and was therefore swept, during bad weather, by angry gusts of southwesterly wind. From the porticoed Ripa ("shore"), various "bridges" stuck out into the water, smaller wharves really, even then built of stone, beside which the ships were moored for loading and unloading. Also on the Ripa was the stone-and-brick custom house (now Palazzo di San Giorgio), with its acutely arched portico and beautiful mullioned windows on the upper stories.

The Lanterna was just as it is today, but it rose on a naked promontory, Capo di Faro, while close to its base stood the gallows. Farther to the west were the homes of the fishermen of San Pier d'Arena, the shipbuilders' docks, then the mouth of the Polcevera. To the east of the port stood the suburb of the woolworkers on the banks of the Rivotorbido, the hill of Carignano, with the Renaissance dwelling of the

*Below: The city and port of Genoa, in a view by Cristoforo de'
Grassi, 1597, which is the copy of an earlier work dating from
1481 (the jetty is being extended). Opposite: The Lanterna and
the lighthouse on the jetty in the Genoa of the* Chronica
mundi *by Hartmann Schedel. On the page opposite the title:
The imaginary world of the Turks, detail from* Preaching of
St. Mark *by Gentile and Giovanni Bellini.*

Fieschi (which no longer exists) and
the bed of the Bisagno.

The most amazing, and if you like, "modern," detail was outside the city itself, namely
the number of villas inhabited by the nobility, and not merely during the summer
months. These residences dotted the river-
banks and hills; the high walls bounding
each property flanked the roads. Little
more than thirty years later, a chronicler
was to say that "from Nervi to Sesto and in
all the valley of Polcevera as far as Ponte-
decimo and up the valley of Bisagno, everywhere was full of admirable buildings, of
gardens and villas, which did give great
delight" (A. Giustiniani, 1537). By shortly
after the mid-1400s over 1,500 properties
were registered in the name of citizens in the
areas containing villas, among which there
were 135 *palatia*, more or less equally divided between the east and the west.

In the port the movement of galleys.
carracks, or the more modest coastal vessels

trading with the Riviera was even then
constant. The routes for Catalonia, Portugal, Sicily, and the east of the Syrian merchants were well traveled, but in the midst
of this busy commerce there was a growing
awareness of a return to more local horizons. The large capitals were increasingly
given over to banking interests and the
more subtle mechanisms of finance, rather
than to the risks of sea trade. All the same,
on the jetties of the port it was possible to
meet old men who could remember very
different times. Since Constantinople had
been taken by the Turks about fifty years
earlier (1453), business relations with Galata, a Genoese city on the other shore of the
Golden Horn, had diminished, but not
stopped. A lessening interest had been
shown for the eastern portion of the Mediterranean (and the importation of spices
had fallen more and more into the hands of
the Venetians), but above all, the Black Sea
had been closed to the Genoese. The Gen-

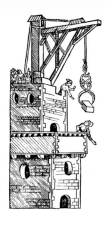

Work in progress,
from Chronica mundi.

oese city of Caffa (Feodosia), set among the
cypresses and Jerusalem pines of the Cri-
mean coast, together with its subsidiary
emporium of Tana (Azof), situated at the
mouth of the Don—from which skins, furs,
Oriental silks, corn, and salt fish were sent
to the voracious capital of the eastern empire, and slaves were sold to Egypt—had
been isolated beyond the straits. Then the
Turks pressed their attack. The desperate
defense of Caffa was useless, and the city
fell in 1475. The only remnant of the Genoese Empire in the east then was the island
of Chios, and it too would be taken, by the
Pasha Piali, in 1566.

Certainly voyages to Constantinople still
continued. The Ottomans had a vested
interest in commercial relations with "free"
merchants, but the risk of attack by pirates
was higher, and it was frequently necessary
to endure the interruption and delay caused
by wars against the "infidels."

Sailing on the Mediterranean one navigated by relying on one's experience with
the coastal waters and on the descriptions
of pilots; the compass was resorted to only
when one was out of sight of land, which
was relatively rare. The *comito* ("commander") and the pilots (generally more than
one) took counsel with one another regarding navigational decisions, "and particularly
what should be done in times of chance"
(this can still be found written in the late
1600s).

In the Genoese merchant navy, when a
dangerous situation arose, two consuls and
two counsels elected by the crew and merchants aboard "*cum ampla bailia*" ("with
ample powers") took responsibility for the
salvation of the ship, men, and cargo. The
decision could be costly. In February 1504,
a ship off the Catalonian coasts *cum procela
valde tempestosa* felt it necessary to throw

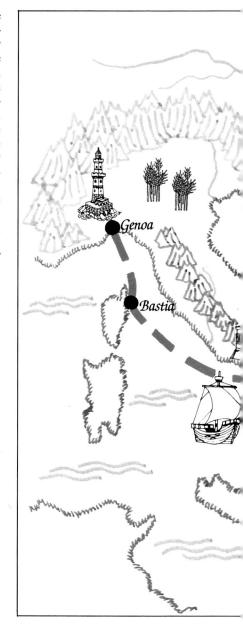

Naples. Opposite: Drawing showing the vanished villa of Poggio Reale in a perspective view by Alessandro Baratta, 1670 (the main building is the quadrilateral one on the left). It was begun in 1487, and in the 1700s the map of the duke of Noja described it as still blessed "with an indescribable delight of gardens, fountains, and groves reaching as far as the sea." Following pages: The city during the 15th century, detail from the Tavola Strozzi.

The Grand Turk's brother

When he had entered Rome through the Portuense Gate from Civitavecchia on March 13, 1489 (a Friday), Gem, brother of the Grand Turk, "was on the back of one of the white horses of his Holiness that are called Chinese, all trapped and barded as when the pope himself rides out on horseback." So reported Burckard, master of ceremonies of the papal court, who recorded the event. It was not a diplomatic mission. On the death of Mohammed II (1481), a dispute had broken out between his firstborn, Beyazid, and his second son, Gem. Beyazid had emerged as victor, and Gem, while attempting flight to Rhodes, was captured by the Knights of St. John of Jerusalem. He had then been sent into France and was finally "entrusted" to Pope Innocent VIII. As long as Gem remained alive, Ottoman aggressiveness toward the western world was halted. The brother of Beyazid II could be used by Christian Europeans to instigate a revolt at any time. When Gem died in 1495, the Turks once again were able to launch an offensive, something they had not done since the death of Mohammed II. The ensuing war, which started in 1499, was directed mainly against Venice and Spain, but ended shortly because the Ottoman Empire had found itself threatened on its eastern front. In the peace treaty ratified in 1503, Venice lost several Greek holdings from its "dominion of the seas," but regained commercial privileges within the empire. With the peace, Christian merchants of every nation could once again return to the Dardanelles.

the cargo overboard.

The voyage to Constantinople took at least thirty days, but it could easily become forty or sixty, depending on the number of stops made at ports and the weather conditions. One departed in May to arrive at the Golden Horn in early July (and make the return voyage in autumn). What kind of experience could it have been to cross a calm Mediterranean between late spring and early summer? The itinerary will be the route of prestigious cruises. At that time one traveled on the sea for a living, out of necessity, in the hope of gain. Whether or not there was also a portion of pleasure, no one can say. But the host of images—light, sea, promontories, islands, and bays—one can imagine seeing from the gently rocking vessel appears marvelous to us.

On leaving Genoa, a stop might be made on the island of Corsica, at Bastia, a place with a typically Genoese appearance. In so doing, one could avoid the capricious currents of the Straits of Piombino. Then it was on to Isola delo Giglio, Civitavecchia, Ponza, and finally Naples. The sailors knew all the safe havens along the coast, and they repeated the names of the saints to whom they were dedicated like a litany to invoke their protection. Naples no doubt looked beautiful under the sun, massed to the north of Castel Nuovo, its port protected by the Molo Angioino, the Vomero hill all green, with the white Cetosa of San Martino at its summit. At the end of the luminous bay rested Vesuvius, covered in vines and woods. The city and the kingdom were by now in the hands of the Spanish. Thanks to the dangerous exploits of Charles VIII, the French had captured the convoy sent to Amboise bearing four thousand kilos of tapestries, carpets, paintings, sculptures in marble and porphyry, the 1,140 volumes

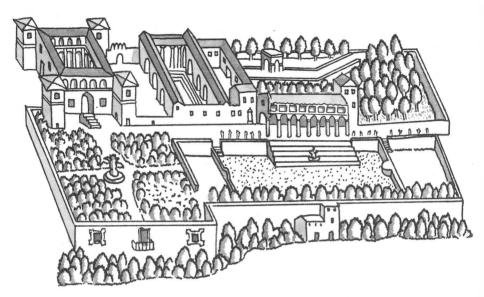

and illuminated manuscripts from the library of the Aragonese kings, and, perhaps, the habit of taking off their hats before the sovereign, something they had seen the Neapolitan gentlemen do. According to Francesco Janis from Tolmezzo, "the profits of the kingdom" lay entirely in the customs duty on sheep to be paid by the migratory shepherds and in the taxes on "Greek wine."

The shores of southern Italy were to be described with a touch of fear; the observation is that of a Frenchman (1552): "All the coast of that sea ... from Naples to Sicily, is shut in by high mountains, at the feet of which there is a beach battered by all the sea winds."

Having passed through the Strait of Messina and completed the long voyage across the Ionian Sea, a landing was made at Modone (Methoni), at the extreme tip of the western coast of Morea (Peloponnesus). Even in Homer's time the city was "rich with vines." At the foot of the fortifications of the little peninsula the sea murmurs blue and transparent; all around are whispering reeds, oleanders, and agaves, the palms, black cypresses and olive trees that Heracles had searched for in the north, beyond the sources of the Danube. In the port, which had ceased to belong to Venice a few years before, new pilots and the dragoman (interpreter, from the Turkish *tercuman*) were taken aboard, and the wait began for a favorable wind needed to round Cape Matapan and pass through the straits to the

north of the island of Citera (Kithira), which in ancient times had the shells of the *purpura* washed up on its beaches. One then passes the last peninsula of Laconia, doubling Cape Malea. On the eastern shore of the peninsula, the bizarre rock of Malvasia was a Venetian stronghold. In Greek it is called Monemvasia because only a slender isthmus (*moni embasia,* "sole entrance") joins it to the coast on which the vines of Malvasia, an extremely popular wine at that time, grew (it is from here that the vines later propagated in Cyprus, Sicily, and Portugal come). Sailing from Cape Malea toward the northeast, one crossed the Cyclades, whose mountains turned purple at sunset, moving under an endlessly limpid sky to the strong breath of the Etesians (which blow from the end of June onward) which cut the "wine dark sea" of Homer with the foam of speed.

Chios (Khios, the very island on which some scholars believe Homer was born) is large, mountainous, and fertile, boasting mulberry trees, olives, almonds, lemons, and vines. The best resin in the Aegean flowed from the lentiscus or mastic, gift of St. Isidore, with which "masticha" was flavored. It is an alcoholic beverage for summer siestas, which becomes opaque when water is added. The Genoese had been rulers of the island since 1261. They had exploited it—the production of silk was the biggest business—and defended a "maona" (a state-guaranteed trade association; the

231

The Aegean. Below: Under sail with a fresh wind, detail from the Gallery of Geographical Maps painted by Antonio Danti, in the Vatican. Opposite: The city of Chios on an Italian map forming part of the collection of Mediterranean islands by Henricus Martellus Germanus, ca. 1490. The island of Chios (Khios), in the eastern part of the Aegean Sea, close to the Greek coast, was under Genoese rule until 1566.

term is Arab in origin), or rather the first of the Genoese maonas, a company whose activity was granted by the state and whose parts were negotiable in the same way as those of a limited company. Then, during the 15th century, all the maonas had been absorbed by the Banco di San Giorgio, the private entity that ran the Genoese state. Beside the port of Chios, the Genoese houses were in the Kastro, on the eastern coast of the island, in view of Asia Minor, with its towers bearing the blazon of the governing Giustiniano family. The Turkish quarter had not yet arisen on the site.

At the entrance to the Dardanelles, ships had to fly a flag indicating they had authorization to trade in the Ottoman Empire. In the strait one sailed for thirty-five miles between the yellow slopes of hills, with fields burned by the sun and dotted with the black tops of trees. At the narrowest point between Europe and Asia there is a gap of only 1,200 meters; after which it only remained to cross the Sea of Marmara. The

Turks call it Kostantiniye; Istanbul is a corruption of the Greek expression "(to go) toward the city." It appeared with its cupolas, its little towers, its belltowers covered with lead standing above the water and the green of the gardens and cypresses, which enfold the low architecture. The gilded cuspids of the minarettes glittered in the sun.

Constantinople is built upon a triangle of hills that extends between the Sea of Marmara and the Golden Horn. It is protected on the landward side by long walls, those erected during the 5th century by Theodosius II. Walls also rise along the shore toward the sea. The Bosporus is so narrow that, in the city, it is said, one can hear the cocks crowing in Asia. The ship moves toward its mooring, making its way in the midst of the comings and goings of the boatmen ferrying people between Constantinople and Galata over the Golden Horn, between Europe and Asia over the Bosporous. The wharves of the port are on the two

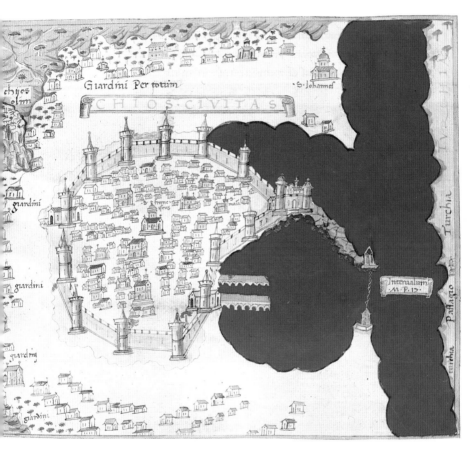

shores of the Golden Horn itself, an arm of sea that extends the river of fresh waters. The Genoese ship moors on the northern bank, before Galata, which the Turks consider a city of "infidels." It is surrounded by walls and crisscrossed by narrow little streets. Along with the Genoese, it is inhabited by Venetians with their *bailo*. Cultured people were to note that the atmosphere was breathless and lazy, opportunistic and ambiguous. It is the prototype of a Levantine port. A 17th-century Turkish writer was to say that its name was synonymous with tavern. There appear to have been two hundred brothels and pothouses, indistinguishable from one another. Few people still inhabit the hill of Pera, above Galata, where the foreign ambassadors had established themselves. On the other side of the Golden Horn, in the capital of the Ottoman Empire, the "Franks"—as the Moslems had called the Europeans from the time of the crusades—became immersed in the exotic. Everyone wore a turban, a felt skullcap

235

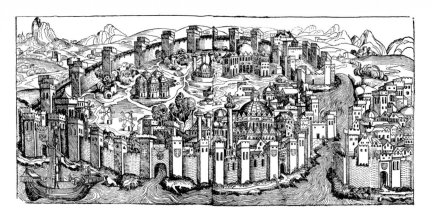

with a muslin scarf (*tulbent*) wrapped around it on their head and babouches on their feet. Styles and colors indicated social status. Moslems wore only yellow, a color not allowed for others. At regular hours all activity ceased for prayer, and the Europeans were soon forced to admit that the Turks gave homage "to their false prophet" more assiduously than Christians did to their god. There are the confraternities of Dervishes and their incomprehensible practices; one of the two leading orders in the city is the *mevlevs*, or "whirling dervishes," so-called because of the dances through which they attain religious ecstasy. Another surprise is the frequency with which baths are taken. A few establishments at certain times of the day are reserved for foreigners. One is also furnished with a massage, a depilation, and a shave. It was forbidden to shave a Moslem with a razor used by an infidel. Traveling salesmen moved through the streets with their goods in a pannier: fruit, vegetables, babouches, earthenware, as well as used objects. Each category of salesman had a specific call. One could also meet tightrope walkers, acrobats (some all the way from India), jugglers, magicians, puppeteers, masters of the shadow theater, bear tamers (this being a gypsy specialty), and vendors of nightingales. In the courtyards of the mosques the public scribes sat awaiting their clients.

The accounts of travelers insist that the individual buildings, seen close at hand, do not correspond with the beauty of the general picture. They describe rows of little houses in brick, wood, and hay covered with lime, with only a few *saray* ("palaces") and a certain small number of "bourgeois" houses, particularly the two-floored *konak*, with a ground floor for servants and slaves and a first floor with closed-in balconies

leaning slightly inward, for the owners. At one point in the external wall these buildings have a little door kept shut with a chain. A water carrier who makes daily rounds with his donkey and his wineskins opens the little door with a key and is thus able to pour the water necessary into the domestic tanks. Those who entered the homes of Turks—a feat not easily achieved—described a large room with many windows and sofas along the walls and an abundance of cushions and carpets. There are no beds, for the residents sleep on mattresses that are removed during the day or on tables. At mealtimes, servants bring food in on a round copper tray, which they set up on a wooden support, and around which one sits cross-legged.

As has been mentioned earlier, not all those living in Constantinople were Turks. In fact, the families who had been there since olden times were predominantly Genoese and Venetian. After the Turkish conquest, the majority of the Greek population had been deported and replaced by Turks from Asia Minor or by other Greeks, from Smyrna, Morea, Sinope, Trebizond, or the archipelago. It was also inhabited by Armenians, Jews, gypsies, Arabs, Albanians, Serba, Moldavians, Wallachians, and Iranians. As in the rest of the empire, the non-Moslems subjects had to pay a head tax and depend in matters requiring jurisdiction on the heads of their respective religious communities: the Greek patriach, the Armenian patriarch, the chief rabbi, and so on. The Greek patriarch was at the Holy Apostles, the Byzantine basilica that had inspired the architecture of St. Mark's in Venice. When the church was demolished he had moved to the basilica of the Virgin Pammacaristos, in the suburbs, between the port of Adrianopolis and the shores of the Golden

It is impossible to imagine, a western traveler was to say, "anything more fascinating" than approaching Istanbul by sea. The singular layout of the city, "similar to a harp or a cornucopia," according to another visitor during the 1600s, is shown in the somewhat amateurish miniature below (15th century), and more convincingly in the woodcut (opposite) from the Chronica mundi *by Hartmann Schedel.*

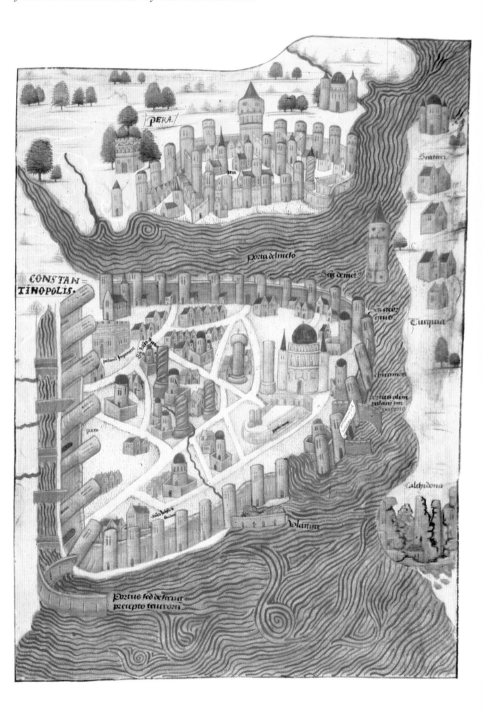

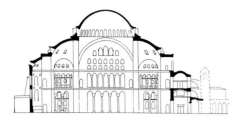

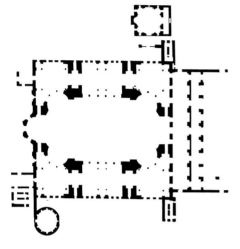

Horn. Many of the Jews there were Sephardic, having taken refuge in the city after being driven from Spain. Thanks to their cultured ways they acted as intermediaries in the dealings between Turks and western peoples. They also had large commercial interests and numbered among themselves the most sought after doctors.

Even then the three most fascinating points of the city, and not only because of their size, were the sultan's palace, the mosques, and the bazaar. The palace, residence of the sultan, seat of government, heart of the empire, is the first structure that can be seen on arriving from the sea. It occupies the eastern extremity of the peninsula, the site of the ancient Byzantine acropolis, and impresses more for the fair gardens running down to the water than for the factories, modest and compact, and soon to be transformed by Suliman. It was then called Yeni Saray, or "new palace"; its modern-day name of Topkapi Saray, "palace of the cannon doors," refers to the cannons that have protected it since the 18th century. One of its best-known buildings at that time was the open pavilion, which Mohammed II had had himself built

and in which he spent long hours alone watching the sea and the city. It was later closed and used as a storage facility for those articles that went by right to the sultan when their owner died without an heir. Regarding the harem, which formed one section of the palace and remained shrouded in mystery, unsatisfied curiosity generated gossip among the foreigners; it was said that there were no fewer than three hundred women confined there, though they were rotated out: "not one day passes without one entering and another leaving." The most important woman in the harem is the *valide sultan*, the mother of the sovereign. Then there are the *kadin*, the legal concubines who have presented him with a son, the *ikbal*, or temporary favorites, and finally the slaves, or *cariye*.

Not far from the sultan's palace, close to the hippodrome, several companies of janissaries are garrisoned, the soldiers feared as much by the sultan himself as by the enemy. When, in their garrisons, they upset their cooking pots, it was a sign of revolt, and anything could happen. The obelisk of Theodotus still stood in the hippodrome— it had been brought there from Carnac and shortened by six meters in order to allow it to enter the ship—as did the obelisk of Constantine Porphyrogenitus, which had been stripped of its plates of gilded bronze during the sack of the city by the crusaders (1204), and the bronze column formed by three snakes entwined. This had been set up at Delphi before the Temple of Apollo in memory of the battle of Platea; the heads of the three serpents held up a tripod and a golden bowl. Basin and tripod never arrived in Constantinople, but the three divided heads of the snakes, which had disturbed the Christians as they had the Moslems, were still there (as can be seen in several

Below: Interpretations of Santa Sophia in Constantinople from the Libro di Giuliano da Sangallo, *or* Barberini Codex, *in which the Florentine architect drew for almost thirty years (1485-1514). Opposite: Plan and elevation of the same church. This great Justinian work, which marked the beginning of the imperial Roman architectural tradition, continued to inspire the Turkish architects who built the mosques of the sultans.*

Istanbul

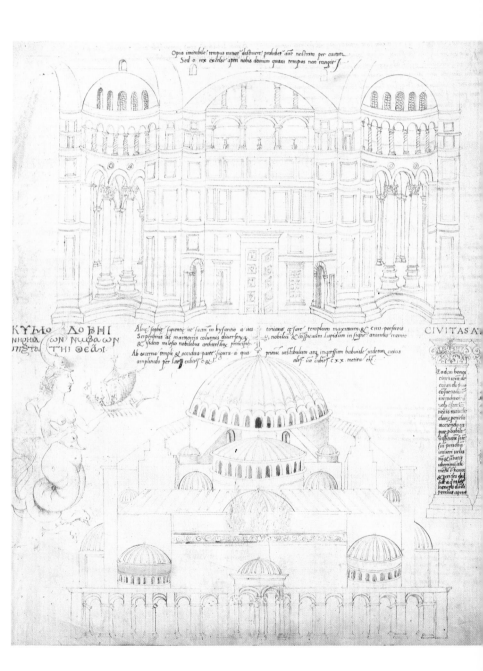

On the shore "two hundred pothouses and in each one five or six hundred good-for-nothings engaged in revelry, who make uproar alongside singers and musicians." So the Turkish writer Evliya Çelebi said of Galata. Opposite: Galata, a Turkish miniature from the Book of Roads, *which describes the stages of an expedition to Persia by Suliman (first half of the 16th century). Below: A Turkish horseman, drawing attributed to Dürer.*

Turkish miniatures).

Mohammed II had entered Constantinople on a Tuesday, immediately gone to Santa Sophia and ordered its transformation into a mosque. By the following Friday, he had already presided over prayers there. The immense structure, with which Justinian claimed to have surpassed Solomon, rose above the tops of the cypresses, perhaps plastered a red color, as has been suggested to restore it today. The interior was resplendent with the marbles removed from pagan temples, such as the eight green columns that the architects Antemio of Tralle and Isidoro of Mileto had taken from the temple of Artemis in Ephesus. The minarettes were two, not four, as can be seen today, one built by Mohammed II, the other by Bayezid. All the famous sultanate mosques of Constantinople descend from Santa Sophia, from the late-Romanesque special concept of a vast hall covered with a cupola. At the moment of which we are

speaking there existed—along with Santa Sophia, which was still waiting to celebrate its millennium—the mosque of Mohammed II, built on the perimeter of the church of the Holy Apostles, with the eight madrasahs around it, and the mosque of Bayezid (1501-5), which was just being completed. Sinan, who was to be the greatest of all Turkish architects, indeed one of the greatest architects in any style or form, was not yet 20 years old and was working as a mason, or perhaps was in the army. He was to build in Rumelia before Suliman ordered him to the capital to build his mosque. Madrasahs were also to stand around the mosque of Bayezid. Architecturally speaking, they consisted of a porticoed courtyard surrounded by cells and by a hall for teaching and prayer; in substance they are colleges in which young men continue their studies after primary school. Like colleges elsewhere, each one had its own prestige, which lends itself to the career of those who have studied there. The madrasah of Bayezid opened the way to positions of the greatest importance.

The bazaar is still a long way from being completed. In the end it would include sixty-six roads, would have eighteen gates that were closed at the set of the sun, and would contain 3,000 booths. However, the old Bedesten, constructed by Mohammed II, was working. The name reveals that it was originally the bazaar of the cloth merchants, but already, beneath its cupolas, there were six hundred luxurious booths, hung with brocades and damasks, selling jewels and precious stones (guarded in two thousand safes), as well as gold and silver objects, carpets, furs, and porcelains. In a street not far from the mosque of Bayezid the booksellers were concentrated. These were sellers of hand-written books, because

the only printing house in Constantinople was a Jewish one, founded by Spanish refugees in 1494. Close to the Bedesten was the slave market, set up in the form of a caravansary, a courtyard surrounded by rooms in which the slaves were kept. The two sexes were kept separated from one another. The law forbids the seller any attempts to beautify female slaves—Russian, Caucasian, Polish—in order to facilitate their sale; nor can he take back the clothes they are wearing.

Food markets were scattered in all parts of the city, the greedy belly of the empire.

However, foreigners were amazed by the frugality of the people and the low cost of foodstuffs. The Fleming Ogier Ghislain de Busbecq, Charles V's ambassador to the sultan, was to note with amazement (1555) that "what a Fleming would spend in one day would be sufficient to keep a Turk alive for twelve." The market offers sheepskins from the Balkans and Anatolia (4 million were imported each year), grain from satellite Danubian principalities, rice from Egypt, chickens from Thrace, and fish from the Bosporus. Yogurt was produced in the surrounding countryside.

241

From Seville to Antwerp

Early in the 16th century, the economic ties between Seville—the great port and shipbuilder for voyages to the newly discovered lands across the Atlantic—and Antwerp—the commercial and financial center of Flanders, then collecting the inheritance of Bruges—became increasingly important. Here an Andalusian shipowner crosses France during a moment of peace to reach the city where circumstances and geography were multiplying wealth.

**Seville ● Córdoba ● Toledo ● Saragossa
Barcelona ● Aigues-Mortes ● Marseilles
Avignon ● Lyon ● Beaune ● Autun
Paris ● Arras ● Antwerp**

On the page opposite the title: Ships on the Guadalquivir in a detail from Vista del puerto y la ciudad de Sevilla *by Sanchez Coello (16th century). "You are not a city but a world, in you can be admired what is lost in others, a part of Spain more important than all the rest." So the 16th-century poet F. de Herrera wrote of Seville.*

The admiral had navigated the ocean *as inquietas ondas apartando*, "dividing the restless waves" (Camoes). On returning from the newly discovered islands, he had gone to Seville on Palm Sunday (1493), where he had participated with emotion in the rites of Holy Week and in the processions marked by the hollow roll of drums. Several of the confraternities that today bear the baroque *pasos* (a wooden figure representing the Passion and the Lamenting Virgin) on their shoulders through the streets were already in existence in the 1300s. On Easter Day, Columbus finally received the letter from Ferdinand and Isabella summoning him to court in Barcelona to give an account of his voyage and to plan for the future.

By now, many years had passed. In Seville, Columbus had watched the preparation of the fleets for other journeys. In the monastery of Las Cuevas he had lain in chains after the ill-fated third voyage.

The moment appeared singular. In 1506, the immense cathedral, which had been in construction for an entire century, was finally being consecrated on the site of the mosque, in the shadow of the minarette with its fine arabesque brickwork. The cathedral was not yet called Giralda, as its steeple had not been adorned with *el Giraldillo*, the statue that turns in the direction of the wind, from which its name was derived.

Isabella had died in 1504, saddened by the knowledge that the heirs to the throne of Castile were her weak-minded daughter (Joanna the Mad) and her German-Flemish son-in-law (Philip the Fair, a Hapsburg), ignorant of the Spanish world and considered by her to be inept. The admiral had also died (May 19, 1506), worn-out, and, perhaps, surpassed. However, with the formation of the Casa de Contratacion (1503),

the port of Seville set out to gain a total trade monopoly with the New World. During 1506, twenty-three ships were to set sail; by mid-century this number would reach over one hundred. The Venetian ambassador Andrea Navagero was to remark that "so many of them go to the Indies that the city is left poorly inhabited and almost in the hands of women."

The widower Ferdinand was doubtlessly displeased with the impending Hapsburg-Flemish succession. The treaty he had signed at Blois (1505) with Louis XII of France stipulated that the princess of Aragon was to marry the grandson of the French Germaine de Foix, opening an avenue for a change in succession if a son were to be born.

The resolution of the knotty problem of the Spanish succession is now known: Philip went to Spain in 1506 to take up the inheritance of his wife, who died within the year, and Joanna's mind became totally deranged. The son of Germaine de Foix, born in 1509, was to live only a few hours. A great many crowns were about to descend upon Philip's child growing up in Ghent, the Hapsburg later to ascend the Spanish throne as Charles V.

Nevertheless, thanks to wool exportation, the Castilian economy developed increasingly stronger ties with Flanders, which had the inexplicable capacity for attracting "risk capital" (including that of the Fugger and Welser families). Such was the context in which the journey of an Andalusian shipowner across France to opulent Antwerp should be envisioned.

To protect Andalusian horse breeding, the use of riding mules had been prohibited, so the shipowner left Seville on horseback. The high sun of Andalusia cast shadows across the city he was departing. The left

Antwerp

Arras

Paris

Beaune

Lyon

Aigues-Mortes

Avignon

Marseilles

Saragossa

Barcelona

Toledo

Cordoba

Seville

bank of the Guadalquivir was surrounded by Roman, Arabian, and Castilian walls that followed the lines of the present-day *rondas* and *paseos*. The Moorish influence was stronger than it is today. Tortuous and narrow little streets unexpectedly widened into irregular squares or ran into dead ends. The outwardly modest houses hid marvelous interior patios, arching porticoes, flowing fountains, and lush, verdant gardens. The Calle de lo Sierpes, well-known to visitors today, held a prison. Almost a century later Cervantes began to write *Don Quixote de la Mancha* there. In the light of summer evenings, it may already have been customary for artisans to sit opposite the cathedral and read romances of knighthood to one another (the most famous of these romances, *Amadis of Gaul*, had already been compiled, but was published in Spanish only in 1508).

The port on the Guadalquivir was watched over by the Arabian Torre del Oro (tower of gold), so-called because of the color of the tiles that decorated it. There was general rejoicing when the fleet descended the river with the tide in its favor and headed for the Indies, which had not yet become "refuge and shelter for the desperate of Spain, church for the bankrupt, safe-conduct for murderers ... common deception to many and particular remedy for a few" (Cervantes, *Novelas ejemplares*).

On the other side of the river, the barrio of Triana, reached by crossing a bridge of boats, was the hang-out of ruffians and lawless types, who drank in taverns with vine-hung pergolas. It was also the home of hardworking artisans who manufactured soap and painted majolica tiles (*azulejos*), which were to be taken as far as America.

It was in Seville that the novel *Comedia de Calisto y Melibea* was published in 1501 in an enlarged and more complete form than the first 1499 Burgos edition. Written in dramatic form and later known as *La Celestina*, after the name of the principal character (an old woman whose artful devices make it possible for Calisto and Melibea to meet against the will of the girl's parents), it came to be considered a basic Castilian theatrical text, but it was written not to be acted, but, on the contrary, to be read in public. This work by Fernando de Rojas, a converted Jew, is rife with bitter pessimism. All the characters die: Celestina, the procuress to whom Calisto turns when refused by Melibea, is murdered by the two accomplices with whom she refuses to divide the reward, and they are immediately put to death by the law; Calisto accidentally falls off a wall; and Melibea commits suicide by hurling herself from a terrace.

The voyager would cross Andalusia by following the Guadalquivir upstream toward that other great city, Córdoba. Its land is fertile: Botero was later to call it "granary, orchard, cellar, and stall of Spain." It consisted of gently undulating

Córdoba in the 16th century (from Civitates Orbis Terrarum *by Georg Braun and Frans Hogenberg, 1572). An anonymous Milanese merchant who visited the city in that period wrote of a "very pretty stone bridge" with 17 arches 302 feet long: the famous "Roman bridge" over the Guadalquivir, perhaps dating to Augustus. Opposite: Ships in the Guadalquivir beneath the Torre del Oro.*

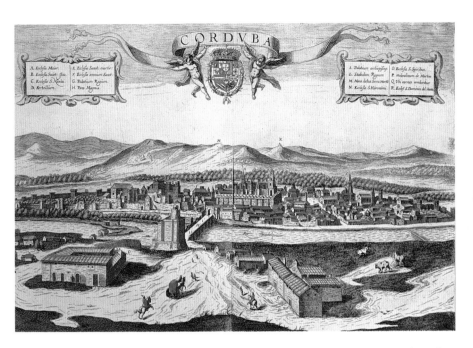

lands with vineyards and olives (although the widespread growth of olive trees occurred later). At the right season it was possible to encounter large flocks of sheep (it is estimated that there were about 2.5 million sheep in all of Spain). In accordance with a law dated 1501, all the lands in which migrating flocks had pastured were to be reserved as pastures in *perpetuo.*

Situated at the foot of the Sierra Morena, Córdoba was on the right bank of the Guadalquivir. Just downstream of a sharp bend, the river was traversed by an ancient bridge that was more Arabian than Roman. In the center of the stream the old Arabian mills were still working. The second largest mosque in the world, exceeded in size only by that of Mecca, stood just beyond the bridge. Seneca, a Córdoban, would have been intrigued by the fact that the mosque occupied the site of a temple dedicated to Janus, and later a Visigothic church of St. Vincent. The columns from the nineteen naves were from all corners of the known world at the time of construction, and even the emperor of Constantinople had donated building materials. It had been used as a church almost three centuries earlier (1236), but the 15th-century Christians showed admiration and respect for this Arabian masterpiece with its 850 columns. Later, a part of the mosque was to be destroyed to construct the Crucero. The interior of the large mosque revealed changing perspectives at every step. Flights of columns rose in every direction, their colors shifting from the gray of granite to the green and violet of jasper. The smooth surfaces of their trunks ended in shadowy capitals of Roman, Byzantine, and Arabic design. The red and

Right: Drawing of a nave of the cathedral-mosque of Cordoba. Opposite: The entrance to the mihrab, the octagonal santuary where during the Islamic epoch one could find a Koran decorated in gold, pearl, and rubies, several pages of which were believed to be by the hand of the caliph Othman.

white stones of the multiple Moorish arches provided another striking contrast.

Once the Sierra Morena had been crossed, the traveler would pass through La Mancha and proceed across New Castile toward Toledo. The countryside was vast and arid: "If a lark wishes to cross Castile," it was said, "it must carry its grain with it." Francesco Janis of Tolmezzo noted that its houses were built of sun-dried mud, the wood needed to bake lime being scarce.

Toledo appeared on a hill surrounded on three sides by the "slow, golden Tagus" (Cervantes). The Catholic Kings' habit of peripatetic governance prevented it from becoming the capital city of Spain, but it nonetheless remained that land's historical and religious heart. (Madrid at that time was little more than a village; it was only later, in 1560, that Philip II was to make it his capital.) The panorama was already dominated by the Alcazar, a four-sided fortress with square towers facing onto the Tagus, the Alcantara bridge over the river, and the castillo of San Servando. Ferdinand and Isabella renovated the western side.

Construction of the cathedral had been underway since the 1200s. Aleman had completed the gothic stalls of the choir, and the conquest of Granada had been carved on the dossals. In the Capella Mayor, the celebrated gateway was missing. The Churrigueresque Transparente, one of the most genial architectural inventions of the 1700s, had not yet been built. Work had just been completed (1504) on construction of the grand retablo in carved, gilded, and painted wood. The historical value of the combined artisanship of Burgundian, Flemish, and Spanish masters would be realized only later. When Tetzel traveled through Toledo as part of the entourage of the Bohemian Lev z Rozmitalu, the only object he considered worth mentioning was "the most precious Bible that can be beheld in all Christendom." A French work of the 13th century, possibly a gift from St. Louis, "with text and glosses written in golden letters and the pages opposite illuminated with figures," the Toledo Bible has remained in the cathedral to the present day.

The city's oldest synagogue, with five naves of horseshoe-shaped arches, Moorish-style geometrical plaster decorations, and pavement divided by ancient *azulejos*, had been transformed into a church—Santa Maria la Blanca—just one hundred years earlier. In 1476, Juan Guas had erected San Juan de los Reyes, considered the most representative example of the isabelino style, in which the symbols of monarchy were a decorative fabric.

Recently, Enrique de Egas had begun construction of the hospital of Santa Cruz (today the museum of Santa Cruz), with funding from Cardinal Pedro Gonzales de Mendoza. The facade was to become a beautiful example of the plateresque style, in which Moorish symbols entwined gothic and Renaissance motifs in fanciful superabundance to create the empression of the exuberant energy of Castile during the reign of Isabella. (It is significant that the name of the style derives from *platero*, "silversmith.")

The traveling shipowner proceeded from Toledo by way of the long road to Aragon. "A most wild country," noted Francesco Guicciardini, an envoy from Florence (1512), "in which no form of lodging can be found, nor can a single tree be seen, but all is full of rosemary and sage, it being an extremely arid land." It was a quite different terrain in the plain of the Ebro River, near Saragossa, which consisted of rows of trees and *tierras de riego*, irrigated lands. The pleasant landscape suggested the intense, but not vain, labor of farmers. Saragossa, surrounded then by walls, was on the right bank of the river. In the gothic Seo (in Aragon and Catalonia *seo* or *seu* is the name of the cathedral church), a teeming mass of workmen had just begun construc-

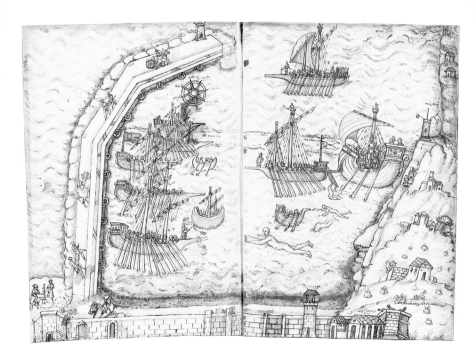

tion of the dome on its polygonal base (1505). Nuestra Señora del Pilar was considered to be the oldest church dedicated to the Virgin Mary in Christianity. Its foundation was believed to have been built by the Apostle James, to whom "the Madonna, seated upon a pillar" (the *pilar*) had appeared, as Francesco Janis diligently notes. However, the building was not as it appears today, since four belltowers and ten domes around a larger central dome were added at the end of the 1600s.

Both churches were in the district of the city close to the river and were also near the Roman stone bridge, the Ponte de Piedra, newly rebuilt at the time in which the Andalusian shipowner would have passed over it. The Aljaferia, the palace of the princes of Aragon and, earlier (11th century), the Moorish kings of Saragossa, was just outside the walls to the west. By way of a grand staircase built in 1492 in the flowered gothic style, one ascended to the apartments of the Catholic Kings. Today, one tower is named del Trovador: this character, the same as the hero of the opera by Verdi (*Il Trovatore*), is legendary, a fictitious medieval personage created by a 19th-century writer.

Moving on, the traveler crossed Catalonia. In the turbulent years of 1465-67, Roz-

mitalu, the Bohemian baron, and his following rode through this poor and devasted country, at the mercy of bandits and rogues and fearing for their lives. The crossbowmen of the Santa Hermandad had not yet imposed order on the roads, repressing robberies, murders, arson, and rebellions with summary justice. This organization, a recreation of the ancient town militia, also known as *hermandades*, was established by the Catholic Kings in 1476 and then disbanded in 1498 because it placed a heavy burden on the taxpayers.

Barcelona was the end of the Spanish part of the shipowner's itinerary. The city's oldest part is today known as Barri Gotic. Rondas have now replaced the walls, and the famous Ramblas descending to the port are from the 19th century. In the square at the sea end of the Ramblas, the Dressanes can still the seen, arsenals that were originally constructed for the conquest of the Balearic Islands (the most recent enlargement was completed in the 16th century).

The principal monuments of the city in the early years of the 16th century are still standing, although subjected to later additions and renovations. In Placa Sant Jaume, the Casa de la Ciutat, or Ajuntament, faced the Generalitat in which the "*corts catalanes*" had their seat. The gothic cathedral

250

"The people of Barcelona," Tetzel wrote in the summary of the journey of Baron Lev z Rozmitalu, "are said to man as many ships as the Venetians." Opposite: The port of Barcelona from the Armoriale, *a Castillian codex from the 16th century bearing the coats of arms of several families and the portraits of the counts of Barcelona. Below: The* Moresque, *colored drawing by Christoph Weiditz made during his travels in Spain in 1529.*

was situated at the highest point of the old city, or Mons Taber. The Placa del Rei was at the center of the royal palace, where Ferdinand and Isabella had received Columbus at the moment of his triumph.

Francesco Janis compiled various facts regarding Barcelona, some of which are of general interest. The city had cobbled streets and drainage pipes, and, for this reason, was always clean; in fact, Janis noted, "the more it rains, the cleaner it is." There were beautiful walls. The private houses were constructed of stone. Every house had a well. Nobody traveled by foot, but, rather, rode on mules. Both in the city and in the suburbs there were numerous convents. The nuns, Janis reported, "have great license to live; they all go around on the backs of mules, and gentlemen follow after them

without shame, and they may take husbands."

The city produced a good quantity of cloth, and it was possible to meet "many noble traders and artisans in great number, although not of great wealth." In the fifteen or so years between the shipowner's imaginary trip through Barcelona and the subsequent testimonial of the traveler from Tolmezzo, the economic decline of the city probably became more noticeable. However, business had a tradition of prosperity. It had nourished the Mediterranean empire of Aragon and Catalonia; its Taula de Cambis ("table of exchange," or bank) had been in existence since 1401. A prosperous Magna Societas of merchants presently controlled approximately half the foreign trade. Nonetheless, the center of commerce was

moving, albeit slowly, toward the Atlantic. Members of the older mercantile dynasties, as in the other merchant cities of the Mediterranean, could reap profits without risks. But the merchants of Barcelona still rode daily on the backs of mules to the Lonja, a vast gothic hall that had been completed in 1393. The term *bourse* did not yet mean "market," but the Lonja, or Loggia, was in practice just that: a business center. Brokers passed in and out among the columns among the groups of chatters, the meditative, the careful, and the diligent. They listened, passed on information, and arranged contracts between those potentially interested in a prospective deal: they were the *corredors d'orella*, intermediaries by ear.

The next stage of the shipowner's journey, from Barcelona to Marseilles, could be undertaken by sea. Coastal trade in the Mediterranean was always heavy. Janis, who had embarked at Naples, refers to a part of this voyage, which he took in the opposite direction. Leaving Marseilles to starboard, he passed two days and two nights "without sighting land, *sed coelum undique et undique puntus.*" Then on the horizon rose the outline of the Perpignan mountains. On the fifth day the anchor was dropped at Salou, much farther southwest than Barcelona and, during the Middle

Ages, the most important port in Catalonia. The pasengers aboard went ashore "half dead" and continued their journey toward Barcelona by land. These records help bring to life the experiences of travelers in those times.

In any case, this Mediterranean route could be dangerous. Sudden storms in the Gulf of Lyon, blown by gusts of the Mistral out of a clear sky, were unfortunately all too well known. There is a ring of truth in the discomforts Cervantes' passengers suffer sailing by galley from Cartagena to Genoa in the *Licenciado Vidriera (Novelas ejemplares)*: "they suffered two storms, one that drove them all to way to Corsica and another that chased them to Toulon in France. Finally, dead tired, soaking wet, and with bags under their eyes, they reached port."

The imagined stopover at Aigues-Mortes brings a powerful sense of history to the traveler's itinerary, for even today it strongly evokes the past. A border of walls and towers was reflected in the waters of the lagoon to the west of the uncultivated delta of the Rhone. Halfway through the 13th century, St. Louis started building this powerful military establishment, and the fleets of two ill-fortuned crusades had departed from it. At the end of the century, Genoese hired laborers completed the quad-

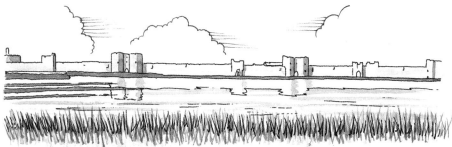

rilateral peripheral walls, which enclosed
an inhabited area with orderly perpendicu-
larly crossing streets. It evoked an atmosphere of "geometrical" medievality, different
but no less characteristic of the times than
the dense maze of tiny streets typically
associated with this period. In the first half
of the 1400s, Aigues-Mortes had been the
base for the overseas trade of Jacques
Coeur, the richest man in France in his
time. However, the sea was now receding
because of coastal silting, and the port was
receiving less use. Before entering the port
of Marseilles the ship passed two tiny islands
of naked rock and a cliff on which the
Chateau d'If, the prison of Dumas' *Count
of Monte Cristo*, was soon to be erected by
Francis I.

The canon De Beatis, who wrote the
diary of the European journey of the cardinal of Aragon, describes how Marseilles
appeared at that time, at the foot of white
calcareous hills, with wooded thickets nearby from which land breezes carried the
odors of Provence seaward. The city, nestled
on a plain between gently rolling mountains,
was long and narrow in form. Its port was
"secluded and extremely safe," protected by
the mountains, and "its mouth as narrow as
a hand's throw, upon which are built two
towers which can be closed with a chain."
The two forts, which can be seen today,
date from the 1600s. On the northern side
the Tour du Roi René (1447-52) still stands.
The city was situated on the northern side
of the port. At the end where La Canebière
now runs inland was the site of the hemp
works, which is recalled by a present-day
street name in Provençal. On the southern
side, in contrast, stood an arsenal "of the
capacity of nine galleys." Beyond the arsenal, closer to the mountains, stood the
monastery of Saint-Victor, whose fortress-
like church and crypts still exist. De Beatis
there visited "the oratory where the glorious
Magdalene went before doing penitence" in
the Massif de la Sainte-Beaume. He saw the
seat carved in rock where the saint rested
and deduced from its length that "she was
a big woman." On the southern side, at the
summit of the rocky spur where the 19th-
century Notre-Dame-de-la-Garde stands, a

prominent symbol of the contemporary skyline of Marseilles, there was only an isolated 12th-century chapel surrounded by countryside.

Once within the borders of France, a long road stretched before the shipowner from Seville across the countryside, as he gradually traveled from the sunny Mediterranean toward a more northern climate.

No traveler of the time failed to be impressed by the sight of Avignon, once the seat of the pope and which, after being abandoned by the curia, still belonged to the church, which would maintain ownership until 1791. The setting in the Rhone valley is one of the most beautiful vistas in Provence. The city, according to Tetzel, had three notable sights: a beautiful bridge, a fine perimeter of walls, and a beautiful—or, as he later adds, "immeasurably splendid"—palace. These are still standing, with the exception of the bridge, the Pont St-Benezet, which retains only four of the twenty-two arches it once boasted (the destruction

took place in 1660). The canon De Beatis also took careful note of the women, who were "of great beauty" and dressed in the French manner. His interest was also caught by the fresco of St. George (which can no longer be seen today), painted by Simone Martini and commissioned by Francesco Petrarch. The fresco depicted the warrior-saint freeing the princess from the dragon. The princess appeared on her knees, her hands clasped in prayer and uplifted to heaven. "Many claim that she is our lady Laura [the woman who inspired Petrarch's love poems] as she really was," De Beatis wrote, as "she has the air of a gentle country lass."

Proceeding northward from Avignon, it is possible to see as far as Valence across a wide plain where the Rhone flows and there are "many vines, good wines, some almond trees, and also those of the olive" (De Beatis). As Francesco Janis tells us, "one navigates said Rhone as far as Lyon." At Lyon foreigners could repose at their ease. Many merchants and businessmen either resided there or gathered there for the trade fairs. The silk industry, which had started in the 1400s, was in a phase of prosperity.

When did the traveler, lifting his eyes up from the road to the surrounding countryside, realize that the Mediterranean ambience had vanished? By the time he had reached sweet, abundant, verdant Burgundy, the atmosphere had certainly changed.

In the Côte d'Or (Burgundy), the vineyards of Beaune are still enclosed by an irregular perimeter of walls. The Milanese merchant whose testimony we have relied upon often recalled "a hospital of much beauty" run by about twenty monks who took good care of the sick. It included eight chambers for the rich, who would travel there from a distance, and a ward with

thirty-six beds, all "with curtains of fair white cloth, which would be honorable for any gentleman." This hospital, the famous Hotel-Dieu, was founded in 1443 by the chancellor of the duke of Burgundy, Nicholas Rolin. The typically Flemish taste of its architecture, with high roofs covered by brightly colored enamel tiles laid in geometric designs, cuspid-shaped attics, and porticoes surrounding the courtyard in plain wooden pillars, were reminiscent of the period in which the region was ruled jointly by the dukes of Flanders and Burgundy, who separated after the death of Charles the Bold. It is likely that the shipowner from Seville visited the hotel to see the polyptych of the *Last Judgment* by Rogier van der Weyden (still there today), for Flemish art was greatly admired even in Spain. He may have also been told to visit the birthplace of the great chancellor, Autun, and it is possible that he made a scenic detour to this town, which is situated in the lovely countryside of the Arroux valley. At

Autun, the powerful and cultured Rolin had a palace, now the home of the Musée Rolin, and had commissioned a painting for the cathedral of Saint-Lazare, of which his son was bishop. The painting, depicting himself kneeling in prayer before the Madonna, is known as the *Madonna of Chancellor Rolin* and is one of the most celebrated pictures in the Louvre today. The artist, Jan van Eyck, had worked in the service of the duke of Burgundy Philip the Good and was already considered "the king of artists, whose perfect and minute works will never fall into oblivion" (J. Lemaire, 1510). As a man of the 1400s, the Sevillian traveler might have been able to understand all the symbolic allusions contained within the punctilious "realism" of the painting. The city on the river, overlooked by a loggia with a classically styled triple arch (vain attempts have been made to identify this city as one of a number of cities visited by van Eyck), may have been intended to signify the *civitas dei* ("city of god"). The garden in front of the loggia is the *hortus conclusus,* sign of the Virgin, taken from the Song of Songs. The iris prefigures the royalty of Christ, recalling the dynastic fleur-de-lis of France and Burgundy. The two men watching the river in sentinel fashion are guarding the Redeemer, the hope of the world. The peacocks symbolize the promise of immortality—an ancient belief held that their flesh was incorruptible—and the peacocks' tails, covered with eyes widely opened in circles, are the image of the night sky.

The epoch of Chancellor Rolin had ended, and the rule of the duchy was divided between France and the Hapsburgs. In

France, through which the Sevillian traveler passed en route to Hapsburg Flanders, the monarchy was solid and appeared more and more as the center of movement of the state. Louis XII was a popular king in spite of several questionable or unfortunate enterprises. In a treaty signed in Blois in September 1504 with the Emperor Maximilian, he had promised his daughter Claude in marriage to the grandson of the Hapsburg, who would later become Charles V. It was the betrothal of children, but there was the prospect that following the death of Louis the French would have to pay an extremely heavy bridal dowry, relinquishing the regions of Milan, Genoa, Burgundy,

and Brittany. Louis XII immediately had the betrothal nullified by the States-General, from whom, in recognition of the narrow escape, he gratefully received the title of "father of the people."

What were the impressions of the Sevillian traveler on the road to Paris? Several years later the canon De Beatis was to record that the nobles, "free from every payment and imposition," when not employed at court retired to their country castles "where they live at small expense," and could revel in hunting. He was also to speak of the "poor, tyranized, and mistreated country people, more like dogs or bought slaves," but in the end he traces the first 16th-century version of the *douceur de vivre*: gentleman, plebeians, merchants, and people of whatever state or condition "as long as they are French, they expect to triumph and live merrily," they are so dedicated to drinking, eating, "and luxuriating" that one does not know how they can "ever do anything good."

Once beyond Paris, the Sevillian shipowner would arrive at Arras in Artois, the city that gives its name to the tapestries that were first produced there. A peculiar feature of this city, noted in the writings of the anonymous Milanese merchant, is that it was partitioned into two sections by a wall and moat: the smaller area, approximately one quarter of the total city, was the *Cité* of the kings of France; the larger area, or the *Ville*, belonged to the archduke of Burgundy, who at that time may have been Philip the Fair, heir to the Spanish thrones.

On the flat plain on the right bank of the Scheldt, the final destination of our traveler, Antwerp, finally appeared. In the last phase of his journey, the shipowner would have traversed a terrain marked by windmills, somewhat reminiscent of his homeland, but with a noteworthy difference. Again we rely on the account of the Milanese merchant, who informs us that in Flanders and Bra-

bant the wind blows for at least three hundred days a year, and by means of an ingenious mechanism it was possible to turn the mills in any direction "to accommodate them to the wind," an advantage with respect to the Spanish windmills with their stationary brick towers.

Our Sevillian shipowner may have traveled to Antwerp to learn about the economic and social character of the Flemings, whose destinies were becoming increasingly connected to those of his countrymen. The city, as he found it, was in rapid expansion: "every day it becomes more beautiful," the Milanese merchant tells us, and within the span of only a few years at least eight hundred new houses had been built.

One could see attractive streets, squares, and the rich homes built of stone. The first Bourse was to be built in 1515, the second in 1531 (the 19th-century building is a reproduction of it). The guildhouse of the Corporation of Butchers (1501-3), a gothic structure of white stone and brick, had recently been completed. The cathedral of Notre-Dame was under constant expansion, and at that time one of the towers was unfinished; the second, which was to reach

a height of 123 meters, would be built
somewhat later (1521-30). Another careful
recorder of the times, De Beatis, was to note
"several most commodious channels of water," the "fair port where there is an infinity
of boats," and, during a visit to the fish-
mongers one morning, forty-six sturgeon,
some so large that the local hand carts
would have been unable to load more than
two at a time, along with blue-fish and
salmon. De Beatis also recounts that he,
together with his master the cardinal and
their entourage, found themselves "all in
admiration" of the enormous volume of
merchants and of the quantity and opulence
of the various goods for sale.

Antwerp owed its prosperity to the progressive silting-up of the port of Bruges.
The transfer of trade to the mouths of the
Scheldt had already begun after the first
decades of the 1400s. English trade had
shifted from wool export to the production
of woolen cloth, and British merchant ad-
venturers had established their warehouses
in Antwerp. In a short time, the British
would export as much as one hundred
twenty thousand rolls of cloth per year. In
addition, there was the trade of pepper and

**Witnesses of the times and places:
A Milanese merchant**

*This manuscript from the British Library
in London has only recently been published. It is a lively account of a journey
through western Europe which, after
analysis of its various chronological references, must have been made in the years
1517-19. The author was an unknown
Milanese merchant or banker (at the time
many men were both) possibly connected
in some way with the bank of the Borro-
meo family, well-known for its intense
international activity. The starting point
of the journey was Milan. Traveling via
Mont Cenis, the merchant reached Lyon
and Paris. From there he visited Flanders,
stopping in Bruges, Holland, and Brabant. From Calais, he crossed the Channel
to England, visiting Canterbury, London,
Southampton, and Greenwich, where
Henry VIII was in residence. Back on the
continent once again, the Milanese returned to Bruges and Brussels, traversed
France, and, entering Spain at Roncesvalles, went on a pilgrimage to Santiago
de Compostela. He made a grand tour of
the Iberian peninsula, covering Toledo,
Córdoba, Granada, Seville, Cadiz, Valencia, and Barcelona. The road back to
Milan passed through the Alps at Col de
Genevre after visits to Carcassonne, Toulouse, and Avignon. Several details sug-
gest that the journey was made on horseback, in carts, and on riverboats, common means of transportation. The traveler was cultured and had widely read. He
was an acute observer, and his descriptions included historical references, both
ancient and modern.*

other spices. In 1503 the city wharves had
seen the first arrival of Portuguese ships
carrying those Oriental products that until
then had been brought to the Bruges by the
Venetians.

The opening of the sea route to the Indies
made Antwerp the center of spice distribution throughout central and northern Europe. The atmosphere of enterprise and
prosperity that began to make itself felt in

Below: Boats on the Scheldt and the city of Antwerp, anonymous painting from the first half of the 16th century. Opposite: The port of Antwerp in a drawing by Dürer. Of his visit to the large Flemish city, the German artist recalls the "Procession of Our Lady," with the participation of magistrates, the clergy, religious orders, confraternities, members of all the arts, carts, and groups interpreting evangelical episodes; it took two hours for them all to pass.

the city was to be described competently—and with the envy of a Venetian—by the ambassador of the Most Serene Republic Marino Cavalli several decades later (1551), by which time Antwerp had reached its peak and was considered the greatest port and richest market in the world. Cavalli listed trade with Spain, Portugal, England, Germany, France, the Baltic, Italy; he calculated that all in all, the transactions were worth almost 2.5 million golden ducats. All forms of goods were bought and sold: spices, sugar, jewels, lead, copper, oranges, oil, dried grapes, wine, timber, grain, linen, wools, canvas, fustians, velvets, and draperies of silk and gold. "There is so much money being exchanged," wrote Cavalli, "and the price of everything is so great, that there is no man, however low or lazy he may be, who is not rich for his class."

261

The ambassador

From Vienna to Moscow

On the far side of wide rivers and endless forests, new cathedrals with bizarre domes rose amid the red walls of the Kremlin. The eastern frontier of Europe was changing, and the ambassadors who ventured there returned with reports like the tales of explorers.

Vienna ● Krakow ● Lublin ● Brest Minsk ● Smolensk ● Moscow

On the page opposite the title: Thus can one imagine the process of a diplomatic mission directed toward the most mysterious of the European states at that time, Muscovy; a detail from the painting by Hans Memling known as The Seven Joys of Mary, *1480, donated by the Buyltinks, husband and wife, to Bruges cathedral so that it could be set in the chapel of the Corporation of Tanners. On the river close to the bridge are floating mills.*

Sigmund von Herberstein, diplomat in the service of the Hapsburgs, was born in Carniola and thus spoke, apart from German, Slovenian, a Slavic language. This was of great use to him when Maximilian I sent him on a diplomatic mission to the "Grand Prince of all the Russias," Vasily or Basil III, son of Ivan the Great, conqueror of Novgorod, and father of Ivan IV, better known to history as Ivan the Terrible. Having grown up in a bilingual country was even more useful to Herberstein when consulting the ancient Russian chronicles that, together with his personal memories, form the source of his *Rerum Moscoviticarum Commentarii*, one of the works by which the countries of western Europe began to learn of the mysterious world that lay to the east. It was a world of vast spaces, and these the lord of Moscow was gradually gathering to himself, taking advantage of the ebb in power of the Tartar Khanates and the crisis in the Hanseatic League, which had in turn caused a weakening in the merchant city republics of Pskov and Novgorod. The people encountered in this enormous land were beautiful, drunken, barbaric, and deceitful—or, at least, so they are described—but also very pious: "Perjury and blasphemy are not to be heard there, and they give the Lord God and his saints such great reverence and honor that wherever they find the image of a crucifix they reverently bow down unto the ground." The Dutch theologian Albert Pigghe of Kampen (Albert Campense) wrote these words for the benefit of Pope Clement VII. The people were considered servile in an Oriental sort of way. The grand prince was soon to be known as *car' samoderzec*, the Slavic equivalent of the Greek *basileus autokrator*, which was the title of the king of Byzantium. But *car* ("czar") was also the title by which

the Byzantine diplomats had, without hesitation, honored the Tartar khans, heirs of Genghis Khan, whose dominion in Russia had only just—and not yet entirely—come to an end and for whom the lord of the Kremlin nourished a hatred as bloodthirsty and ruthless as the methods both he and

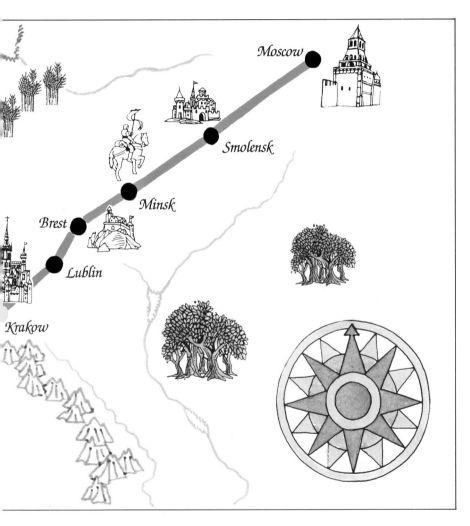

they used to wield power.

Baron Herberstein carried out a second diplomatic mission to Moscow, but the itinerary outlined here does not correspond to any of the four routes that the baron followed during his two round-trip journeys, each of which was dictated by necessities of the moment. Instead, the itinerary given here follows geographic logic.

Vienna itself was a borderland. Situated at the edge of the wooded hills of the Wiener Wald (Vienna Woods), the last fading remnants of the corrugated line that forms the Alps, Vienna looks out from its

Vienna. In 1278, the city came under the power of the Hapsburgs, who quickly made it their residence and under whom it grew. The city on the Danube had once been a Celtic settlement, a Roman military frontier post, and a free imperial city thanks to the privileges conceded it by Frederick II; here, a view of the city from the Chronica mundi *by Hartmann Schedel. Opposite: The road, a detail from the* Portrait of Benedetto di Tommaso Portinari *by Hans Memling.*

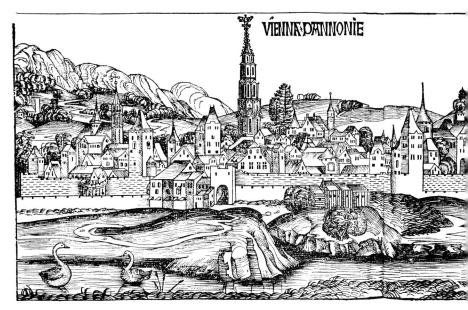

VIENNA·PANNONIE

eastern side, along which the Danube descends, toward the vast plains of Hungary, which spread out as far as the mountain chain of the Carpathians. But if one goes up the Morava River, a left-hand tributary that reaches the Danube just below the city at the Morava Gate, between the Sudeten and Carpathian mountains, one heads up to the Polish lands in which the upper courses of the Oder and Vistula diverge. The plain that gradually takes shape is even more immense and extends unbroken northward, ploughed by great rivers, as far as the freezing waters of the ocean. To the east it goes as far as the Caspian Sea and then on to even vaster lowlands. At Vienna, the Alps and the steppe seem to set their diverse breaths one against the other.

The city is located where the Wien, a small river descending from the Wiener Wald, joins one of the arms of the Danube (today this is the Donaukanal). The great blue river was at that time in a savage state: it spread through the plain of Marchfeld, flooding it, dividing into various arms that separated small islands (the principal branch is now called the Alte Donau). Maximilian, the fifth of the Hapsburgs to wear the imperial crown (which continued to be borne by his family after his death until one came who did nor care for the title of Charlemagne), had been able to return to Vienna in 1490 after his adversary, the Hungarian Matthias Corvinus, who had conquered and held it for five years, died there. The city itself was small, but life seems to have been prosperous, or at least it was thus observed by Enea Silvio Piccolomini (later Pope Pius II), who, being born in a well-to-do Viennese family, should have been a good judge. In Am Hof Square, site of the principal residence of the dukes of Austria, noble knights had for centuries competed in tournaments. Now the Ma-

266

Even more so than today, the Innere Stadt consisted of tortuous streets and tiny squares around the Cathedral of St. Stephen. The church itself, with its high, steep roof constructed to allow the abundant winter snows to slide off it, was dedicated to the patron saint of the diocese of Passau, upon which Vienna itself had been dependent until the year 1480. The church had been renewed in a gothic style by the Margrave Rudolph, busily emulating his father-in-law, the emperor Charles IV of Luxembourg, who, in Prague on the Hradschin, had had a gothic cathedral built by the French master Matthew d'Arras. Some of the older men could show their grandchildren the pulpit on the outside of the cathedral from which, halfway through the 15th century, St. John of Capestrano had preached a crusade against the heathen Turks. Many

riensäule rises from it, the 17th-century column to the Virgin with four angels fighting a lion, dragon, serpent, and basilisk, which is to say, war, hunger, heresy, and plague, the four scourges of humanity. The Prater was the site of headlong hunts on horseback by members of the court. After Maximilian's second marriage, to Bianca Maria Sforza, the court's favorite pastimes included the performance of tragedies, featuring choruses, masks, and theatrical performances with songs and dances in the Italian manner. In the area today taken up by the Schönbrunn palace, there was nothing but a mill. The little church of the fisherman, Maria-am-Gestade ("Mary on the banks"), dominated what was at that time the bed of the Donaukanal. The Graben, the beautiful baroque road-square, on the other hand, marked the line of the moat forming part of the Roman fortifications, which had lasted up to the 12th century.

of these same grandchildren would themselves live to see the city besieged by the Turks in 1529. The tower on the southern side, which the Viennese call the Steffel, had been completed in 1459. It was already 136 meters high, and during the second siege by the Turks, which took place in 1683, rockets were launched from its top as a signal to the army coming in support that the town still held. On the opposite side, construction of the Adlerturm ("tower of the eagle"), begun in 1467, had recently been left incomplete (1511) due to lack of funds.

The imperial castle, the Burg, the construction of which started in the 13th century, was later to be absorbed into the Hapsburg palace (Hofburg); it corresponded to the eastern wing looking onto the court known as *In der Burg*, its Renaissance doorway guarded by a drawbridge. Here, the family guarded the two priceless treasures of the dynasty, a unicorn's horn two and one half meters long (in reality the tusk of a narwhal) and an agate washbasin three quarters of a meter in diameter. This last, dating back to the 14th century, had

been taken as spoils at Constantinople in 1204 by crusaders and had passed into the hands of the Austrian house through the Burgundian heritage: no one had any doubt that it was the Holy Grail. The Kapuzinerkirche, in whose crypt the Hapsburgs were to be buried generation after generation, had not yet been built. The court chapel was the Augustinerkirche, the interior of which was at that time also gothic (Johann Sobiescki intoned the *Te Deum* in it after the libertion of Vienna from the siege of 1683, and it was also used for the celebration of the marriage by proxy of Marie Louise to Napoleon, during which twelve rings of different diameter were prudently blessed, as no one could give exact indications as to the size of the imperial ring finger).

The university was in the area still known as the Universitätsplatz. Founded in 1365, it was the second oldest in the German world; it had now become the most important. In 1445, the humanist Enea Silvio Piccolomini had held a famous lesson there on the exemplary value of ancient authors and classical poetry, marking the start in Vienna of a new culture. In contrast, in the

Following pages: Pieter Brueghel, The Reapers, *detail. This is one of the five remaining pictures from a series depicting the twelve months, possibly never completed, or perhaps comprising only six paintings, as the months are joined in pairs (in which case, instead of representing July or August, as it is thought to do, the picture would refer to the two-month period July-August, or, according to some, August-September).*

Markt, which corresponds to the Forum of the Roman city originally on the spot, called Vindobona, it was perhaps still possible to see—as it had been throughout the Middle Ages—the cage in which bakers accused of selling bad bread had been locked. Such miscreants were dunked three times in the Danube. Bakers could also be heroes in Vienna: there was, for instance, the one who (according to legend) managed to kill a basilisk by placing a mirror before its eyes; on seeing its own ugliness, the monster died of absolute fright (there is still a House of the Basilisk on the Schonlaterngasse; the basilisk is a natural concretion protected by a niche in the face of the building. It is said to have been there for about eight centuries).

A short distance from Vienna, continuing up the valley of the Morava, one entered the lands of the Jagiellos, the eastern European dynasty—its founder was a grand prince of Lithuania, a pagan—that came within reach of, but missed, a great destiny. It was in 1516 that Ladislaus Jagiello, king of Bohemia and Hungary, died at Buda and was succeeded by his son, Louis II. Less than a decade later Louis lost his life in the disastrous battle of Mohacs (1526), in which the Turk Suliman I conquered Hungary. Hungary was not taken back from the Turks quickly, but the crowns and kingdoms passed to the Hapsburgs, who, through opportune marriages, had been preparing for the acquisition.

Having crossed Moravia, which formed part of the kingdom of Bohemia, one entered Poland. Here the king was Sigismund I Jagiello, brother of the late Ladislaus. The grand duchy of Lithuania, which extended from the Baltic into White Russia and the Ukraine, was dynastically linked to Poland.

The wide open lands of Poland and

*Krakow. In the church of St. Mary, the sculptor from
Nuremberg Veit Stoss left the great altar bearing the* Seven
Consolations of the Virgin *(detail opposite). Stoss had his
workshop in the Polish city for twenty years; on returning to
Nuremberg he found himself condemned for forgery (1503);
released thanks to the intervention of Maximilian, he did not
regain the esteem of his fellow citizens, who all the same
appreciated the works he had done in his homeland.*

Lithuania were used to produce grain, hemp, wood, pitch, and leather, the basic materials on which western civilization depended to sustain the speed of its development. Among other things, these were needed for navigation. Under Sigismund, who conquered the Teutonic Knights, the Poles had thrown down the obstacles that had kept them away from the Baltic. By way of this sea and the rivers flowing into it, the market sucked up products bearing signs of all the toil of laborers but brought profit exclusively to a class of landowners who identified themselves with the nobility. Even more than the nobles, whose estates stretched as far as the eye could see, these landowners were little more than misers. In a structure left over from and forever falling back into the Middle Ages, possession of land, the privileges of the nobility, and service during war among the knights all formed an indestructible circle that would in the long run bring Poland to tragedy. The middle classes, when they existed at all, were excluded from the right to buy land, from marriage into the nobility, from having any say in the kingdom's diets, and from obtaining holy orders or benefits. Historical transformation follows distorted paths, but here it could not even take full advantage, in terms of economic development, of the increase in prices of exported goods. The nobles grew richer, and their influence on the crown increased. The monarchy remained weak due to lack of money—the landowners had the right to export duty free—and due to the impossibility of forming the backbone of an administration—elsewhere taken by the middle classes—and so the military structure lingered on very much in the spirit and practice of feudal knights. The Lithuanian-Polish giant, the grain empire— as it has been called by

historians—was immense, but appeared powerful only because no one had as yet tested its muscle.

The imperial ambassador passed through this land on horseback, immense views all around him. "City of great fame, metropolis of Poland Minor" (or "Little Poland"). This is how Krakow is described in the *Descrizione della Sarmazia europea* ("Description of European Sarmatia"), published in Krakow in 1578, by the Veronese Alessandro Guagnino, a soldier who had fought for the Poles in their wars against the Muscovites. The city was washed by the Wista, "a navigable river by which all forms of merchandise are transported," and from the beginning of the 13th century it was the capital of the kings of Poland. The castle, on the low hill of Wawel, 236 meters high, had been enlarged and renovated in the Renaissance style by Sigismund. The Florentine Francesco della Lora had recently completed the courtyard, with its greatly admired loggia. The arrival of Bona Sforza, the king's bride, had brought many Italians to the city, including a number of artists. On the Wawel was also the cathedral, in its 13th-century version. The kings of Poland received their crown under its vaulted roof amid the tombs of their predecessors.

The city's major church, St. Mary's, was in the Rynek, the central square and marketplace. Worshipers were amazed by the great altar, sculpted and painted by the German Veit Stoss, who had worked in the city up to 1496. It was a truly moving work, thanks to the realism of the late gothic figures depicted in heavily colored and gilded wood. Dedicated to the Madonna, its most important scene was that of her death, with Mary and the Apostles depicted larger than life (the altar is now in a museum). Around and above could be seen the

*Krakow. Below: A street in the city with a blacksmith's
workshop; opposite, the founding of bells; two miniatures
from the* Behem Codex, *a collection of privileges and statutes
of the city and the regulations of its guilds, illustrated by a
local artist, around 1505 (Balthazar Behem, who gives his
name to the codex, was the scribe and municipal notary who
compiled it). Worthy of note in the first of the two miniatures
are the people dressed in Oriental clothing.*

Seven Consolations of the Virgin (Annunciation, Nativity, Adoration of the Magi, Resurrection, Ascension, Pentecost, Incoronation).

The buildings around the square were to gain their monumental size during the following decades and in the 1600s. The lion of St. Mark indicated the homes of the Venetian merchants. The university had its seat in a gothic building put up in 1364. Only slightly younger than that of Prague, it was at that time at the apex of its fame and its function as a promoter of culture. Copernicus had recently studied there. Travelers from southern Europe passing through Krakow noticed that food in the city was extraordinarily inexpensive (but wine was inordinately costly), and that one met many people in the streets dressed in Oriental style, with caftans and turbans. This was due in part to the influence of distant countries, beyond forest and steppe, to trade, and to the presence of merchants; but it was also a popular fashion. The development of the city was a consequence of its position at the intersection of ancient highways. One stretched from the shores of the Black Sea through Leopolis and on

through Silesia and the countries of western Europe, while the other, starting at the Morava Gate from the Adriatic, reached the Baltic. In a certain measure, the city was a crossroads where goods, men, and the atmospheres or echoes of more or less the entirety of Europe of that period could meet, often together with elements from the Turkish East and Tartary.

All around, where the circle of walls enclosed the city for over three kilometers, there are now gardens. The sense of limitless space that crept into the soul when traveling across the Polish landscape was linked to the fearful awareness that Tartar horsemen, eager for absolute destruction, might appear on the horizon with each new spring.

To reach Muscovy, one rode northeast, at first following the course of the Wista. Lublin, a city in central Poland, was en-countered on a river called the Bystrzyaca, a tributary of the Wieprz, in its turn a tributary of the Wista. The greatest surprise in this city was perhaps that of finding Byzantine frescoes in the gothic 15th-century Church of the Trinity. These date back to 1418 and are the work of Russian artists who painted at the court of Ladislaus.

Brest (known as Brest-Litovsk), situated on the Bug, another tributary of the Wista, was a "walled city with fortified bastions, banks, and dikes, founded on the plain in the midst of marshes" (Alessandro Guagni-no). The traveler now found himself crossing Lithuania, a region that until recently was part of the Soviet Union. Baron Herberstein drew a strongly colored picture full of social preoccupations: the people were poor, oppressed by slavery; the knights enter homes of the village folk, sometimes with great

Poland and Muscovy. Opposite: This engraving from Chronica mundi *is intended to be a synthesis of the Polish landscape and is largely imaginative; however, several characteristics are significant; the country village with thatched roofs, the well with its balance-beam, the emphasis laid on the waterway (probably the Wista) and its entry into the Baltic. Right: Muscovy in a map dating from the 1500s: rivers and forests.*

following of servants, and do as they please, taking whatever they wish, and are even allowed to beat up the master of the house. The authorities make no decisions, take no action for the individual unless they receive gifts, for which reason the ambassador cites the cynical bon mot of the official: in Lithuania, every word is gold.

Minsk, in White Russia, is mentioned by Herberstein only as a "castle." Smolensk is the first city on the itinerary to be in the possession of the grand prince of Moscow, the Russians only recently having conquered it from the Lithuanians. Here flows the Dnieper, which cultured travelers gave the classical name Borysthenes. The castle was judged extremely strong; it contained a church dedicated to the Virgin and so many wooden houses that it almost appeared to be a city. It was defended by a moat surrounded by sharpened stakes. In the suburbs outside the castle walls were scattered ruins of stone monasteries. The surrounding countryside was a valley with gentle, fertile hills followed by vast forests, possessing an inextinguishable reserve of furs.

Not surprisingly, travelers make much mention of the Russian climate and the bitterness of the winters. Crops would sometimes fail to reach maturity, and in some years traveling peddlers with their trained bears were found frozen dead by the wayside. Travelers overtaken by the dark were found dead in their carts. Wild bears emerged from the forests and, driven by hunger, forced their way into village houses. Fleeing peasants perished from the cold.

However, in the western portion of the country, the economic resources were well known. There are, for example, the reports of Paolo Giovio, of Como in Italy, who, having lived at the papal court, was one of the most well-informed men of his time. He

mentions grain, linen, hemp, leathers, "most noble furs, the value of which, thanks to the incredible greed and delicacy of men, has grown so great that the lining for a coat is sold at one thousand gold ducats." Along with these products, there were beeswax and honey. Giovio obtained his information from a Russian ambassador in Rome, Dmitrij Gerasimov, who, in order to give credence to the notion that honey was not produced in hives but was gathered in the hollow trunks of trees, told him the story of a peasant who, while in search of honey in the forest, fell into the trunk of a fallen tree and was submerged "up to his breast in a deep well of honey." He subsisted on this honey for two days and then managed to escape by clinging to the back of a she-bear that had come to feed there (from the *Libellus de legatione Basilii*, 1525, in the 16th-century Italian translation published

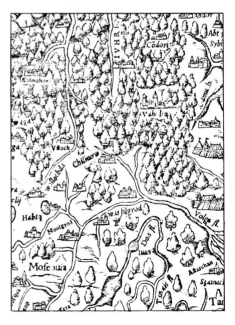

in the works of Giambattista Ramusio).

On the road to Moscow, Baron Herberstein gathered and studied impressions from which he was to sketch a portrait that is perhaps less amazing to us than it was to his contemporaries. What follows are some of his random observations. Dress: long and without folds, with tight sleeves, the belt tied to the right (the Tartars, who wore a similar dress, tied theirs to the left), and a "Russian" shirt, worked with various colors around the neck, and with buttons of silver or gilded copper. The priests married, according to the rules of the Orthodox church; one had to be married in order to become a deacon; priests who were widowed could no longer administer the sacraments but could perform religious service as long as they led a chaste life. Icons were in every home, placed in the most respected position. People paying a visit bare their heads upon entering a home and look around until they find the image, where they make the sign of the cross three times with bent head before greeting, embracing, and kissing the master of the house. It is believed that no woman can keep herself honest and good unless she is shut up in the home; wives and young girls rarely go to church, even more rarely do they speak to friends, and then only to elderly people, although on special holidays the recreation of the spirit is allowed by letting them play innocent party games in pleasant fields full of flowers.

What can be said of these opinions of the national temperament, if not to note that even in those days the well-known faculty for generalizing impressions was rife? Herberstein had a heavy hand, and to him the Russians appeared to prefer the state of slavery to liberty; in the upper classes everyone claimed to be the servant of the prince; in the lower, if a master on his deathbed frees his servants, the latter, for money, give themselves into the service of other masters. Albert Campense draws a positive judgment by negation: among them, cheating, adultery, and rape are considered "abominable wickedness"; public whores are never or scarcely ever seen, blasphemy and perjury are unknown, and "all vices which are against nature are totally unknown to them." The Venetian Ambrogio Contarini, in Russia from 1476 to 1477, states that "the men are of great beauty, and likewise the women, but they are bestial people." In particular, "they are great drunkards, and of this fact they do make much vaunt, and despise those who do not do likewise." They do not get drunk on wine, of which they have none, but on "the honey drink, which they make using the leaves of a certain flower, which is certainly not a bad drink and the most so when it is old."

Finally, there was Moscow, the red towers of the Kremlin and the cupolas of the recently completed churches rising above its brick walls. Situated among immense forests of lush green, Moscow was built primarily of wood. Many houses were built

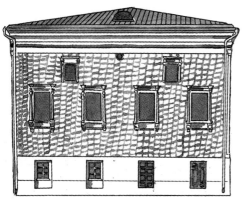

Below: In this plan of Moscow (from Braun and Hogenberg) the walled part is the Kremlin; the city, built of wood, continues outside. In the detail it is possible to see sleds on the frozen Moscova, archers on horseback, as well as "Polish bison" and aurochs. Opposite top: The sea captain, from the Ständebuch *by Hans Sachs. Opposite bottom: The Diamond Palace (Granovitaja Palata) in the Kremlin, built to hold the treasure of Ivan III.*

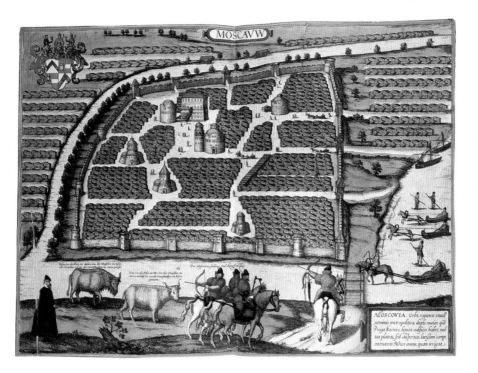

around a large courtyard and were surrounded by kitchen gardens. In the vain attempt to prevent recurring fires, the homes and workshops of smiths and other artisans who made wide use of fire had been relegated to the city's outskirts, scattered among fields and lawns. This helped make the city look much larger from a distance than it actually was.

There were no walls around the city, with those of the Kremlin enclosing only the citadel. On this subject Ambassador Herberstein informs us of a usage pertaining to the public order: the squares were barricaded with beams and patrolled by guards at night. Late-night wanderers who ran into these guards were beaten and ended up in prison unless, of course, they were persons of note, in which case they were accompanied home.

On the river, the Moscova, many mills were at work for the public good, and merchandise was transported along its course. As stated by Ambrogio Contarini, however, at the end of October the river "freezeth over," and on its surface "stalls are set up bearing all manner of goods" along with "bazaars of all nature." There is sale of "corn and fodder, cattle, pigs, wood, hay, and every other necessity." There are also horse races and other entertainments, but sometimes, he adds, "people break their necks."

The only portion of the city that would

be recognizable today is the Kremlin, the construction of which lasted thirty-one years (1485-1516). As can be read in the Italian translation of Herberstein's *Commentarii*, published in Ramusio, "the defenses of that castle, along with the prince's palace, have been built in the Italian manner by Italian workmen whom the same prince had summoned and whom he richly rewarded."

Were Maximilian's ambassador to return to the Kremlin today, he would recognize the walls and towers, three cathedrals, and a brick palace. Along with these there were in his time numerous other wooden churches. The cathedral of the Assumption of the Virgin (Uspenski Sobor) had been built by the Bolognese Aristotele Fieravanti between 1476 and 1479, using as a model the cathedral built by Vladimir, which he had gone especially to see. The completed work was "unique in height, luminosity, accoustics," as stated by a chronicler. "Its like was never before seen in the land of Russia." The czars were crowned there. The second cathedral was the collegiate church of the Annunciation (Blagovetcenski Sobor), built between 1484 and 1489 by masters from Pskov. It was here that the czars were baptized and married. The third was that of St. Michael the Archangel (Archangelski Sobor), raised by the Milanese Massimo Novi between 1505 and 1509. It was here that the czars were buried. The palace, the Granovitaja Palata, had been built in stone by order of Ivan III to serve as a stronghold for the treasury; Moscow had been completely burned down, and not for the first time, when the prince was 12 years old. The architect, another Italian, was Marco Ruffo, who designed the first floor as a single room, the vault of which rested not only on the surrounding walls, but on a single central pillar.

On his arrival in Moscow, the Venetian Contarini had been housed in the very same building as "Master Aristotle, which was almost adjacent unto the palace of my lord, and was a most commodious house" (he was later moved). The Bolognese architect had come to Russia together with his son Andrea and an assistant, who is cited in the documents as "the boy Petruska." He started by having to raze a series of walls. This was done first by undermining and then propping them up with trunks of wood, which were then set alight, so that the Muscovites—who looked on the foreigner with undisguised haughtiness—were astonished: "That which took three years to build, in less than one week was already in pieces." Another Italian architect, Pietro Antonio Solari, from Milan, is the author of the better part of the Kremlin's towers. His last work was the Spasskaia, or "Tower of the Savior," which opens into Red Square toward the picturesque and colorful St. Basil (which was built a good deal later) and via which the large automobiles of Soviet authorities once entered the square. While it was being built, a spring suddenly burst forth, flooding the worksite. Solari got wet while trying to take emergency measures, caught a bad cold, and died.

Around the city were great monasteries, including the famous monastery of the Holy Trinity (Troitsa Lavra), the first Russian communal-life monastery, founded by the peasant saint Sergius of Radonezh in 1354, who had performed many miracles and was buried there. The populace gathered there on certain feast days, and even the grand prince visited it frequently. At that time, the monastery housed that most famous of Russian icons, "the Trinity," full of subtle religious significance. It had been painted around 1425 by the monk Andrej Rublev.

The Trinity of the Old Testament *represents the biblical episode of the three angels visiting the old man Abraham and promising him the birth of Isaac: while sitting in front of his tent, by the oak trees of Mamre, in the heat of the day "Abraham lift up his eyes and looked, and, lo, three men stood by him" (Genesis 18:2). When Rublev painted this icon, Masaccio was painting the frescoes in the Brancacci Chapel.*

Moscow

Chronology

1446 Filippo Brunelleschi dies
1447 Nicholas V (Parentucelli) is elected pope; already grand prince of Lithuania, Casimir IV becomes king of Poland
1450 Francesco Sforza takes possession of Milan
1451 successor to Murad II, Mohammed II becomes sultan of the Ottomans
1452 in Mainz, Johannes Gutenberg begins printing the "24-line Bible"; Lorenzo Ghiberti completes the third door (Paradise Gate) of the baptistry in Florence; Frederick III is crowned emperor in Rome in the last imperial Roman coronation
1453 Mohammed II conquers Constantinople; at Castillon, the French defeat the English, lead by Talbot, completing the expulsion of the English from France, to whom only Calais remains
1455 Calixtus III (Borgia) becomes pope; the Wars of the Roses begin in England
1458 The humanist Enea Silvio Piccolomini (Pius II) is elected pope
1461 the king of France, Charles VII, dies; he is succeeded by his son Louis XI; Edward of York has himself proclaimed king (Edward IV), while Henry VI is a prisoner in the Tower of London
1462 on the death of Basil II, Ivan III becomes grand prince of Moscow
1463 the start of the war of Venice against the Turks, which continues until 1479
1464 death of Cosimo de' Medici; Paul II (Barbo) becomes pope
1465 the League of the Public Weal is established in opposition to Louis XI of France
1466 the Second Peace of Torun between the Order of Teutonic knights and Poland gives Poland access to the Baltic Sea
1467 death of Philip III the Good, duke of Burgundy, who is succeeded by his son, Charles the Bold

1468 commercial block of the Hanseatic cities formed against England
1469 marriage between Isabella, heiress of Castille, and Ferdinand, heir of Aragon: this partnership is the foundation for the union of the Spanish crowns; the two heirs succeed to the throne respectively in 1474 and in 1479
1470 Henry VI is reestablished on the throne of England (Edward IV, with the help of Burgundy and the Hanseatic cities, regains power the following year)
1471 Sixtus IV (Della Rovere) becomes pope
1472 marriage of Ivan of Moscow to Sophia, niece of the last Byzantine emperor: Moscow becomes the "third Rome"; death of Leon Battista Alberti
1474 Peace of Utrecht between England and the league of Hanseatic cities; the Hanse, providing assistance to Edward IV, is given given back its commercial privileges in England
1476 the duke of Milan, Galeazzo Maria Sforza, is assassinated; he is succeeded by the boy Gian Galeazzo under the regency of his mother, Bona of Savoy
1477 Charles the Bold dies before the walls of Nancy, ending the independence of the duchy of Burgundy; marriage of Mary of Burgundy to Maximilian I; Sandro Botticelli paints *La Primavera*
1478 in the anti-Medicean conspiracy of the Pazzi in Florence Giuliano de' Medici is assassinated and Lorenzo is wounded
1480 Ludovico Sforza becomes the tutor of his grandson Gian Galeazzo and de facto ruler of Milan; the Turks occupy Otranto
1481 the sons of Mohammed II, Beyazid and Jem, fight for succession, the former gaining control; in Portugal, John II ascends the throne
1482 the Treaty of Arras is signed between Louis XI and Maximilian I, settling the

The first imaginary itinerary in this guide is set in 1446, the year of the journey from Florence to London made by Gerozzo di Jacopo de' Pigli, business associate of Cosimo de' Medici; the last takes place in 1516, the year of the first mission to Moscow of the baron Sigmund von Herberstein. This brief chronology recalls some of the events in Europe between these two dates.

Burgundy inheritance
1483 Charles VIII is crowned in France; on the death of Edward IV, the duke of Gloucester has himself proclaimed king (Richard III)
1484 Innocent VIII (Cybo) accedes to the pontificate
1485 with the Battle of Bosworth Field the Wars of the Roses come to an end; Henry (VII) Tudor defeats Richard III; Matthias Corvinus, king of Hungary, conquers Vienna
1488 Bartolomeu Dias rounds the Cape of Good Hope; the *guerre folle* in France
1489 Venice takes Cyprus from Catherine Cornaro
1490 on the death of Matthias Corvinus, the Hapsburgs return to Vienna
1492 fall of the kingdom of Granada, last Moslem potentate in Spain; the "discovery of America": Christopher Columbus crosses the Atlantic and explores the islands of the Caribbean; death of Lorenzo the Magnificent; Alexander VI (Borgia) becomes pope
1493 death of the Emperor Frederick III, who is succeeded by his son Maximilian
1494 the expedition by Charles VIII of France, an attempt to conquer to kingdom of Naples, begins the long Italian Wars; the Medici family is forced out of Florence; Sebastian Brant publishes *Das Narrenschiff (The Ship of Fools)*
1495 on his return to France, Charles VIII fights the battle of Fornovo; in Milan, Leonardo begins the painting of the *Last Supper* in the refectory of the Grazie; Manuel I becomes king of Portugal
1497 departure of the Portuguese expedition led by Vasco da Gama that will circumnavigate Africa and reach India; John Cabot, on behalf of the king of England, discovers Nova Scotia and Newfoundland
1498 Louis XII (Orléans) succeeds Charles

VIII on the throne of France; Michelangelo sculpts the *Pietà* in St. Peter's; Girolamo Savonarola dies at the stake
1499 Louis XII of France invades Italy to claim the duchy of Milan; with the Peace of Basel the independence of the Swiss cantons is recognized de facto; Copernicus is in Rome teaching at the university
1500 Pedro Alvares Cabral discovers Brazil
1503 death of Alexander VI and, after the brief papacy of Pius III (Todeschini Piccolomini), Julius II (Della Rovere) is elected pope; Bramante builds the little temple of San Pietro in Montorio; the Spanish defeat the French at Garigliano and take Naples
1504 Raphael paints the *Sposalizio*
1506 death of Philip the Handsome of Hapsburg
1508 Michelangelo begins painting the frescoes of the ceiling in the Sistine Chapel
1509 the Venetians are defeated in the battle of Agnadello by the forces of the League of Cambrai; Henry VIII succeeds his father on the English throne
1510 Martin Luther visits Rome
1511 Erasmus writes *The Praise of Folly*
1512 Selim I succeeds his father Beyazid II; the Medicis return to Florence
1513 Leo X (Medici) is elected pope; Machiavelli writes *The Prince*
1514 death of Louis XII of France; he is succeeded by Francis I
1515 Francis I triumphs at Marignano
1516 Thomas More writes *Utopia*; Charles V becomes king of Spain

Bibliographical notes

Those interested in reading further about travel in Europe during the 15th century will find the following books of interest.

Baron Lev z Rozmitalu
The Travels of Leo of Rozmital through Germany, Flanders, England, France, Spain, Portugal and Italy, 1465-67, translated from the German and Latin and edited by Malcolm Letts; Cambridge, published for the Hakluyt Society at the University Press, 1957.

The Cardinal of Aragon
André Chastel, *Le cardinal Louis d'Aragon, Un voyageur princier de la Renaissance,* Paris, Librairie Arthème Fayard, 1986 (includes the text of the *Itinerary of the Cardinal Luigi d'Aragon* written by Antonio de Beatis). De Beatis's diary has been translated into English as *The Travel Journal of Antonio de Beatis: Germany, Switzerland, the Low Countries, France and Italy, 1517-1518,* translated by J. R. Hale and J. M. A. Lindon, with an introduction by J. R. Hale, The Hakluyt Society, London, 1979. The introduction presents an interesting overview of Renaissance travel literature.

The anonymous Milanese merchant
Un mercante di Milano in Europa, Diario di viaggio del primo Cinquecento, edited by Luigi Monga, Le Edizioni Universitarie Jaca, Jaca Book, Milan, 1985 (the introduction includes notes and a bibliography of travel diaries of the early 16th century). Two interesting accounts of pilgrimages to the Holy Land are presented in *Viaggio in Terrasanta di Santo Brasca,* 1480, con *l'Itinerario di Gabriele Capodilista, 1458,* edited by Anna Laura Momigliano Lepschy, Milan, Longanesi, 1966.

Interesting texts concerning northern Europe and particularly eastern Europe (Poland and Russia) are included in the celebrated work by Ramusio: Giovanni Battista Ramusio, *Navigazioni e viaggi,* edited by Marica Milanesi, Turin, Einaudi. Volume III, 1980, includes the commentaries by Sigmund von Herberstein on Moscow and Russia and the travel account of the Venetian ambassador Ambrosio Contarini. Volume IV, 1983, includes the journey and shipwreck of Piero Quirino, a Venetian gentleman, the same shipwreck described by Cristoforo Fioravante and Nicolò di Michiel, who were present, the description of Sarmatia by the Veronese Alessandro Guagnino, and the books of Matteo di Micheovo on Sarmatia. As for Sigmund von Herberstein, he published his description of Moscow in Latin (Vienna, 1549) and German (Vienna, 1557). The Latin version has been reprinted as *Rerum Moscoviticarum commentarii Sigismundi Liberi Baronis in Herberstein, Neyperg & Guettenbag,* Frankfurt, 1964; it is also available in English as Sigmund von Herberstein, *Commentaries on Muscovite Affairs,* edited by O. P. Backus III, Lawrence, University of Kansas, 1956.

Also of interest are:
Mercanti scrittori, Ricordi nella Firenze tra Medioevo e Rinascimento, edited by Vittore Branca, Milan, Rusconi, 1986. This includes the memoirs of the great traveler Bonaccorso Pitti. *Alle corte di cinque papi, Diario 1483-1506, di Giovanni Burcardo,* edited by Luca Bianchi, Milan, Longanesi, 1988, is a partial Italian translation of *Johannis Burckardt capelle pontificie magistri ceremoniarum libri notarum ab anno MCCCCLXXIII usque ad annum MDVI.*

Index of places

A

Aare, river, 186
Adda, river, 135
Adige, river, 153, 161
Aiguebelette, 139
Aigues-Mortes, 243, 252-53
Aix-en-Provence, 148
Alb, region, 157
Allier, river, 141
Amboise, 133, 141, 143, 147, 230
Amiens, 128, 199, 216
Ancona, 192
Andalusia, 246
Angers, 133, 141, 148
Antwerp, 93, 96, 243, 244, 258-61
Aosta, 87
Apennines, 78, 82, 84
Aragon, 121, 136, 249
Arc, river, 138
Ardennes, 89, 93
Arno, river, 79, 80
Arosa, 130
Arras, 93, 243, 258
Arroux, valley, 255
Artois, 258
Asturias, 129
Augsburg, 153, 155, 157, 158, 160
Auron, river, 121
Autun, 243, 255
Avigliana, 138
Avignon, 243, 254
Azay-le-Rideau, 142
Azof, 228

B

Baghdad, 114
Balearic Islands, 250
Balkans, 241
Barcelona, 243, 244, 250-52
Basel, 171, 182, 184, 185, 186
Bastia, 230
Bavaria, 157
Beaune, 243, 254
Bergen, 102, 171, 172, 174, 175
Bern, 185
Berry, 121, 141
Besançon, 77, 89
Bilbao, 127
Bisagno, river, 227
Biscay, bay of, 121, 127
Blois, 133, 143, 244, 256
Bohemia, 156, 269
Bologna, 84, 182
Bolzano (Bozen), 153, 160
Bornholm, island, 107

Bosporus, 225, 234, 235, 241
Boston, 199, 208
Bourges, 117, 121
Brabant, 93, 258
Bremen, 104
Brenner Pass, 153, 157, 160
Brenta, canal, 161
Breslau (Wroclaw), 103
Brest (Brest-Litovsk), 263, 276
Brittany, 133, 134, 148, 257
Bruges, 77, 78, 86, 92, 93, 94-96, 99, 102, 103, 172, 243, 259-60
Brussels, 77, 93
Buda (Budapest), 269
Bug, river, 276
Burgos, 117, 121, 126, 127, 246
Burgundy, duchy of, 78, 86, 89, 90, 92, 121, 254, 255, 256, 258
Byfjord, 174
Bystrzyca, river, 276

C

Cafaggiolo, 82
Caffa (Feodosia), 228
Calais, 199, 215
Cam, river, 209
Cambrai, 223
Cambridge, 199, 208, 209
Candia (Crete), 172
Cantabrian Mountains, 125
Canterbury, 199, 214
Carinthia, 159
Carnac, 238
Carniola, 264
Carpathian Mountains, 266
Cartagena, 252
Carter Bar, pass, 201
Casentino, 80
Castaneda, 128
Castile, 121, 125, 126, 127, 128, 136, 244, 248
Catalonia, 136, 249, 250, 252
Cesena, 163
Chablais, 87
Chambéry, 133, 138
Chambord, castle, 143
Chantilly, 187
Charité-sur-Loire, 121
Chenonceaux, castle, 142
Cher, river, 142, 147
Chinon, 141
Chios (Khios), island, 225, 228, 231, 234, 241
Citera (Kithira), island, 231
Civitavecchia, 230
Clavijo, 124
Coblenz, 171, 180
Cologne, 155, 171, 178, 180, 182
Constantinople (Istanbul), 225, 227, 228, 230, 234, 238, 240, 268
Córdoba, 121, 129, 243, 246-247
Cosenza, 106
Côte d'Or, 254
Covigliaio, 82
Cyclades, 231
Cyprus, 231

D

Danube, river, 157, 231, 266, 269
Danzig, 101, 102, 107-8, 110
Dardanelles, 225, 234
Daugava (Western Dvina), river, 110
Delphi, 238
Dnieper (Borysthenes), 277
Domesnes, cape, 110
Don, river, 228
Dora Riparia, river, 138
Dordogne, 122
Dornach, 184
Doubs, river, 89
Dover, 214, 215
Dresden, 166
Durham, 199, 202
Dvina, river, 110

E

Ebro, river, 125, 249
Edinburgh, 199, 201
Elba, island, 80
Elbe, river, 104, 171, 175
El Padron, 130
English Channel, 215
Ephesus, 240
Erfurt, 180
Essex, county, 210

F

Falster, island, 107
Faucille, Col de la, 89
Fenland, 208
Feodosia, 228
Fermignano, 137
Finis Terrae (Finisterre), 120, 130
Firenzuola, 82
Firth of Forth, 201
Flanders, 84, 86, 88, 93, 102, 114, 127, 169, 243, 244, 255, 256, 258 Fleet, river, 209, 212
Florence, 77, 78-82, 86, 96, 171, 182, 186, 187
Fornovo, 200
Fosse, river, 204
Fourvière, 139
Franche-Comte, 89
Franconia, 157
Friesland, 103
Friuli, 186

G

Galata, 227, 234, 235
Galicia, 117, 118, 120, 124, 128, 174
Geneva, 77, 78, 88, 139
Geneva, Lake of, 87, 88
Genoa, 96, 102, 225, 226, 230, 252, 256
Ghent, 77, 93, 94, 99, 244
Gien, 141
Giglio, island, 230
Gog Magog Hills, 209
Golden Horn, 230, 234, 235, 238
Göttingen, 103
Graben, 160
Granada, 121, 124, 248

285

287